IN DEFENCE OF COUNTRY

Life Stories of Aboriginal and Torres Strait
Islander Servicemen & Women

Aboriginal History Incorporated

Aboriginal History Inc. is a part of the Australian Centre for Indigenous History, Research School of Social Sciences, The Australian National University, and gratefully acknowledges the support of the School of History and the National Centre for Indigenous Studies, The Australian National University. Aboriginal History Inc. is administered by an Editorial Board which is responsible for all unsigned material. Views and opinions expressed by the author are not necessarily shared by Board members.

Contacting Aboriginal History

All correspondence should be addressed to the Editors, Aboriginal History Inc., ACIH, School of History, RSSS, 9 Fellows Road (Coombs Building), Acton, ANU, 2601, or aboriginal.history@anu.edu.au.

IN DEFENCE OF COUNTRY

Life Stories of Aboriginal and Torres Strait
Islander Servicemen & Women

NOAH RISEMAN

Australian
National
University

PRESS

Published by ANU Press and Aboriginal History Inc.
The Australian National University
Acton ACT 2601, Australia
Email: anupress@anu.edu.au
This title is also available online at press.anu.edu.au

National Library of Australia Cataloguing-in-Publication entry

Creator:	Riseman, Noah, 1982- author.
Title:	In defence of country : life stories of Aboriginal and Torres Strait islander servicemen and women / Noah Riseman.
ISBN:	9781925022780 (paperback) 9781925022803 (ebook)
Series:	Aboriginal history monograph.
Subjects:	Aboriginal Australians--Wars--Veterans. Aboriginal Australian soldiers--Biography. Australia--Armed Forces--Aboriginal Australians.
Dewey Number:	355.00899915094

Cover design and layout by ANU Press.
Cover art: *Private Arthur 'Darky' Butler* by Bruce Fletcher, www.awm.gov.au/collection/ART40563/?image=1.

Contents

Contents

List of Figures

Preface and Acknowledgements

From 2009–13 I had the privilege of travelling across Australia to interview Aboriginal and Torres Strait Islander men and women who served in the Australian armed forces. I conducted 33 interviews in total with men and women who had served in all three services (Army, Air Force and Navy) between the 1950s and 1990s. These were whole-of-life interviews, asking a range of open-ended questions. It was important to learn about the speakers' entire lives to understand how military service affected their life trajectories, whether reinforcing childhood plans or providing them with new personal and professional opportunities. Some of the interviewees spoke at length about their times in the armed forces, while others dwelt more on their pre- or post-service lives. Such variations indicate that for some interviewees, being an ex-serviceperson and the time they spent in the armed forces was a defining feature of their identity; for others, it was one step in a much longer personal journey.

Every interview was unique. It may be more appropriate to refer to the questions as prompts, because it was the participants whose life stories drove the directions of the interviews. Oral historian Lorina Barker describes her own similar experiences interviewing members of an Aboriginal community as yarnin',[1] and that is a fitting way to describe the conversations. Several interviews left me (and sometimes the speaker) in a state of shock, just needing to decompress. I heard stories of racism, troubled childhoods, post-traumatic stress disorder and losing friends in war. I also heard stories of perseverance, overcoming hardship, community support and, unanimously, genuine respect and love for the Australian Defence Force. I learned something from every interview and am grateful to all of the participants for sharing their life stories.

Unfortunately, it is not possible to publish all of those interviews; this book contains a sample that I selected because they represent a diverse array of experiences in life and in the Australian military. The words are the speakers'

---

1   Lorina Barker, '"Hangin' out" and "Yarnin'": Reflecting on the Experience of Collecting Oral Histories', *History Australia* 5, no. 1 (2008): 09.1–09.9.

own with minimal editing. Where I have made changes, it has been primarily to preserve the flow of the text or to structure the paragraphs into a coherent narrative. All interviewees provided input into the editing process and reviewed the final texts of these chapters. I, like all other oral historians, acknowledge that something is lost when reading an interview transcribed into text. The pauses, the laughter, the facial expressions and the changing intonations of voice cannot come across in a written text. I therefore encourage the readers to listen to these interviews; those, where marked, are available from the National Library of Australia and can be accessed online.[2] Those not in the National Library are being deposited into the Australian Institute for Aboriginal and Torres Strait Islander Studies.

Though the words in these chapters belong to the interviewees, there are other people who played a role in preparing this book whom I must thank. At the top of that list are the speakers themselves for giving their time not only for the interviews, but also carefully reading these chapters, providing comments and ensuring that their words were not misrepresented. Thank you also to the three research assistants who helped with interview transcription: Sari Braithwaite, Christin Quirk and Rachael Lorenz-Stockdale. I appreciate the thoughtful feedback Dr Sam Furphy and Dr James Bennett provided on the manuscript. Colleagues at the Australian Catholic University (ACU) have been supportive throughout this entire project and have provided important advice along the way: Shurlee Swain, Nell Musgrove, Ellen Warne, Maggie Nolan, Hannah Forsyth, Melissa Bellanta and Cath Bishop. A special thanks also to Naomi Wolfe from ACU, who has provided significant support as a friend and colleague, and has been especially important at providing cultural advice. Richard Trembath has been my collaborator on this project, so I thank him for his hard work which complements these interviews in our monograph, *Defending Country: Aboriginal and Torres Strait Islander Military Service since 1945*. Funds supporting this project came from Australian Research Council Discovery grant DP110101627, an Army History Research Unit grant, the National Library of Australia and an Australian Catholic University Faculty of Arts & Sciences Early Career Research Incentive Award. Gratitude also goes to the Australian Catholic University for providing financial support for this publication.

Finally, as always, I need to thank my family and my loving partner, Michael, for their ongoing support. Michael in particular had to endure several bouts of my research trips away from Melbourne and hearing me ramble about these amazing people I was meeting for my work.

Aboriginal and Torres Strait Islander readers are cautioned that this book contains names and images of persons who are deceased.

---

2   Sue Gordon: nla.gov.au/nla.oh-vn5018270. John Schnaars: nla.gov.au/nla.oh-vn5018258.

Abbreviations

2IC	second-in-command
AASM	Australian Active Service Medal
ACT	Australian Capital Territory
ADF	Australian Defence Force
AIF	Australian Imperial Force
Anzac	Australian and New Zealand Army Corps
APC	armoured personnel carrier
ATSIC	Aboriginal and Torres Strait Islander Commission
ATSIVSA	Aboriginal and Torres Strait Islanders Veterans and Services Association
AWAS	Australian Women's Army Service
AWM	Australian War Memorial
AWOL	absent without leave
BAE Systems	British Aerospace Systems
BARK	Brothers Act of Random Kindness
BCOF	British Commonwealth Occupation Force
BMA	Brigade Maintenance Area
CEO	chief executive officer
CSM	company sergeant major
DDG	guided missile destroyer
DFRP	Defence Fuel Remediation Program
DUI	driving under the influence
DVA	Department of Veterans' Affairs

ETP	Electrical and Technical Power
FaHCSIA	Department of Families, Housing, Community Services and Indigenous Affairs
GP	general practitioner (doctor)
GPS	global positioning system
ICC	Indigenous Coordination Centre
IED	improvised explosive device
IET	Initial Employment Training
ILUA	Indigenous Land Use Agreement
IMT	Infantry Minor Tactics
INTERFET	International Force for East Timor
IRC	Independent Rifle Company
LGA	local government area
LINC	Local Indigenous Network and Communities
LLB	Bachelor of Laws
LNG	liquefied natural gas
LP gas	liquefied petroleum gas
MP	Military Police *or* Member of Parliament (contextual)
NAIDOC	National Aboriginal and Islander Day Observance Committee
NAOU	North Australia Observer Unit
NASA	National Aeronautics and Space Administration
NCO	non-commissioned officer
NGO	non-governmental organisation
NPA	northern peninsula area
NTSRU	Northern Territory Special Reconnaissance Unit
OH&S	occupational health and safety
OISR	Operator of Information Systems and Radios
OLA	Open Learning Australia
PIR	Pacific Islands Regiment
PNG	Papua New Guinea
POW	prisoner-of-war
PTI	physical training instructor
PTSD	post-traumatic stress disorder

R&R	rest and relaxation
RAAF	Royal Australian Air Force
RAN	Royal Australian Navy
RAP	Regimental Aid Post
RAS	replenishment at sea
RPG	rocket-propelled grenade
RSL	Returned and Services League
RSM	regimental sergeant major
RTB	Recruit Training Battalion
SAE	Service Assisted Evacuation
SAS	Special Air Service Regiment, Australian Army
SLR	self-loading rifles
STI	sexually transmitted infection
TAFE	Technical and Further Education
TI	Thursday Island
TNI	Indonesian National Armed Forces
TO	traditional owner
TPI	Totally and Permanently Incapacitated Veteran
TSLI	Torres Strait Light Infantry Battalion
UNTAET	United Nations Transitional Administration in East Timor
VCP	vehicle checkpoint
WOD	warrant officer disciplinary
WA	Western Australia
WAAAF	Women's Auxiliary Australian Air Force
WRAAC	Women's Royal Australian Army Corps
WRAAF	Women's Royal Australian Air Force
XO	executive officer

1

Introduction: A Long History of Service

On 10 November 2013, a ceremony in Adelaide dedicated a war memorial to all Aboriginal and Torres Strait Islander men and women who have served in the Australian armed forces. The memorial was the culmination of years of hard work from Indigenous and non-Indigenous supporters alike. One of the themes permeating the dedication speeches was about how during both the First and Second World Wars, Aboriginal and Torres Strait Islander service personnel fought bravely for Australia yet returned home to continuing discrimination. Indigenous contributions to Australia's military history for the most part went unrecognised and became forgotten in the national story. At the ceremony, Frank Lampard, the Deputy Chair of the Aboriginal and Torres Strait Islander War Memorial Committee, delivered an impassioned speech in which he declared to resounding applause: 'I'm proud to say that lack of recognition ends today!'

The memorial in Adelaide represents one of several initiatives in the new millennium to commemorate Aboriginal and Torres Strait Islander military service. For instance, members of the Perth-based organisation Honouring Indigenous War Graves regularly travel to gravesites of Indigenous diggers to perform ceremonies and place commemorative headstones. In Redfern, a Coloured Diggers March has honoured Indigenous servicemen and women every Anzac Day since 2007. In the major capital cities the Department of Veterans' Affairs now organises commemorative services during Reconciliation Week. In January 2014, the Sydney Festival showcased the new play *Black Diggers*, depicting the experiences of Aboriginal servicemen in the

First World War. The play has since toured to the other capital cities. The theme of NAIDOC Week in 2014 was 'Serving Country – Centenary and Beyond'. In 2015 the artwork *Yininmadyemi – Thou didst let fall* was dedicated to Aboriginal and Torres Strait Islander military service in Hyde Park in Sydney. These high-profile examples complement commemorative activities in local Aboriginal and Torres Strait Islander communities across the country. Indigenous Australians have always known about their kin's contributions to Australia's defence. These events are all contributing to an awakening among the non-Indigenous community about the histories of Aboriginal and Torres Strait Islander military service.

Aboriginal and Torres Strait Islander people have been protecting this country since time immemorial. They defended it valiantly when Europeans arrived; they resisted invasion, dispossession and massacres. Frontier wars waged from the time of the First Fleet in 1788 through to the 1930s in central Australia. These wars were still being fought when the Australian colonies federated in 1901 and the Commonwealth excluded Aboriginal and Torres Strait Islander people from participating in the new nation as equals.[1]

While many Aboriginal people were still fighting on the frontiers of northern and central Australia, others were fighting for the British Empire in the Boer War from 1899 to 1902. At least 10 Aboriginal men signed up and served as regular soldiers. Approximately 10 other Aboriginal men were employed as trackers. Little is known about these men, though there are indications that some may have been left in South Africa at the end of the Boer War because of immigration restriction constitutive of the White Australia Policy.[2]

When the First World War broke out in 1914, Aboriginal men were among the thousands quick to sign up for military service. However, regulations barred the enlistment of persons 'not substantially of European origin or descent'. Some men managed to skirt these rules due to recruiters looking the other way or by pretending to be Italian, Indian or Māori (who were permitted despite not being European). In March 1917, the need for manpower drove the Commonwealth to loosen the regulations and to permit men of mixed descent to enlist. It is difficult to determine the precise number of Aboriginal men who served because the Australian Imperial Force (AIF) did not record the race of enlistees. The Australian War Memorial (AWM) has been working since the 1990s to compile lists of Aboriginal service personnel from each conflict, relying primarily on family names and Indigenous community input but also through records such as state

1   See Henry Reynolds, *Forgotten War* (Sydney: NewSouth Publishing, 2013); John Connor, *The Australian Frontier Wars: 1788–1838* (Sydney: UNSW Press, 2002); John Chesterman and Brian Galligan, *Citizens without Rights: Aborigines and Australian Citizenship* (Cambridge: Cambridge University Press, 1997).
2   See John Maynard, '"Let us go" … it's a "Blackfellows' War": Aborigines and the Boer War', *Aboriginal History 39* (2015): 143–162.

Aboriginal Protection Boards, correspondence in Department of Repatriation files and newspapers referencing Aboriginal service personnel.[3] Currently the AWM estimates that by the end of the First World War, over 1,300 Aboriginal men had served in the AIF. Most reported being treated as equals while in the AIF, but upon their return to Australia most were denied veterans' benefits, continued to live under restrictive protection acts and confronted prejudice. Notwithstanding the protest of Aboriginal activists – many of whom served, were related to veterans or had lost family in the war – the status of Aboriginal Australians had not improved substantially by the 1930s.[4]

When the Second World War broke out in 1939, much of the First World War experience repeated itself. Once again some men enlisted and once again regulations officially excluded persons 'not substantially of European origin or descent'. The larger scale of the conflict and direct threat to Australia from late 1941 changed the status quo. Regulations were ignored because Australia needed any able-bodied person who could serve. This time Indigenous women also served in the new women's auxiliary services, providing an opportunity for many of them to escape the limitations of domestic service imposed during the assimilation era. Again, those men and women who served in regular enlisted units reported that they were treated as equals, whether they served in places as diverse as Greece, Libya or New Guinea. In 1989, historian Robert Hall estimated that 3,000 Aboriginal people and 850 Torres Strait Islanders enlisted in the Second World War; now the AWM has identified approximately 5,000 Aboriginal and Torres Strait Islander servicemen and women.[5]

Northern Australia became a frontline in the Second World War after Japan swept across the South Pacific, dragging Aboriginal and Torres Strait Islander residents of the Top End into the conflict. Even before Japan entered the war, authorities recognised the possibility of an attack and enlisted Indigenous people to defend the country. The first formal Indigenous unit was the Torres Strait Light Infantry Battalion (TSLI), formed after May 1941. The TSLI was a group of approximately 440 regularly enlisted Torres Strait Islander men whose job was to patrol the Torres Strait and to provide mechanical and logistical support for ships passing through. Commanding officers and visitors praised

---

3   See 'Indigenous commemoration for the Centenary', Australian War Memorial, online, available from www.awm.gov.au/1914-1918/indigenous-commemoration/, accessed 13 February 2015.
4   See Noah Riseman, 'Enduring silences, enduring prejudices: Australian Aboriginal participation in the First World War', in *Endurance and the First World War*, eds. Sarah Murray, David Monger and Katie Pickles (Newcastle upon Tyne: Cambridge Scholars Publishing, 2014), 178–195; Timothy Winegard, *Indigenous Peoples of the British Dominions and the First World War* (Cambridge: Cambridge University Press, 2012); Philippa Scarlett, *Aboriginal and Torres Strait Islander Volunteers for the AIF: The Indigenous Response to World War One* (Macquarie, ACT: Indigenous Histories, 2012).
5   See Robert Hall, *The Black Diggers: Aborigines and Torres Strait Islanders in the Second World War*, 2nd ed. (Canberra: Aboriginal Studies Press, 1997); Robert Hall, *Fighters from the Fringe: Aborigines and Torres Strait Islanders Recall the Second World War* (Canberra: Aboriginal Studies Press, 1995).

the unit for its professionalism and effectiveness, yet its members received less pay than non-Indigenous men serving alongside them. The Queensland Chief Protector of Aborigines quarantined part of their wages, and that pay became part of what is now referred to as 'the stolen wages'. It was only in 1982 that surviving members of the TSLI received back pay – valued by then at over $7 million.[6]

Another all-Indigenous force was the Northern Territory Special Reconnaissance Unit (NTSRU), formed in February 1942 at the same time that the Japanese began bombing Darwin and northern Australia. From February 1942 to April 1943, anthropologist-turned-serviceman Dr Donald Thomson organised and commanded a group of 51 Yolngu men in Arnhem Land. He trained the NTSRU to use bush warfare to ward off potential Japanese invaders, relying on their own knowledge of the land and weaponry such as spears instead of guns. The NTSRU patrolled Arnhem Land and constructed outposts but received no payment except for basic trade goods such as fish hooks, wire and tobacco. The force disbanded in April 1943 when the immediate Japanese threat had passed, and other white units arose to patrol the Top End. It was not until 1992 that surviving members of the NTSRU and families of deceased veterans were awarded back pay for their service.[7]

While the TSLI and NTSRU were the only *formal* Indigenous units in the Top End, there were other Aboriginal men and women employed by the Army or Air Force. Some worked in labour camps, moving ordnance, constructing shelters, preparing food and cleaning. Others worked with local Army or RAAF servicemen clearing and constructing runways, moving supplies or serving as coastwatchers. There were some instances when Aboriginal or Torres Strait Islander men rescued crashed Australian or American pilots. A Tiwi Islander captured the first Japanese prisoner of war on Australian soil whose plane crashed after the first bombing raid on Darwin. Aboriginal and Torres Strait Islander residents at missions were also the victims of Japanese bombings. The North Australia Observer Unit (NAOU), a scouting unit operating from Queensland to Western Australia, employed local Aboriginal men as trackers. Women had to protect their families when men left to join forces such as the

6   Hall, *The Black Diggers*, ch. 3; Hall, *Fighters from the Fringe*, 135–153, 173–191; Elizabeth Osborne, *Torres Strait Islander Women and the Pacific War* (Canberra: Aboriginal Studies Press, 1997), 103–122.
7   Noah Riseman, *Defending Whose Country? Indigenous Soldiers in the Pacific War* (Lincoln, NE: University of Nebraska Press, 2012), chs 1 and 2; Donald Thomson, *Donald Thomson in Arnhem Land*, compiled and introduced by Nicolas Peterson, rev. ed. (Melbourne: The Miegunyah Press, 2005), ch. 6.

Torres Strait Light Infantry Battalion. For all the duties that local Indigenous men and women performed, they received little recognition or pay, primarily because they were not formally enlisted in the Australian armed forces.[8]

After the Second World War, once again veterans returned to the discriminatory policies and legislation operating across Australia. Yet the period from the end of the war through to the 1970s would see gradual reform to Indigenous affairs, with Second World War veterans some of the key activists for change. The military, too, reformed its policies gradually. Immediately after the war, commanders reinstated the rule about members being substantially of European origin or descent, meaning only a few Aboriginal or Torres Strait Islander men served in the British Commonwealth Occupation Force (BCOF) in Japan. In 1949, partly under pressure from Indigenous veterans and the Returned Sailors', Soldiers' and Airmen's Imperial League of Australia (currently Returned and Services League or RSL), the Army finally lifted its colour bar. The Air Force and Navy followed suit when the *Defence Act* was amended in 1951. Through the 1950s, while the services did not promote Indigenous enlistment, they did at least permit it on a case-by-case basis. Indigenous men served in the Korean War and Vietnam War; Indigenous women enlisted in the women's services. During the periods of National Service (1951–59 and 1964–72), Aboriginal people's status was ambiguous. Aboriginal people could always volunteer, but the *National Service Act* specifically exempted Aboriginal people from compulsory National Service. Yet the regulations accompanying the Act excluded many Aboriginal people of mixed descent from the definition of 'Aboriginal', making them indeed liable for National Service. There were inconsistent applications of the law across and within states. Notwithstanding internal and external pressure to remove discriminatory provisions from the *National Service Act*, the clauses remained on the books until the repeal of the Act in 1973.[9] The final discriminatory provisions of the *Defence Act*, exempting Aboriginal men from compulsory call-up in a time of war, were finally removed in 1992. Even while these latent discriminatory clauses were still in legislation, throughout the post-war era Aboriginal and Torres Strait Islander men and women served in all services, all conflicts and peacekeeping missions.

The Australian armed forces, functioning collectively as the Australian Defence Force (ADF) since 1976, have evolved in their policies and practices towards Aboriginal and Torres Strait Islander service since lifting the colour bar. Reports

---

8   See *No Bugles, No Drums*, produced by Debra Beattie-Burnett, directed by John Burnett, 49 min. Seven Emus Productions in association with Australian Television Network, 1990, videocassette; Osborne, *Torres Strait Islander Women and the Pacific War*.

9   See Noah Riseman, 'Equality in the ranks: The lives of Aboriginal Vietnam veterans', *Journal of Australian Studies* 36, no. 4 (December 2012): 411–426; Noah Riseman, 'The curious case of Mervyn Eades: National Service, discrimination and Aboriginal people', *Australian Journal of Politics and History* 59, no. 1 (2013): 64–80.

on the extent to which Indigenous service members reported racism vary across individuals, services and eras. One worrying pattern, though, is that reports from ex-service personnel suggest an increase in racism in the forces since the end of the Second World War. Those more likely to experience racism were those who served in the 1980s and 1990s, those with darker skin and those in non-combat units. Those men and women who experienced racial vilification recall that the ADF did not have adequate racial vilification rules until the 1990s. Since then, the ADF has actively implemented rules against racial vilification. In the new millennium, the ADF has also set up programs to recruit Aboriginal and Torres Strait Islander members and has been an active proponent of Reconciliation.[10] The 2011 ADF census reported that 1.7 per cent of Army, 1.6 per cent of Navy and 0.8 per cent of Air Force members identified as Aboriginal or Torres Strait Islander, constituting 1.4 per cent of the total ADF. This equates to over 700 serving members of the permanent ADF.[11] A more comprehensive history of Indigenous service since the Second World War is available in the monograph *Defending Country: Aboriginal and Torres Strait Islander Military Service since 1945*, co-authored with Richard Trembath.

The story of Aboriginal and Torres Strait Islander military service is about more than just wars, rules and regulations, ranks, homecomings and statistics. It is about people. It is about lives and experiences: motivations to serve, employment opportunities, mateship, prejudice, readjustment, post-traumatic stress disorder, family, interactions with civilian Australia and community. This book presents a snapshot of life stories of the thousands of Aboriginal and Torres Strait Islander men and women who served in the armed forces during the post–Second World War era. The histories are presented in the storytellers' own words, expressing their own reflections about their lives and the role military service played. Some of these stories are confronting, such as the trauma witnessed in war zones or abusive childhoods as members of the Stolen Generations. Other stories are inspiring, revealing Indigenous ex-servicepersons contributing to community development at the grassroots or national level. Many of these stories of military service are not about conflict, as there were many men and women who served in the Australian armed forces in non-combat roles or during eras when Australia was not engaged in overseas conflicts. These eight life stories cannot be said to represent all Aboriginal and Torres Strait Islander ex-service experiences.

---

10   See Noah Riseman, 'Racism, Indigenous people and the Australian armed forces in the post–Second World War era', *History Australia* 10, no. 2 (2013): 159–179; Australia, Department of Defence, 'Defence Reconciliation Action Plan 2010–2014: Reconciliation through our people', December 2009, available from www.defence.gov.au/CODE/_Master/docs/drap/DRAP2010-14.pdf, accessed 14 September 2015; Australia, Department of Defence, 'Australian Defence Force Indigenous Employment Strategy 2007–17', available from www.defence.gov.au/fr/publications/ADF%20IES%20-%20External%20Version_04Dec08.pdf, accessed 3 July 2012.
11   Australia, Department of Defence, 'Department of Defence Census 2011 public report', Canberra, Roy Morgan Research, May 2012, 44.

They were chosen, though, because they present multiple perspectives on military service and draw from diverse backgrounds: men, women, Aboriginal, Torres Strait Islander, Army, Navy, Air Force, veterans of Vietnam, Gulf War, Somalia, East Timor, peacetime.

Sharing stories and learning about Aboriginal and Torres Strait Islander histories is at the heart of the Reconciliation process. Service in the armed forces has been a shared history between Indigenous and non-Indigenous Australians, yet it was not necessarily an experience universally the same. Through learning about Indigenous service people's life stories, we can understand both the common bonds between Indigenous and non-Indigenous diggers and the ways that Aboriginal and Torres Strait Islander servicemen and women experienced military life differently. The stories in this book are only one contribution to a much wider process of sharing histories. Hopefully they will generate more discussions about Aboriginal and Torres Strait Islander military history and add to the ongoing awakening of non-Indigenous Australians to that past.

2

Community Advocate

Mabel Quakawoot[1]

Mabel Quakawoot is a Baialai (Byele) and South Sea Islander woman. Like so many other black women raised during the assimilation era, she had few employment options and worked as a domestic servant after she left school. It was the retired RAAF pilot whom Mabel worked for that inspired her to sign up for the Women's Royal Australian Air Force (WRAAF) in 1957. She left the WRAAF when she married and raised a family in Mackay, Queensland. After her children were old enough, Mabel became involved in many community initiatives, particularly around education for disadvantaged youth. In 2014, after this interview, she was elected to the Working Party for the National Australian South Sea Islander People. Her story provides insights not only into how Indigenous women experienced life in the armed forces but also how the armed forces often represented an escape from domestic service and the limitations imposed on Aboriginal women in assimilation-era Australia. It is also the life story of a humble person, happy to give back to all members of her community – South Sea Islander, Aboriginal, Torres Strait Islander, and non-Indigenous.

---

1   This interview was recorded in Mackay, Queensland, on 5 June 2011.

I was born in 1937; I'm now [2011] 74 years of age and still going. Growing up, we lived on a farm outside of Rockhampton that was given to my grandfather on my mother's side after he came over here as an indentured labourer. The people gave the farm to him when they left to go back to England. He could not own the farm because he was an indentured labourer, so he had to then put it in the names of his children; the farm is still in our name to this day. He was called an alien. If he had died without family he would have been just an alien. A lot of the people who came from the Pacific Islands were aliens and died as aliens, and were buried in the alien part of the cemeteries. He managed not to be sent back when a lot of the other Pacific Islanders were because his family was here and his last boss didn't want him sent back. He put in an affidavit to say that this man was very good and he wanted him to stay in Australia.[2]

My grandparents were from Vanuatu. My mother's father came from Pentecost Island and my father's father came from Tanna Island in the Pentecost group in Vanuatu. My [maternal] grandfather, he went to his grave with great big whip marks all across him, but they didn't speak of it. The last person that owned him didn't whip him. My father's father was also like that, but he was a good horseman. Therefore, instead of working in the cane fields like my mother's father did, he was with the cattle. He drove with the cattle and things like that. He married an Aboriginal lady; therefore we have the two bloods running through our veins. He mixed with a lot of Aboriginal people because his wife was Aboriginal, but we grew up mainly with my mother's family; therefore we were brought up mainly South Sea Islanders. We went to visit our grandparents, my father's mother and father. We went, but they were a lot older because my father was 20 years older than my mother. But you wouldn't have noticed that they were 20 years apart. We were mainly with my mother's family.

My father was born in Gladstone, on Boyne Island. They lived on Boyne Island and went to school from there. At the present moment that's the island that is our grandmother's ancestral place – Curtis Island, where they're putting all the great big gas things now, which is very sad because they've ruined the island. We brought some bones back from Scotland to bury on that island. That is our burial grounds, but we don't get buried there.

My family life as a child was loving, strict, and we knew that we couldn't be disobedient. I was the eldest of nine; there were seven girls and two boys. It gives you extra responsibilities and they still make sure that the responsibilities are there. I still have to make decisions for all of us now. Whether they take my

---

2   For a history of the South Sea Islander labour trade in north Queensland, see Tracey Banivanua-Mar, *Violence and Colonial Dialogue: The Australian-Pacific Indentured Labor Trade* (Honolulu: University of Hawai'i Press, 2007); Raymond Evans, Kay Saunders and Kathryn Cronin, *Race Relations in Colonial Queensland: A History of Exclusion, Exploitation and Extermination*, 3rd ed. (St Lucia, Qld: University of Queensland Press, 1993), 147–234.

decision or not is another thing, but they run it past me and that's as it's always been. I had a lovely, lovely childhood. A lot of people looked at us like we were snobbish, but we weren't snobbish. It was just our father was very strict and we had to do things properly. I knew that when I went into the Air Force, I couldn't shame my family. I respected my family right to the hilt because Dad taught us that no matter where you are, you still have family and you still have people who care for you. That's how he brought us up, every one of us, and we still care for each other – each and every one of us, together.

I went to school on a horse. If we didn't put the horse in – and there used to be three or four on a horse going to school – we had to walk and it would be about four miles. We went to school with no shoes on. It was a one teacher school and there were mainly all South Sea Island kids. There would be about two or three white children in the school and we were taught by a white teacher. I only went as far as what would now be grade 10, but it was scholarship. I did my scholarship and I passed that. I loved school; out of the nine of us, not one of us did not like school. Dad made sure that we were all educated, even if he had 'seven bloody girls', as he used to say.

We learnt all the needlework and everything like that because when my mother was growing up that was all that was taught to her mother, so she taught it to all her children. But we didn't do any weaving like they did because my mother's father didn't learn anything from any Aboriginals because there was a distinction between the two races, which I found very hard. It still exists today in certain parts of the areas even though they have now intermarried a lot, with white as well as with the other cultures. But we're accepted in, if we wish to be accepted. I'm not saying that everyone accepts you. They accept you if you wish to be accepted, and we accept them if they wish to be accepted. That's a distinction I'd like to make between the coloured races because in Mackay there are the three different races. There's South Sea Islander, Torres Strait Islander and Aboriginal, and the three races live quite harmoniously together, but we don't tread over each other's lines.

Tradition from the South Sea Islands was important to us. My grandfather took a piece from my ear and he put it in my hand.[3] He did that because he was the eldest, my mother was the eldest, and I was the eldest. So that came down to the eldest one in each family. I didn't do it to my daughter even though she was the eldest too. Being South Sea Islanders there were certain parts of Joskeleigh that we were not allowed to walk, because they had devil men. We were very respectful of where we went.

---

3 Mabel is describing a South Sea Island cultural practice where her grandfather removed a small piece of flesh from her ear.

Community life was fantastic. Everyone looked out for each other. They weren't backward in rousing on you and telling you, 'You're a naughty girl and you better not do that because I'll tell your mother'. We had a lovely life. Christmases were all spent all together; families came. At night-time, before the Christmas dinner, we went to different friends, or friends came to us. Lunchtime on Christmas was always just family only. We used to go fishing and swimming and those things because we lived just outside of Rockhampton at a little place called Joskeleigh. It's quite well known in the South Sea Islander circles and in any history books.

Yes, there was racism, but we were always told that it was their bother not ours because we couldn't help how we were born, what colour we were. There was no use losing our tempers over it. I was very fast and I went to run in races, but this fellow took exception to me being dark. He said that he didn't want his daughter to travel with the nigger on the train, so I was left out of that and I never went back to run again. I was 14. I didn't run, but his daughter didn't make the team either. I remember another incident when my sister was walking home from school and this little girl said, 'Oh! You're a blackfella'. My sister said, 'Oh well! At least I'm black all over not speckled and spotted like you'. It was a little red-headed girl that had freckles all over her face. The girl ran home and told her father and he came tearing down and wanted to give my sister a hard smack. That was one thing that stood out in my mind, but otherwise there was nothing that I can remember. Even in the Air Force, I seemed to have been accepted by all – except when some American airmen came over and they didn't want to sit in the mess with a nigger. The Commanding Officer told them that they could go down to the hangar and their meals would be sent down there – and they did.

My father used to work at the meatworks and my mother, before she got married, used to do housework for different areas, like station owners. When she got married, that just ceased altogether because you were not allowed to work when you were married. The same applied when I got married. I could have gone and had a job at Qantas, but my husband said, 'No. No one else's wife is working'. That was years later, 20 years after my mother stayed at home. We owned our own home, which was very prestigious for black people to own their own home in that day and age. Mum had a beautiful carpet on the floor and beautiful lounge chairs. My father was very proud of that home. We helped, my brother and I, to pay for that house because we went to work early.

My father worked in the meatworks nearly all his life. I can remember when the Depression was on, he'd go away from home and he'd stay away. When the Second World War was on – I was about five – Mum was home with whatever kids there were; I think there were four of us then. The Americans came around to have their way with her, I suppose. But she had a double-barrelled shotgun; she just would stand there and tell them to go. One night, these white Americans came to rattle the door and it was an old wooden door that had a bolt thing that you just bolted in. She just let one barrel of the shotgun go at the door, and they never came back anymore.

There were a lot of young dark girls that had babies to the white Americans, but they wouldn't allow the black Americans to go anywhere near anyone. Well, this is what I surmised later on when I joined the Air Force because that was still the same attitude that the white Americans had. I don't think that most of the relationships between the Americans and South Sea Islanders were consensual because they were not seen out together. They weren't out walking together anywhere. As a child you don't know that this is being implanted in your brain, but it gets implanted in your brain to do that. The children of white American men and South Sea Islander women were accepted by the community, yes. But if they did something wrong they'd say, 'Oh, that half is American'. You wouldn't let the mother hear you saying that. So, I suppose there was a little bit of racism within there, but if the girl was in trouble they would help the girl, or the boy.

After I left school I did housekeeping for about four years in Rockhampton because they didn't believe that dark people could understand reading and writing and be in an office. I wished I had gone and challenged them, but that would be cheeky of me in those days. They gave me very menial tasks, like scrubbing the floors and washing the walls and making beds and things like that, which I did quite happily. There were two lots then: there were the rich and the poor. There was no in-between. The white people that were there, they were like us. They'd go out and have to work, and they had the same menial tasks if they were classed as poor people by the ones who had money. That's all they allowed them to do. Well that's how I saw it anyway.

Until I joined the Air Force at about 19 years old in January 1957, I went to work for these really nice people. One was a fighter pilot in the Second World War and he was the one who gave me the incentive. He said, 'You have enough brains to join the Air Force', and I heard that; I thought it was quite funny, but it was really great because they believed in me, even though I didn't believe in what I was doing. I put in an application to join and I had to have an aptitude test. I passed my aptitude test and so I was in the Air Force. My father reacted with, 'You can't be true!' He said, 'They don't take blackfellas in the Air Force. Army, yes, but not in the Air Force'. I said, 'Well I have been accepted to go and do an aptitude test'. Then, when I was accepted it was just unreal. My father could not believe it. I think that in his mind, the girls who went and joined the services were bad girls – they'd go to bed with anyone or whatever. That was in his mind, but it was never like that. I think he felt like that because you were going into a white man's world; he thought that you were just fair play for the white man. He never ever said it, but that's what I thought was going through his mind. He wanted to protect me more than anything else. In those days it was 21 years of age that you had to be before you could join, or sign any forms. The Aboriginal people didn't even have the vote. I went and I forged my father's signature and I got in – and he never knew. He would be very angry if he found out! My brothers and sisters thought I was mad because I was going away from home. But that was it.[4]

I did not know what I was getting myself into. The fighter pilot I worked for didn't talk about that. He just said, 'You've got the brains to join something'. He said, 'Scrubbing floors is too menial'. He just thought that I was bright and he planted the seed and it grew. When I joined the Air Force we had to have tests to see what mustering we would come under. I came under a mustering of a teleprinter operator – that's like a telegraphist. I worked with signals. I heard later from a cousin of mine that was in the Air Force who said, 'You must have mustered one of the highest musterings'. I said, 'Well, I didn't know'. When we sat for our aptitude tests in Brisbane, I passed and then we went to join the Air Force. You had to sit to see what mustering you went into and because they don't know who you are, you just send this form in and you're just given a number. So my number came up that I passed and that's where I was sent: to Ballarat to do signals. It didn't worry me because I just thought that was great.

At training I remember marching. Marching was something that you had to do. You had to make sure you carried everything in your left hand because you had your right hand to salute. Your shoes had to be polished and the seams on your stockings had to be straight and all these things. Then after six months, they became second nature to you; you just did it. You also had to do chores, like making sure your beds were made. We learnt how to make bed rolls in case there was a war and all these things. But, you know, I thoroughly enjoyed it. Men had to go through the same training if they came into the signals; the men did the same as the women. But there were other things that women were not allowed to do, like go down to the hangar and they weren't allowed to fly the planes. But they had women transport drivers. They had to pass a very rigid test; they had to learn how to change a wheel and all that. But they weren't allowed to touch the aircraft, from what I can remember.

Life in the Air Force was getting up and making sure everything was done properly because if you didn't you'd get confined to barracks. I went through to Point Cook to do four weeks and then we went to Ballarat to do the radio training. We were there for six months and that's when we had to learn everything.

---

4   The Women's Royal Australian Air Force (WRAAF), formed in late 1950, was the successor to the Second World War Women's Auxiliary Australian Air Force (WAAAF). Women were employed in WRAAF in non-combat roles to free up male labour. The WRAAF was disbanded in 1977 as women were integrated in the regular Air Force. There is currently no published history of the WRAAF, but the history of the WAAAF is available from Joyce Thomson, *The WAAAF in Wartime Australia* (Melbourne: Melbourne University Press, 1991); Clare Stevenson and Honor Darling (eds), *The WAAAF Book* (Sydney: Hale & Iremonger, 1984).

We had to learn to type and to do every single thing to go into the field. Five of us completed the whole thing. We women were not allowed to train with the men, who were training in a different building. We had a very strict, nasty fellow that was on top of us. He was just nasty, as if women were just awful, but we used to play tricks on him. We'd wait outside until the last minute and his face would be all red because he was coming in. Then we'd hide the papers so we couldn't type, and silly things like that. There'd be no typing paper or we'd hide the thing across the top of the keys so you couldn't see the keys. There was no such thing as electric typewriters. You had to use those old ones that you had to press and you had to memorise the keys, so we'd hide those things to cover the keys. He'd be just ropable; he'd just go ballistic. We put a pair of fluorescent women's scanties up on the flagpole one Monday night and we had a full dress parade on the Tuesday morning. The poor orderly sergeant pulled the pants down to change the flag from the ensign to the full flag. He nearly freaked when the pants came down because we had all the bigwigs there on parade in Canberra. He just ripped the pants from the line and the boys got into trouble for putting the pants on the line – and we didn't. We didn't say a word! It was fun. And then the strangest part about it? After that, my sister went and married his son. She was in Canberra as a dental assistant and she met his son down there. Oh, it was really interesting.

At the barracks in Ballarat there were administration people too and I would say, in all, there would have been about 27 women and there would have been almost 1,000 men. The women all lived in the same quarters and we had a great big sergeant; she was big in size, as well as big in voice. She would make sure that we were all in bed every night. She just looked after her trainee WRAAFs as if we were her little chickens. It was really great fun, but she was very strict. She wouldn't allow any rot or anything like that to go on. When we went to the mess to eat, the women had a separate area to eat in.

I remember one story – I hadn't gotten my posting as yet and a friend of mine had been posted to somewhere in Melbourne, but she didn't have a suitcase. She took my suitcase to take her clothes away and then she sent me a telegram to say that she'd put it on the train to come back. I was in the post office with this telegram and this fellow came in and said to me, 'Oh, you've got a telegram. What's it about?' Now this was a training station and I thought, 'Top Secret'. So I said, 'Oh, it's just to tell me that I'd won the Golden Casket in Queensland'. I think it was £15,000 at that time. He said, 'What!?' I said, 'Yes, I did'. Then I had to go off as we were having a top-secret viewing in a theatre of what not to do. They were looking for me all over the base. The Commanding Officer even had the press come out to interview me and when they found me, they said, 'Quick, quick, quick, the Commanding Officer wants to see you'. I went down to the office and he said, 'Come in, come in. You've won all this money'. I looked at him and I said, 'What?!' He said, 'Yes, you've won all this money'. I said, 'No, I haven't. I just told this private bloke that I'd won this money because he was sticky-beaking into my business'. He said, 'Well, I better go and send the press away'. I said, 'What? You've got the press out here?' He said, 'Yes, to take your photo and everything because you've won all this money'. I said, 'Oh my goodness gracious. That's ridiculous!' I just shot out. When we went to tea that night I had many proposals of marriage; it was not funny. I was so embarrassed because it was just a lie. One fellow had his meal coming along and he was looking over at me and making eyes at me. We had big poles in the middle of the mess and he walked into the mess pole with all his soup and everything went everywhere. Oh, it was shocking. It was terrible. I felt terrible and they said, 'Well, it serves you right for telling lies'. I said, 'No. That fellow was sticky-beaking and this is supposed to be a top-secret area'. So yes, it was fun. But the funniest part about it was that I was the only dark person there.

After about six months in Ballarat, a recruit arrived who couldn't sew. They gave her this pair of shorts that was too long for her legs, so she couldn't run. Seeing as I could sew, I stitched them up quickly. One side was coming out and I was telling her it was coming out, but she was running along and crying because she got homesick so much. She said, 'These shorts are coming undone'. I said, 'Well, pull the whole lot down'. It was so funny. She was running because we had to get all these needles and then we had to go and do exercises; she was the person who had three left feet. I felt sorry for her. She was so uncoordinated, but she's a lovely person. She married the cook from Canberra and then he joined the police force. Some of the WRAAF that I was in, there were women who married men from the Air Force.

The only time I went out with the men was when there were six or eight of us all going out together. I never, ever went with one of them by myself – only when they took me on a special coffee trip, because I would trust those people. I think I still have the thought of my mother shooting that door. The men always wanted to be seen with me in uniform in town. It was a thing with them. It was a little pet thing that I just went along with because I used to have my coffee and have a meal and go out for dinner. I thoroughly enjoyed it. It was something new for them. It was really strange, but I could get a nice meal in town without having the mess food. I was being treated differently not because of the race, but because of the colour. There was one fellow whose family had a cattle station or something. While I was in Canberra, he used to like to take me to the big top restaurants in there because his family had a cattle station. He'd just say, 'Watch their faces. Watch their faces'. I'd get dressed up to the nines and the two of us would walk in and everyone would turn around and look. He said, 'Oh geez, I just love that'. But they were really nice people.

The women were never an issue. In those days, you were not allowed to be in the Air Force as a lesbian. You had to get out straightaway and all that sort of thing. We did have a couple of them, which to me, now when I look back, we were really shocked when we found out. We went into this meeting. I wasn't the only one thinking that we knew everything about sex, but we didn't know that. We didn't know about two men or two women. When we came up there was another girl from north Queensland who was with me and she said, 'Do you understand what they're talking about?' I said, 'I have no idea whatsoever'. She said, 'Are they telling us that … ?' I said, 'I don't know'. Then I thought, 'Well, how stupid'. This was just the two of us speaking after the meeting. She came to see me about 10 years ago and we sat and laughed about the silly things. We were so naive — and then there's real little innocent. They were telling us about the different sexual things that you could catch. We never had a clue because she grew up further north than I was and I think they were more backward than we were! As far as those sorts of things go, it was just husband and wife, and that was it. There was nothing else, until we came across it in the thing afterwards. We'd meet up, probably in Melbourne or Sydney somewhere, and they'd say, 'Oh, we've got two of those sorts of people in our place'. And they'd say, 'Yeah, but they don't touch you; do they?' I said, 'No. As far as I'm concerned, they're quite nice people'. It was part of the training to get us to understand homosexuality, but we didn't look at it as sexuality. We just looked at it as a thing that they were telling us about. It was really weird when I think of it now. I'd like to be a fly on the wall down in the barracks just to see — although maybe I wouldn't like to. The men had that training too, in separate things. These are raw kids from the bush; I suppose the city kids probably knew all about it, although maybe they didn't because everyone had a family life then, didn't they? Families were together in those days. If you joined the Air Force, you probably came from a good family.

But in the Air Force, I thoroughly enjoyed myself. We'd drive from Canberra to Sydney and have a whole weekend in Sydney. We wouldn't do the same things in Canberra as we did in Sydney because that was like home base and we didn't want the Air Force there to know. No one in Sydney knew who we were once we got all dressed up and we sprayed our hair and we wore all these clothes. We went out and we walked into this place in Queanbeyan. They started playing the song 'Beatnik Fly'. It's all about people called hippies now. Well, that's how we were all dressed — in all these sorts of clothes. This lady that was sitting at the next table to us said, 'I cannot stand these university types!' So the Air Force got away with something else. We used to have fun going out. We never, ever went to Duntroon, but to Fairbairn and the Navy base in Canberra we'd all go and have a party. The girls from Duntroon would go across to the Navy or come across over to our wet canteen and have a party there.

We were all friends together. We all played softball as the combined services. We played hockey, netball and that as combined services, but then we also still played those things against each other. The Army played the Navy and the Navy played the whatever, but then we'd combine all together. The thing was they'd choose a team out of there to play netball or hockey or softball or whatever. You had to have so many sports under your belt before you could get a blazer – and I got a blazer. I've still got the blazer at home, but it won't fit me now. I have fantastic memories from the sports because you made a lot of friends that were there for life. This lady came up to me in the street about 10 months ago and she said, 'Were you ever at Fairbairn Air Base?' I said, 'Yes'. She said, 'Oh, I was the Navy Madam'. Well, they were all madams. We didn't connect being a madam with anything rude because we were just so naive. There was one with really white hair who was the madam of all the Air Force in Australia. She was the 'head serang' and it was great because you'd never see her unless she was there at your air base to do an inspection.

I've only seen three of the crew that we were with in Ballarat since. I don't know who's died or who's still alive. I've seen a lot of the other ones who had other musterings, but we were the main ones. They used to call us the 'gaga' people because we couldn't talk about anything that we did at work. I remember when I had my first child, I went into hospital and this nurse came along and she said to me, 'Oh, you were in the Air Force, were you?' I said, 'Yes'. I was coming out of anaesthetic and she said, 'What did you do in the Air Force?' I said, 'Now, that would be telling'. I didn't say another thing about it and she said, 'My God. You must have been brainwashed'. I said, 'No, it's just preservation'.

I still can't say too much. Signals, yeah – I was in the Department of Air in Canberra. That is where I worked, taking and sending messages. The only other thing was if you didn't have your little card to leave, they'd ring the security. Like if you dropped it somewhere where you were working and you couldn't find it, they wouldn't let you out. You'd have to find your card before they'd let you out. That's how secretive it was. I think it's still like that. So when we met up with this friend of mine and the other fellow that was there with us that day, the three of us could talk freely. You see, when I got married, they sent me a telegram with all the coded messages and I had to decipher it to see what they said. Sort of silly things like that that you did that stayed within the signals area. It went to the people who you knew.

We were over in the Administrative Block in Canberra, opposite the Old Parliament House; the Army was there, the Air Force was next to it, and the Navy was over here and we were all in there. One time, one of the Army chaps decided to clean the machines and then he lit a cigarette afterwards. You were allowed to smoke inside then, and he lit a cigarette and everything just went up! Everything just went *schwoom* and this fire started. Then the Air Force got in it and they knew we had to cover everything first and lock it down before the photographers came in. The Navy had to do the same. Then we went to help the Army to see what needed doing there because that was where the fire was, but we closed all of ours up first. We had to crawl on the floor to get out because the smoke was thick, and we helped other people when we were out there because the fire had gone through. It was myself and this girl that came from up further north who did all those things automatically. We just did it and when we got outside, everything was fine. We helped everyone else and when everything was all over, both of us fainted. Oh, he did get into trouble; he would have because that was the Army. The senior men went in and made sure that everything was closed up before the photographers got in to take photos of the fire. They put us in hospital for a week. It was terrible. It could have been worse, but everything was done so quickly between the three services.

It was predominantly men, but we women were getting paid less. There wasn't anything we could do about it. Women do the same work as men; we had to do all the same things as the men. Everything; even when we moved across over to Russell Hill, next to Bugs Bunny. We used to call that big thing on the hill Bugs Bunny; that's the American War Memorial. The two women – there was only myself and this other girl from further north – the two of us had our times off together. Women could only do daytime work, not night-time work as the men did, so we were safe in that way. We were lucky. The men were very good to us. They treated us like ladies. They didn't treat us any different. They expected you to do exactly the same work as them. You had to pull your weight and everything, but when you were out you were ladies. You weren't WRAAF women. I found that so nice because when you were doing something and you didn't send a signal when you were supposed to, they would go mad on the men before they'd say, 'Did you send … ?' If you said, 'Yes', they'd say, 'God! He's an idiot'.

There was no gender discrimination at all except the lesser pay, yes. To me, there was a job to do and I did it – the same as before I was in the Air Force. If a job was given to you to do, you did it. We were asked by order and those were the things that I wished would come back now. Then there wouldn't be so much of this thing that went on in the Navy with the women,[5] because the men treated the women as ladies when they were out and they had respect for them

---

5   Mabel is alluding to the sexual abuse scandals that have engulfed the ADF and Australian Defence Force Academy since being broken in the media in April 2011. Since then, the ADF has conducted a series of reviews investigating abuse claims dating back to the 1940s. The most prominent reviews are Gary Rumble, Melanie McKean and Dennis Pearce: 'Report of the Review of Allegations of Sexual and Other Abuse in Defence: Facing the Problems of the Past', Canberra, 2011 (also known as the DLA Piper Review); Defence Abuse Response Taskforce, 'Report on Abuse in Defence', Canberra, 2014; Australian Human Rights Commission, 'Review into the Treatment of Women in the Australian Defence Force', vols 1 and 2, Canberra, 2011 and 2012, and follow-up audit reports.

as if they were their mothers. This is how I saw it then, but it was fun. It was fun because you'd come out and because there were only three girls in there; a female Army, a female Navy, and a female Air Force personnel. One was on the front desk; some of them were females and some of them were men. It sort of all depended, but they only had one female from each service on the desk. We went out many a time with the bigwigs with the big flash cars. You could get in the limousines because many a time they gave us a lift back to the base if it was raining, and the car pulled up right in front. It would be the Air Force ones that would give you a lift back and then they'd have to go back to their own base, but they were very nice to us.

The first time I ever saw someone being pulled by their feet off parade was in Canberra in front of the War Memorial. They had to go there and do a service and this fellow fainted; he was pulled off by his feet and Mr Menzies was there. I had quite a lot of encounters with politicians. They were all really nice people and none of them put you down. A lot of them liked to have a photo in there with the Air Vice Marshal Scherger. He's got an Air Force base named after him now: Scherger Air Force Base in the Northern Territory. He was very nice.

There was no racism at all – only coming home on the airplane on a civilian flight out of uniform because not many dark people flew in those days.[6] This air hostess came along and she said to me, 'Would you like a magazine to look at?' I'm a person with words and I said, 'Yes, thank you very much. I'll have something to read'. She just looked at me. That's the only sort of thing because you're out of uniform. They flew us home for free on the civilian planes in those days. I don't think they do it now. Our stamps were 1p each or half a penny each to be posted, whereas everyone else had to pay 5p or 3p or something like that to post a letter. My mother said that when she was writing to us, she'd only pay a half a penny to send the letter because it was to an Air Force base.

There were no dark men in the Air Force that I ever saw, even though I've read later that these men had been pilots. None of them were from Canberra at all and there were none in Ballarat that I saw. I was still the only one because it was unheard of. It was just unheard of, but there were some Aboriginal and Islander women and men in the Army. The minute there was a dark person, they'd want to team you up with that dark person. It was really strange when I got engaged to my husband. Everything had to stop. I had to be moved out of that area altogether and I had to be put in as a telephonist so that I wouldn't see any top-secret stuff going through. But anyway, that's beside the point. I knew that that had to happen, but the thing was when my husband came down to

---

6   For more information on racism in the armed forces during this era, see Noah Riseman, 'Racism, Indigenous people and the Australian armed forces in the post–Second World War era', *History Australia* 10, no. 2 (2013): 159–179.

visit – well, he was my fiancé then – the two of us went into the mess to have Christmas lunch because I couldn't get off for Christmas. It was like we were a pair of people from outer space. Everybody wanted to meet him. I'd consented to marry this fellow and he was darker than I am – very dark.

He was a cane cutter from the Solomon Islands and he had no other bloods in him; Colin was descended from indentured labour. I met him in Rockhampton while I was on leave because his cousin was going with my sister. He said, 'Oh, we're going down fruit picking in Victoria, so I'll come across and we'll see each other in Melbourne'. I said, 'Oh, rightyo'. So I went down to Melbourne and stayed at one of the barracks in Melbourne and we all went out together. When he came to pick me up, he asked me to go out by myself with him, even though he was with some friends from Rockhampton, and even though we had only just met in Rockhampton. I hadn't gone out with him by myself or anything yet. He asked me would I like to go out for tea that night and I said, 'Yes'. I think it was quite funny that he turned up to meet me and he had his shirt on inside out. Years later I said, 'Why did you turn your shirt inside out?' He said, 'You frightened the daylights out of me'. I said, 'Well, if I frightened the daylights out of you, why did you come and pick me up?' He said, 'No, I just wanted to get to know you better'. I said, 'Oh, rightyo'.

We didn't meet again until we got engaged. I went home on leave in September 1960 and he came down and we got engaged. We had a sleep-out on the veranda, but Mum and Dad couldn't have him sleeping out on the veranda outside my door (we had French doors on our house near my room). They decided to put his bed into this other part of the house and they got the bed stuck in the door. They approved of him, yes. Dad approved of him. Then we didn't see each other until he came down at Christmas time – that's when we went into the mess. Then we didn't see each other until the following September and in 1962 we got married. When we got engaged, all the people that he knew here in Mackay were questioned by the people from the Air Force. He's from Mackay and for security reasons they went and questioned everyone: his friends. We got married in May 1962. We'd only been out with each other seven times. The seventh time was when we walked down the aisle.

When I was married in 1962 we had to get out of the Air Force. As soon as I became engaged, I had to switch to be a telephonist; that just entailed having the old things on your ears and you plugged all the things in. Well, we weren't allowed to have the things on our ears because the Air Force thought that those things on our ears were bad for our brain because of the things going into your brain. You just had the speaker thing that hung on your neck and was here in front of you; you just plugged and plugged and did everything like that. There was none of these press buttons. It was manual work. I did that from the time that I was engaged until I was discharged. Then we moved to Mackay and I just stayed at home. Colin was a cane cutter and we lived on the cane farm that he worked on. I had my two children there, five years after we were married. Zelda was born in '67 and Gabrielle was born five years later in '72. My husband didn't want me to go to work. I didn't order him around. There was a strong thing that, 'Everyone else's wife is not working. You're not going to work'.

He's died now, so 43 years we were married. A lot of people thought that it wouldn't last because I'm such a bossyboots and he was so quiet, but then they don't know that his quietness hid something. I'm so loud and demanding and he's one of those quiet ones that just goes and does things quietly – one of those really nice men that wouldn't be nasty or anything. But he'd let it be known when he was not very pleased; he let you know quietly – not with words, but by actions. It's strange because he's one of those people that you'd look across the room and if he was ready to go, and I wasn't, he'd stay – and then you'd know that you've stayed over. He'd do the same to me and just by look we'd know that each other wanted to go home. It was a really weird relationship that one.

Both our girls went to uni and they're both teachers. I had praise about my eldest one. We had Sorry Day not so long ago and she gave a talk at the school about Sorry Day.[7] One teacher told another teacher who told me that it was the nicest Sorry Day speech that she has ever heard anyone give. She said, 'There was no blame. There was no putting down, nothing'. She said something about, 'Everyone is sorry. We are not sorry for one race and they're not sorry for us. Everyone is sorry. So, we'll just leave it at that' – or something to that effect. Like, today is the day that we should all say sorry for something that we have done nasty to someone else, not just for the Aboriginals to say nasty. She said, 'And coming from a dark person, all the teachers just couldn't believe it'. I said, 'Well, that's probably how she thinks'. She said, 'Well, the teacher was very impressed and so was the whole school'. I said, 'Oh, thank you very much'. Yes, when you hear things back like that about your children, you must have done something right, somewhere. I think their dad had the same idea when he heard good things.

When Gabrielle was going to school this job came up in a quarry. These friends of ours started this quarry and they wanted a Girl Friday, so I was Girl Friday. I'd run their kids to school, I'd work in the office; I'd do all the little bits and pieces, like going to pick up things that were needed. I became generally good friends with them. I am still good friends with their children to this day. That was the only time that I was allowed to go to work. My husband didn't

---

7   Sorry Day has been observed annually on 27 May since 1998, the first anniversary of the handing down of the *Bringing Them Home* inquiry into the Stolen Generations. It is a day for reflection about the historical mistreatment of Aboriginal and Torres Strait Islander people.

want me to apply for a job. That was just something that I did and from there I went on. When they left there, I didn't like the new fellow. I used to do the weighbridge, and carry the explosives and everything from town. When they left, this other fellow came in as the boss of the place and he was a nasty man. He was really, really nasty, but I stayed there because he wanted a girl to train for the office. So I trained this girl. He was nasty to her, too. I left then, after she was trained, and she left too when I left. Then I went in and this job came up to go and teach the special needs kids in about 1980.

It might have been '79 or something and then this job came up. You didn't have to have things in those days to say you'd been to university or anything like that, so I got this job teaching special needs kids. They went from small to 18 years old and then they had to leave. That was in a very special needs school; they had the slow children who could read, but they were slow readers. There were some very disabled ones there also. I did that for 21 years until they put all the special needs children into mainstream schools; I forget which year that was. That was the saddest day for those children, as well as for the teachers, because they put them in there and they were like kids in a zoo. The other kids who went to school were poking fun at them in the bigger schools. It was really sad. It's a bit better now, but the teachers in those high schools were not trained to be special needs teachers. That was one of the things that I think the government should have looked at before they moved them across. They just moved them across one Christmas holidays and just moved them over. I went and taught at the high schools then with the special needs kids. I taught them sewing, science, maths, English, and reading. I was like a personal aide to them in the mainstream schools. Then they gave me 10 or 12 kids to teach myself. I was so used to teaching them that they put them all together in my class and I had to take them to do all their work and everything. Those kids still remember me to this day. But, that was my job and I did it to the best of my ability. Even now, I get asked to go back and teach them, but that's only on a voluntary basis. To me, that was lovely.

Then I just left there and then I went to TAFE. After all this, I finished teaching one Friday afternoon and Monday morning I started at TAFE as a sewing, cooking and English teacher. I did that for seven years and then I decided I'd retire. I think I was 65, 66 years old. My husband was working at TAFE then because I told him that he couldn't be pushing these great big cane bins all his life. He got a job there as a cleaner and I said to him, 'Look, just looking at your report cards, you shouldn't be doing that. You've got a few more brains than that'. So he went there as a cleaner and learned the computers.

It was in 1967 when the Aboriginals had the Referendum; that was the year my first child was born. Before then, I was fighting for that. I signed a lot of papers in my time. I didn't march or anything, but I acknowledged that I wanted change for the Aboriginal people, like voting and things like that. That's what I wanted and I made people aware of it. Some people in Mackay here, and my husband also, didn't know what I was talking about. For instance, my sister also had a son in 1967 and she was down in Sydney in the hospital. By this time, she was a triple certificate nursing sister, and it was very bad down there in Sydney. They put her into this little back room out the back where all the rooms and everything were. They'd go out there and they'd talk about all these patients and everything; she'd know what they were talking about. So she said to her husband, who was a white person, 'Would you like to bring me in my certificates, please?' He said, 'Yes, rightyo. What, what do you want them for?' She said, 'Just bring them in, please'. She set them all up on her desk and the nurses came in, then the doctor came in and they all had a look. They moved her directly from there into another room that was much nicer because they realised that she could understand everything that they were talking about because she was a triple certificate sister. She'd done midwifery and general nursing, and those sorts of things in the operating theatre. That was her part with the racism – sort of subtle racism.

I still say that subtle racism continues here in Mackay. It's the little subtle things, like I went to the bank just after I was married. I went into this branch and the girl behind the counter kept serving all the white people before she served me. When I went up to the desk to wait for her to serve me, she'd serve the next person who came in. I just said to this other lady, 'Excuse me? Is this the manager's office? Just here?' She said, 'Yes'. So I just walked in. I pushed the door open and I said, 'Excuse me, don't you serve dark people in this bank?' He said, 'What?' I said, 'I've been waiting out there for almost an hour or more to be served and the girl there is serving every other person who is white before me'. So he came out. At that time, I had little jobs that I did. I was cleaning in the bank and saving money because my daughter had just been born. I was saving money to put away for her education. The thing is, he came out and he said, 'Oh, it can't be'. I said, 'Well, just watch'. So I went back out and stood there. He was watching as she served people before she served me. He walked out and told her to pack her things; she had to now go because he didn't want that sort of thing causing racism in his bank. She looked at me and she started crying because I'd reported her – but she wouldn't serve me. She wouldn't even listen to me when I said that I was next. I felt sorry for her, but I'm hoping that it taught her a lesson. That's all I can say about that. That's the first lot of racism I'd seen here in Mackay, but after that I didn't have any. Oh well, I can't help it. I was born black. I can't help that.

When I first went to teach at the high schools, this Year 8 boy came in and he looked at me and said, 'I just can't stand blackfellas'. I just looked at him and I said, 'That's your problem, not mine'. After that, I took him right through school. He was one of the special needs kids that couldn't read properly and I took him right through grade 10 or grade 11 and did all the things with him. I taught him to spell, taught him to do his homework, taught him to write essays and do all those things. I'd completely forgotten about him after he left school, and one day I was waiting for my husband at TAFE and I saw him and he asked me if I came there every day. I said, 'Yes. I come to wait for my husband'. About a week later he bought me a great big bunch of flowers with chocolates and everything in it and he said, 'If it wasn't for you, I wouldn't be where I am today. Thank you very much'. He was an only child. I always say that racism is learnt; it's learnt from home or wherever it's learnt from. I've seen him since and he came and introduced me to his wife and his children. You're just thankful that I wasn't nasty back to him because I could have been. I could have reported him and he would have been in big trouble, maybe. Yeah, but that's a bit of racism that I got from the school kids. The only other time was when my children went to the primary school and when they went to high school. My daughter said to this girl, 'Oh, have you seen so-and-so?' – they were looking for this girl. And this girl just turned around and looked at her and said, 'Well, is she black or is she white?' My daughter was shocked. She said, 'Mum, I never thought of people either black or white.' She said, 'They just had a name and that's their name'. I said, 'Well, there are all kinds to make the world'.

I became active in the schools, fighting for the Aboriginal kids in the schools. Like a lot of schools, they decided they'd have all the Aboriginal kids there because the Aboriginal kids got money to go to school. That went to do projects for them, but a lot of the schools kept the money and spread it across the schools, which I didn't like. A lot of the parents were not really good money managers. I'm not trying to put them down or anything; I'm saying a truth. There were a lot of white people that were not good money managers, too. The Aboriginals were more or less brought to the fore, to show them up. At the special school, I took the money from the kids and put it into a trust fund in the bank, so that when they wanted to go away on trips they could go on trips. We had to go through all the proper channels to do this, but they had their own sleeping bags, they had their swimming togs, they had their towels, they had everything. We kept it there at the special school so that when things came up that they had to go on, we had the things there and they could go and we paid their fare. We paid everything. At the end of the year, they could have that money back. They had money to spend at Christmas, whether Mum got it or Dad got it or whomever, but that was their money and we gave it back to them. We'd start again the next year. I was called horrible names by the dark people because I did this to them. Because see, Mum or Dad was taking the money and going to put it on the pokies or something. I knew that, so I just decided to do it this way, so as those kids have something. It was tough love. That's because I wanted them to have the same opportunities that I had. My parents never held back on anything.

When it was my mother's turn to make a cake to raise money for our hockey association, she'd make the cake. She wouldn't come, so we'd take the cake and raffle the cake. She used to make beautiful sponge cakes and everyone – even from the other clubs – would come and want to buy her sponge or her ticket in the raffle. I wanted the kids to have the same opportunity – especially the dark kids that were handicapped because they had a harder job to hoe.

We sent our children into a town school, a big school that had 500 or 600 children, rather than send them to the school down the road that had 20 kids or so. We could have sent them down there, but when they went to high school, they would find it very tough because they were nurtured there in the small school. My husband said, 'Oh, you're mad! I went to the same school, you know?' I said, 'No'. In this day and age, they have one mark against them before they even start and that's being black, but they can't deny you your brains. If you've got your brains, you're up there with the best of them. If you can use your brains to the best of your ability, you go for it! It doesn't matter what colour you are or anything. I think that's what got me into the Air Force in the first place – because this fellow had told me that I had enough brains to get in. Well, that's why we sent our children into a big school to start off with. Still, when my daughters went to university, they said that I had kept them wrapped in cotton wool, because going to a big town was entirely different than staying here in Mackay.

I would like to have one of my children join the Air Force. The youngest one went and did Air Cadets for about six years and she became pretty high in the Air Cadets. When it was the last year she wanted to join the Air Force. She went from here to Townsville to do the final Air Cadets. She went up to the Air Force base in Garbutt in Townsville and she passed everything, but they wouldn't let her join because she was only 16. She said, 'Well, I'm the same person as what I'll be when I'm 18'. Still, they wouldn't let her join. She said, 'Well, they can stick it', and just walked away and left it. She finished and she went down and did science at the university in Brisbane and became a teacher.

The Aboriginal kids these days don't know the fights that the dark people went through to get them to where they are now. They had Sorry Day. They have Reconciliation and all this sort of business. I even fought for the Reconciliation for the South Sea Islanders and things like that. I'm one of those people that doesn't like being at the forefront. I like to be just doing things and helping them raise some money so as the ones who were the leaders can go and do it. I'm really like that. The protest that I had when they put out the bicentenary book in 1988 is that there's not one mention of Aboriginals in the diary book. The only person that's mentioned that's black was a fellow that came out on a boat. He was an American Negro. I've kept the book, just so I could see the racism that went on and that's what I didn't like. Otherwise, I went and did my voting. I was a quiet protester. That's what I was because my husband was a Solomon Islander and he didn't like those things. But myself, with my father being Aboriginal and South Sea, I had to stand for my rights. I quietly did it, without making a big show.

My one scream was when [Queensland Premier] Anna Bligh gave Curtis Island to the mining companies and they said that the Aboriginals and the companies have all come into an agreement. I thought to myself, 'Well, I never saw any bill of sale for that land. There is no bill of sale, is there?' They're frightened to do what the Americans have done. They've given their [Native American] land back with an apology and that is their land, whereas the Aboriginals have to sign what they call Indigenous Land Use Agreements (ILUAs).[8] It's not even worth the paper that it's on because once that's been signed, the mining companies just move in and take it. It is ridiculous. The sooner there's a fight for that, I will march for that. I don't want these mining companies in here because they are ruining the land of the Aboriginals. I would fight against them because I'm a director with the Port Curtis Coral Coast Corporation. I went to this meeting and I asked the LNG companies, 'Now, excuse me. How much will it be making in approximately a month?' They were giving us $2 million for down in Gladstone as a one-off thing and they would make $16 billion a month. They're raping our country and I told that man that was sitting there, 'Do you mean to tell me that you're paying us $2 million? You're raping our country and you're taking $16 billion out?' I said:

> For that money, I would like to see hospitals, schools, accommodation and everything like that in the areas where you are for elderly people, for homeless, for all the Australian people. It may be that we have to sign the ILUAs, but that land is used also by white people, Chinese, whatever. We're all Australians, and you're here working for this great big conglomerate and taking our money, our resources and selling it overseas and giving us peanuts. We're not monkeys.

I sat down and the whole hall of about 200 people just screamed. I felt so embarrassed, but I was so angry at the time that this LNG Company was doing this.

The whole meeting was filled up with Aboriginals as well as native title people, South Queensland Native Title. Now, why did we have to have native title land use? Why? We can't own it. It just annoys me. It's all very good for how they go on, but that's something I will fight for. If I have to get up and go and lead someone now, I would do that. I'm just so passionate about it now. I was quietly involved on a personal level in native title in the 1990s. I was with their cause, but I didn't march or become seen. I made sure that I became involved. I knew

8   ILUAs were an initiative of the Howard Government since amendments to the *Native Title Act* in 1998. For more information, see www.nntt.gov.au/ILUAs/Pages/default.aspx.

[Eddie Koiki] Mabo; I knew his wife and I gave them my support for all that [*Mabo* native title case]. Even though my husband and I have different ideas of it, I gave my support. In the end, my husband came around to seeing what I was pushing for. I was pushing for land rights, for recognition. After Mabo won recognition, I became more active after that.[9]

Otherwise, my husband and I were very vocal in the South Sea Islanders organisations, but we didn't go and do the things. There were three ladies and two men that were the ones in the forefront. We supported them. We raised money. We did all the things for them. This would be in the '80s and '90s. It might have been the end of the '70s. To this day, I am still active in that. I go off to things that my daughters do. They're in the two camps; they go for the South Sea Islanders as well as the Aboriginals. There's no one thing for better or for worse. But they lean more towards the Aboriginal rights because they think that the South Sea Islanders got up and they did things. They moved forward quicker because they were made to talk. They brought them over here; they had nowhere else to go, so therefore they were kept down. They had to learn English quicker than the Aboriginals were. The Aboriginals had run away into the bush. The South Sea Islanders had nowhere to run, so that's why they were kept down. They were downtrodden. We built a grass hut out here with all the artefacts in it. We put in all the artefacts for the South Sea Islanders. I tried to help with the Aboriginals and Torres Strait Islanders, but they decided that they were doing it their way. They classed me as a South Sea Islander because I'm married to a Solomon Islander. I don't mind that, but anywhere I can help, I help.

I've only sat on the Murri Court as an Elder twice.[10] In town here, when the young children go in you don't treat them with kid gloves because they're streetwise. You don't hold their parents up as an example of what they should do. But then Aboriginal people didn't like me telling them that because they see me as a South Sea Islander. Those are the little things that I wish I could overcome in their minds. I said what I wanted to say to those children and the other people didn't like it. The Aboriginals didn't like it at all. I'd been up to Townsville to the juvenile courts up there. One little boy came over and he said, 'Can I call you Granny?' I said, 'You may call me Granny', and he came

---

9   The 1992 *Mabo* ruling established native title rights in Australia, which are particular types of rights over land by virtue of traditional occupation since before colonisation. For more information about the *Mabo* ruling and developments to native title since 1992, see Lisa Strelein, *Compromised Jurisprudence: Native Title Cases since Mabo*, 2nd ed. (Canberra: Aboriginal Studies Press, 2009).

10   The Murri Court was established in 2002 as a way for Indigenous Elders to have a role in the sentencing process for particular Indigenous offenders in Queensland. The Newman Liberal National Government scrapped the Murri Court in 2012, though the new Labor Premier Annastacia Palaszczuk reinstated it in Queensland's 2015 budget. See Anthony Morgan and Erin Lewis, 'Evaluation of the Queensland Murri Court: Final Report', AIC Reports Technical and Background Paper 39 (Canberra: Australian Institute of Criminology, 2010).

and snuggled up. He was just 10 years old. It was really, really sad, because that boy came from Doomadgee and that's way up in the Gulf. I wanted to know why was this 10-year-old boy in gaol. What bad thing could a 10-year-old boy do? Why did the judge send him to gaol? Why didn't they take him away from wherever he was there and put him into foster care in another town somewhere? Or something like that? Because they'd taken him from all loving kindness and all that is 10 years old. But that's not for me to decide. Those people that are the great big Aboriginal activists who are lobbying the government for all this money and land, and fighting all the wild rivers or whatever it is, they should go in there and fight for those kids and find out the reason why those kids are in there. They say they want to save the children. Well, why not look in the gaols for the 10-year-old and the 12-year-old? That's my fight, anyway.

The mothers and fathers of the South Sea Islander children look after them, but they're mixing with the wrong type of kids through the courts. There are a lot of South Sea Island kids going through the courts now as adults. You see very few of them going through as children. You see them going through as adults, like 19 or 20-year-olds. Whether they're nine years old or 29 years old, they all need love and acceptance. If you don't give those people that, they're going to go and do wrong things again, no matter whether you're black or white. You have to have acceptance by society.

I remember one time that these skinheads were walking down the street and my youngest daughter said, 'Mum, quick. Get in the car. These are skinheads and they don't like black people'. I looked at these boys walking down and I said, 'All those boys, they can't read and write. And the whole thing is, they join together as a group and that's what they do because they can't read and write. All they can do is go and cause havoc everywhere'. They walked past and they said, 'Oh, hello, Mrs Quakawoot. How are you today?' My daughter looked at me and she said, 'Mum!' I said, 'They all went to special school, darling'. It's like that was because they didn't have anyone to really continue that niceness to them. They'd learn a bit of school and then they'd get moved into another class. That's why I'm teaching reading and writing skills to kids at home now. So that when they get into school, they don't have to sit there at high school and think, 'What is the teacher talking about?' Like me with that woman who was giving this sexual talk about lesbians; at least they'll know what the teacher is on about – not that I teach them about lesbians! I want them to know the reading and the writing of things because no matter what – even if you are good at maths – you still have to read something to learn about that math or that sum.

I'm currently doing this Certificate IV in Business and Governance. I want to ask if I can go into the Indigenous communities to find all the adult people who are illiterate and if I can set up classes in those communities so long as they pay my fare and my accommodation. I don't care if I don't get a wage because I get the pension. I would go into those areas and I would teach them. These are things that Aboriginal leaders should be looking at: teaching adult literacy into these places so as those mothers and fathers can understand what their children are learning. If the mothers and fathers don't know, they can't teach the kids. They have most of the waking days at school. If it isn't in them at home, they won't learn it. This is where I see the government falling down. We're going to have a lot of illiterate people. Like when you get kids going to join the Army now, they can't spell or they can't do anything like that. How are they going to read signals and signs and all that? These are things that I believe in for this country: black, white, red, yellow or what.

I started the cups of tea here in Mackay at the courthouse. It started when I went to court to give evidence once. It was the first time I'd ever been in a courthouse and this white lady was there with only thongs on. It was a cold July morning. She was there with her two small children and she did not have enough money to buy them a drink and the fountain was broken and the kids were hungry. I didn't interfere, but I went home and rang the mayor. I rang the members for parliament, both federal and state. I told them, 'Okay, they say that this is a beautiful town, but this is what happens behind the scenes'. I said, 'Now, you know who I am, both of you. I'm Mabel Quakawoot. I want something to be done about this. I would like to have a room at the courthouse where these people go. I would like to have a room there that they could have a cup of tea and a couple of biscuits and sit down and have a chat if they want to'. Then these other two goody-goody women decided that I was black and I couldn't do it, so I let them take it. We had to wait six years and nothing was done until Tim Mulherin, the member for here, rang me and said, 'Mabel, whatever happened to that cup of tea thing?' I said, 'Well, these two ladies were going to do it'. He said, 'Well, they haven't done a single thing. Do you still want to run with it?' I said, 'Yes'. So he then got a room at the courthouse for me and put a table, a fridge, and a nice lounge and somewhere they could sit. Now we have cups of tea. I put my face in the paper pretending to have a cup of tea. I got many people to come and help, but I only wanted them for Wednesdays, as that was Children's Court days, and the thing was up and running. When we first started it, everyone put in whatever they could, like $5 or $10 or $20 or something, so we could provide the first lot of biscuits and tea and coffee and everything. We did that. It's been going for four years. We have not had to put in another cent because we've put a donation tin there. When they have a cup of coffee, they could donate. See, with things like that you look after the whole community, not just the black community or the white community.

There hasn't been any movement for an apology to the South Sea Islander community. They had Reconciliation and that was only down in Brisbane.[11] There's never been anything else from the Federal Government. Yes, there have been pushes for something, but they don't get anywhere. The feeling is, 'We've apologised enough'. I just think that everyone that you meet doesn't understand the South Sea Island thing. They're so surprised because everyone thinks you're either Torres Strait Islander because of your hair, or Aboriginal if the hair was straighter. I always say, 'Our ancestors were brought over here as indentured labourers, a fancy name for slaves'. This is how I knew it, but there's never been any push. There have been little pockets here and they put things up to say: 'For the South Sea Islanders', but nothing big like the apology to the Stolen Generations was. I wanted to build a great big boat and put a thing down in a hole that you could go down in and show how they were bought here to Australia. But there are some South Sea Islanders that say that I'm Aboriginal. I'm both. That Independent MP Rob Oakeshott, he just couldn't believe that I'm carrying around all this stuff to do with all these things in my head. He said, 'Why don't you write a book?' I said, 'I have started writing a book. It's about the two families and I'm going through each child in those families. It's a long story and I hope it's not published until after I'm dead, so they can't sue me'.

I used to march every year at Anzac Day, but not now because I can't walk very far. I'm also involved in the Brisbane WRAAF organisation. They don't have it here in Mackay and the RSL here in Mackay has closed. They had the Air Force personnel league or whatever they call it here in Mackay, but I didn't join, because they were all men. I started the first Returned Servicewomen's League in Mackay in about 1978. We just raise money and give things to different ones. Every month, everyone takes an item to be raffled, and we buy these cent sale tickets. The money that we raise with the cent sale things, they give that money to a needy cause. It could be anything. And that's what we do with our little bits of money. There are about 37 of us altogether and still growing. We go and we have a meeting once a month and we do all these things. I haven't been to a meeting for ages now because I do religious education at the schools and the days that they have the meetings are the days that I have to go to religious education. But I started it up; I pushed forward for it. We have our meetings and everything in the RSL place, but it's not all Air Force; it's all services.

11   In July 2000, the Queensland Beattie Labor Government 'acknowledged the history of unjust treatment, disadvantage, prejudice and racial discrimination endured by the [South Sea Islander] community and the significant disadvantage the group still faces today'. See 'Queensland Government Action Plan: Australian South Sea Islander Community', Brisbane: Queensland Government, Department of Premier and Cabinet, 19 July 2001, available from www.datsima.qld.gov.au/resources/datsima/publications/archived/qld-govt-assi-action-plan.pdf, accessed 10 February 2015.

My brother and my sister served in the armed forces as well. My brother did two tours over in Vietnam with the Army and my sister was in the Air Force in Penrith, so neither of us went overseas. My sister was in the same mustering as I was and I said, 'How did you get in?' She said, 'They put me in there because of you'. I said, 'Oh, that's a bit of a thing. They shouldn't have put you in there. Why didn't you get in on your own steam like I had to?' She said, 'Well, I did all right'. My sister did the same mustering, but she didn't get sent to the Department of Air. One day we were talking and I said to her, 'Oh, it's a wonder they didn't send you to the Department of Air'. She said, 'No, I didn't have as many brains as you, you stupid thing!' It was just a little banter thing because I got sent to the Department of Air because that was the echelon of the Air Force. But as for my brother, he was a train driver and he almost got to the stage where he could be a stationmaster and he had to sit for this exam. I think that he always wanted to go into the Army, but he never let anyone know, until I went into the Air Force. Then he came home with all the papers and he put them on the table and said, 'Well, there you are, Dad. If you want to go and be a stationmaster, there's all the papers. You fill them in and you go to be stationmaster. I'm off to join the Army'. My father had pushed him into going on the railway and he was so disappointed when he went in and joined the Army. He did two tours over there. He was a demolition expert. They were first in and last to leave, setting bombs and letting bombs go and whatever they had to do.

Being South Sea Islander and Aboriginal, I was never discriminated against by the mainstream RSL, but I tell you what happened to my brother. He came out here in 1967 when he came back from Vietnam and he went into the RSL here in Mackay to have a beer. They told him they couldn't serve him and his three mates. He said he'd been to war and they said they didn't recognise the Vietnam War. As a matter of fact, it has since become quite embarrassing because I'm the only dark person that's been in the services here in Mackay and it's a thing like you're in a fish bowl. Everyone wants to know you and say, 'Oh, yes. Well, she was in the Air Force and she was … '. It becomes quite embarrassing, so I very seldom say it.

Out at the hut here in Mackay there is a stone there on the ground with a plaque that has all the South Sea Islanders who have served in all the wars. They're all there. It was sitting there for years and no one did anything, so I then started having an Anzac parade out there. It was a separate parade, but we got the mayor and the two members of parliament to come out there and give a speech. We kept that going and then, like all organisations, someone else takes over and they let it lapse. At every one of them, I had to speak. There were quite a few Vietnam vets that have come. There's one that I know of who went up when they had to roll the marbles and pick the names out to go to National Service.

They were sent over there and one of them died over there. That was a sad thing, but no one will get up and say this story or when he joined; they just say that he was killed in service. I'd like them to say how and when they joined or that he wasn't in the regular Army. It's up to their family to say that.

There's a thing for the Vietnam vets down near the airport and the library in there that is named after that young boy that went over there. They called it the Bobongie Memorial and the library [after Private Andy Bobongie].[12] Things like that have come through, and I'd like for them to get up, but they don't want to get up. I think they say, 'Oh, there's Mabel spouting again'. If I say so, they get up and do it, but people don't know what they're worth. They're so shy to get up, but anyway that's them. They attend all these things, which is good. So, what happened last year, I was so sad that of all the people who went up to lay wreaths, not one of them went up to lay a wreath for the South Sea Islanders or the Indigenous. I'm going to bring it up at the next meeting because there wasn't a wreath laid for the Indigenous soldiers who were killed in battle. That was the big RSL march in the streets when they go and put all the wreaths around the cenotaph. I want to see one of the leaders from the Aboriginal community and one from the South Sea Islander community to go up.

I think that the majority of South Sea Islanders and Aboriginals are very proud that they served their country. I would tell them (especially the young children) to do their lessons very well because in this day and age to go into the Army, Air Force and Navy, you can learn a trade and you can get paid as you're learning the trade. I would tell the mothers and fathers to do all they can to get them into that because we are a minority and if we don't stand up for ourselves, no one else is going to stand up.

I think we should bring back National Service for the girls and the boys. We have to pick our young ones up and they have to go and join something like that which has discipline and respect. But then, do the people in the armies – the captains and the WODs [warrant officers disciplinary] and all those sort of people – do they want to have that problem on their slate? That they've got all these people who are layabouts, cheeky, disrespectful? Do they want to try and knock that out of them? This is the saddest part because you see the young children nowadays – even in grades 5, 6, 7 – they are so disrespectful to everything. So when they get to 16, 17, if you made it compulsory to join the services and have two years in there, would they come out different people or would you be making them nastier than they are when they went in? These are things, but then I think that the government has to try something so that we don't have all these drug addicts with nothing to do, and that's what happens

---

12   See 'South Sea Islander Honour Roll', www.mackayhistory.org/research/war_memorials/SSI_memorial.html.

with this. They have all this sadness and they have to go and have psychiatrists, so why can't we get them to join the services to do that or something? I think that we should find out some way to make sure that our children are not wasted; not become illiterates. Even as old as I am, if they wanted me to go back and teach the children to read and write, and help out, I would. I would go back and do it at the drop of a hat because there are too many illiterate youngsters around. They can't spell properly and mainly most things now are just ticking boxes. Some of them can't read what has to be ticked in the boxes. So I really think the government should look at taking those children to have a gap year or two gap years. Maybe they want to join, but to have two gap years from, say, 16 to 18. Then they can go and join, go into the university, or something like that so as they're prepared to go into the university to then administer to the rest of Australia. This is how I see it; we've got to get them when they're young. Maybe because I enjoyed myself so much in the Air Force, I just think that we should do something like that.

On reflection, the military is a good thing to join. Not that you could get a good job later on, but it is something that never leaves you. I think you become more proud of your country joining the services than you do if you don't join. You're respected when people know that you've joined the services. I had dared to go and join the Air Force 50 years ago. I can see in people's minds when they find out that I was a black person in the Air Force, and a woman at that. One person said to me years ago, 'You know, the Air Force is a Menzies' Blue Orchids. They didn't have very many black people in there, but you joined and you're a woman, with it, into the bargain'. I said, 'Well, I didn't find that strange. It was just me. You know, I don't look down and say, "Oh, I'm black"'. She said, 'Oh, well, it is different. It's different to know that someone has broken that barrier'. You don't think of things like that. To me, that's not a barrier; that's just something I wanted to do. But she looked at it as a barrier that I'd broken down.

3

The Stolen Veteran

David Cook[1]

David Cook's life story is compelling because of the many incidents of trauma he has experienced. He was a member of the Stolen Generations, growing up in both Kinchela Boys Home and in a foster home in Raymond Terrace outside of Newcastle. He enlisted in the Army at 17 and served two tours of duty in Vietnam, witnessing the horrors of war and suffering post-traumatic stress disorder. He also speaks extensively about the role of race in the Vietnam War, being treated as an equal within the Australian Army while witnessing discrimination in the American Army. After the war, Cook's life spiralled downward through cycles of imprisonment and violence before he reconnected with his family in Raymond Terrace and turned his life around.

When I was in my early years, I lived with my mum and dad up in a place called Ebor where I was born [in 1945], second of five siblings. It's right up on top of the Great Divide, north of here [Newcastle]. My father and my mother worked for different property owners around the place right up until I was around about seven or eight, probably a bit younger. Then we moved, my mum

---

1   This interview was recorded in Raymond Terrace, New South Wales, on 20 January 2010.

and dad. I don't know what happened between them, but we moved to Taree. And one day, the police just came and just took me and my sisters and put us in a home, which for me was called Kinchela Boys Home. I was probably eight, say. I was a bit younger when we left Ebor. The girls got sent along with my little brother to Cootamundra Girls Home. My brother couldn't come with me because he was so young. So, the next four years I spent in Kinchela Boys Home. I didn't know the Welfare treated the whole lot of the Aboriginals the way they treated us, 'cos I was so young. I kept saying, 'Why are they treating me like this all the time?' I thought it was a personal thing with me.[2]

In Kinchela Boys Home we had no schooling. We worked – vegetable gardens; milking cows, baby cows, by hand, making their way to butter – everything was self-sufficient. The only time we ever went anywhere was to play football, and then it was against another Aboriginal team which were in the local area of Kempsey. If you played up in Kinchela Boys Home, if you did something that you shouldn't have done, your punishment was bad. All the boys would be lined up, and the punishment used to happen when you go to lunch, or dinner, or tea. They all lined up, and you have to walk down the line, and they've got to hit you. They can't hit you in the face; they punch you in the chest, in the belly, and if you didn't hit hard enough, you'd go up the end of the line. So if it was your brother coming down and you didn't hit him hard, you'd get the same thing. This is the sort of violence that they taught us in there. Other than that, I wasn't a very violent lad.

Halfway through that four years, or getting around the end of the four years, they sent my little brother up to the boys' home because he was big enough then. In the meantime, my sisters had been adopted by this family called Mrs Smith,[3] and she lived in Allworth. She didn't have a husband but she had a son. Eventually the reason she adopted us was the money – to get money for bringing us up, and because she had no other income. I was probably 11 – 10 or 11.

I started going to this school – St Bridget's in Raymond Terrace. I was pretty good at school even though I had no training in my earlier schooling. I learned pretty quickly, and I stayed there until such time as I was old enough to go to Raymond Terrace High School. I went to Raymond Terrace High School and that's where I decided I was going to join some sort of force – the Army, the Navy, whatever. In Raymond Terrace I was more or less classed in the same class as the foreigners – like the Germans and the Yugoslavs – and we were all hated. So we stuck together. It wasn't until recently that things calmed down in this

2   For a history of the Stolen Generations see Anna Haebich, *Broken Circles: Fragmenting Indigenous Families* (Fremantle: Fremantle Arts Centre Press, 2000).
3   Name changed to protect identity.

town; it was a very racist town earlier in my years here. But I was good at sport, which was a big breaker – cricket, football – that helped a lot. People sort of like sports, and it sort of calmed the waters a bit. But I still wasn't allowed in the hotels and stuff like that.

At home I was always last to do everything. Like, we didn't have any electricity; we didn't have all the mod cons. When I knocked off school, I had to go and get firewood, had to boil the pot with the big copper, fill the bath up so the girls could have their bath, and there was three of them. They all had to have their bath, and then I had to have a bath and I had to use their water. That's how it was all the way through until we moved into Raymond Terrace where we had electricity. I spoiled them by doing all the work for them and stuff. I had to be the one who had to dig the garden and grow the vegetables. I'm the one that had to cut the whole lawn with the hand-push mower. I'm the one who had to do the firewood. If the mosquitoes came, I had to go get the cow dung and burn it. The girls'd go swimming in the summer. They'd clean the house; that was it.

In the meantime I got kicked out of Mrs Smith's home. So then a couple by the name of the Thomases,[4] who used to drive our bus to school, they took me in and his wife, I owe a lot to her. He told me that I wasn't brainy enough to join the Army or the Navy or the Air Force. She taught me after school, a couple of hours after school each day – English, history, and maths – and it helped a lot. When I left school, I got a job in his brother-in-law's sawmill.

Then came the time that I applied to join the Navy and they sent me the entrance forms. I had to go to HMAS *Cerberus* after I went to Rushcutters Bay and passed my exams. I had to go to HMAS *Cerberus* in Melbourne, and I stayed there for three months. But I just couldn't handle the discipline, and I was told service was no longer required. I had a German officer, and I was the only Aboriginal in the outfit, and there weren't many Aboriginals in the forces. It didn't matter what I did, I just couldn't do it right. He just didn't want me in his outfit. I was a blot on his outfit, being black. I was even causing the other guys hassles as well because I wasn't doing stuff right. They had to do the same punishments as I had to do, and they were supposed to get onto me to make me do it right. I remember saying to some of the guys, 'I keep getting knocked to you by this lieutenant. I want you to do it for me'. Well, when they did do it right, some of them said, 'No, mate, that's deeper. That's deeper than what you think it is. He just doesn't want you here'. So, I had no option but to get out of there. But they wouldn't let me out – they said we've spent too much money on you, so you either have to go try for the Air Force or the Army.

---

4   Name changed to protect identity.

When I got discharged from the Navy, the Thomases didn't want anything more to do with me. So, in the meantime, the Smiths had moved into Raymond Terrace. When I went home I went back to see my sisters, and Aunty said that I could come back there. When I went back, I told them that it wasn't going to be for long because I was going to go back to the Army, and no one believed me. I just wanted to get away from home in Raymond Terrace, so I was willing to take anything. If I could take what I was getting at home, I could take anything. I finally did go back to the Army, and I passed the tests, and the rest is history with my war record. It turned out that I didn't have to have too much worries – especially in the Army – and I went through to be a full corporal.

When I got into the Army and I left Kapooka after the recruit training, being in the top 10, I was told that I could go to whatever branch that I want to – Engineers, Infantry or whatever. I picked Engineers, and then I went to the School of Military Engineering in Sydney. After I finished that I got posted to 1 Field Squad, 17th Construction Squadron and they sent us to New Guinea. I was 18 years old when I hit New Guinea in 1963. I did 12 months in New Guinea as a field engineer building toll booths, roads, bridges, like construction mobs do in the Army. That was pretty exciting, and I was pretty happy and so was everybody back home because they knew I wasn't coming back!

I really knew I was going to make something of myself when I got in the Army because I liked it. It was something that I liked doing. It was free; there was no prejudice. There was absolutely none. When we went overseas, New Guinea played rugby league all the way through the region, so I played rugby league with Wewak. It was virtually an Army team because there were hardly any Europeans in New Guinea at the time. I played in Wewak, Malolo, Mt Hagen, Port Moresby, all those areas. We would fly out a DC-3 for our whole football team, and we played. Then the local Papua New Guineans would have a get-together after the game because we couldn't fly out that night because of the clouds and stuff. So we were stuck there overnight, so they put on a party for us and stuff like that. It was really good.

We had the locals cleaning in the canteen and all that sort of stuff. We used to do exercises with their soldiers once or twice a year. They were fantastic soldiers and better than us in the jungle. You could not see them at night-times and stuff, and they could be right on top of you. So they were pretty good at their jobs. No wonder the Second World War guys – the Fuzzy Wuzzy Angels – no wonder they appreciated them so much.[5] But we never had to go to war with them; we just had exercises.

---

5   See Riseman, *Defending Whose Country?*, chapter three; *Angels of War*, produced and directed by Gavan Daws, Hank Nelson and Andrew Pike. 54 min., The Australian National University, Research School of Pacific Studies, 1981, videocassette.

After we did the 12 months there, we came back to the School of Military Engineering. Then they sent us to Borneo for six months to fight the Indonesians in Borneo with a British outfit called the Screaming Eagles. It was 60,000 British troops in Borneo, and there were about 200 to 300 Australians, which were us. We were building a road so the British could get their supplies through. We carried live ammunition and stuff like that, mainly for the animals, like the orangutans and all the fierce animals they have over there. But we never got into any contact with the Indonesians. We were more or less billeted next to the Ghurkhas, and they are good soldiers as well. But we never had much to do with them; our job was to build the road and to go home, so virtually that's what we did.[6] We were only there six months but it was in the winter in Australia, and the British Lions rugby league team were coming down to play Australia. They stopped off in Borneo to visit their troops and the Australians got a team together to play the British Lions in Borneo. It was a pretty close game because they couldn't handle the heat, coming from England. It was a friendly but it was pretty hard. So I played against the British Lions. That's one thing a lot of people can't say.

When we came back to Australia, we were there back home and that was the end of '64. At the end of '65, they asked for volunteers to go to Vietnam. Well, no one knew what Vietnam was or where it was, and we were young, crazy, and full of adventure, so all of us young boys stepped forward. Even the brass didn't know what we were going to do there.[7] All we knew was that we going over with 1 Battalion, 1 Battalion Battle Group, and 105 Battery, and we were going to be attached to these guys. Nothing was concrete of what we were going to do, and we thought it was only going to be a picnic – a couple months here, there, and home. When we got there, it was shocking! It was the rainy season, and we went over on the HMAS *Sydney*. All our stuff was still on the *Sydney* and we only had nothing – just rifles and bullets. It was raining cats and dogs, so we had to borrow tents off the Yanks.

It's the first time I ever saw prejudice so blatantly as when we had to have a shower with the Americans. There, in the US 173rd Airborne, they had black lines and white lines. The whitefellas lived here, the blackfellas lived here. The blackfellas ate in this mess and the whitefellas ate in this mess. Here we are in our outfit, we had three Aboriginals: one Thursday Islander [Bill Unmeopa], me, and Billy

---

6   See Peter Dennis and Jeffrey Grey, *Emergency and Confrontation: Australian Military Operations in Malaya and Borneo 1950–1966*, The Official History of Australia's Involvement in Southeast Asian Conflicts 1948–1975, vol. 5 (St Leonards, NSW: Allen & Unwin and the Australian War Memorial, 1996).

7   Australia's Vietnam War has been written about extensively. For a good general overview, see Peter Edwards, *Australia and the Vietnam War* (Sydney: NewSouth Publishing, 2014); John Murphy, *Harvest of Fear: A History of Australia's Vietnam War* (St Leonards, NSW: Allen & Unwin, 1993).

Coolburra, who came from Arnhem Land.[8] Even the Australians were shocked at the racism there because they've never seen it so blatant. It became apparent that they – the 173rd – come from the South of the USA, and they were shocking racists. But surprisingly, they treated us Aboriginals pretty much the same as they treated themselves. They didn't treat me different because, probably, I was from another country, and that was okay I suppose. They probably knew that I couldn't take anything that belonged to them. But the funniest thing about it was we first went out into the jungle with these guys. When they picked up dead soldiers and put them on the chopper, it didn't matter whether he was black or white; they'd pick him up and put him on the chopper. When they got back to base, they had different morgues. The black man went in the black morgue; the white bloke went in the white morgue. Here we are – we're fighting for democracy, for Christ sake, and equality between people and countries, and they're carrying on like that. I just couldn't believe it.[9]

We ended up building our own canteen to keep away from these racist things because they carried guns into their canteens. What a volatile mix! Guns and beer and drugs; they were heavily involved in drugs. Our commanding officer said, 'I've seen enough of this. We'll build our own'. We were only with them for six months, but the amount of things that we saw and did in those six months is absolutely incredible. The racism sticks with me the most in that. After our six months there they said, 'Rightyo. We're moving. We've got the Australian taskforce coming over. We've got to move down to Vung Tau and clear the area so the majority of our taskforce can move in'.

There was only one major personal issue that I had with the Yanks. We had a day off. We went into the local town in Bien Hoa. There was a bar there called the Cherry Bar where we used to drink. It was getting around six o'clock in the afternoon, and these MPs came in and told us that we had to drink up and get out. Well, we weren't American soldiers; we were Australian soldiers, so we told them, 'Piss off! Got nothing to do with us. We're only here helping you fight the war'. He didn't take too kindly to being told to piss off. He just walked up with his nightstick and knocked all of our drinks off the table. I stood up and I punched him straight in the chest and hit him just above the heart and

---

8   Billy Coolburra actually came from Palm Island. There was a fourth Aboriginal man in the outfit – Frank Mallard. Cook did not realise that Frank Mallard was Aboriginal until, a year after this interview, I told Cook that I had subsequently interviewed Mallard. Mallard's Aboriginality was also unknown to the commanding officer Sandy MacGregor, who published a narrative about their unit in Vietnam. See Sandy MacGregor, as told to Jimmy Thomson, *No Need for Heroes* (Lindfield, NSW: CALM Pty Limited, 1993), especially pp. 81–90. This opens up other questions about racial passing among some Indigenous service personnel.

9   See James E. Westheider, *The African American Experience in Vietnam: Brothers in Arms* (Lanham, MD: Rowman and Littlefield, 2008); James E. Westheider, *Fighting on Two Fronts: African Americans and the Vietnam War* (New York and London: New York University Press, 1997). On Aboriginal reactions to American racism in Vietnam, see Noah Riseman, 'Equality in the ranks: The lives of Aboriginal Vietnam veterans', *Journal of Australian Studies* 36, no. 4 (December 2012): 417–419.

dropped him straight to his knees. After that, MPs came from everywhere out of the woodwork. I don't know where they were but they came from everywhere. It was on – a bar fight. They locked us up; they handcuffed us all together and marched us down the street, about seven or eight of us. You had MPs both sides of us, walking us down to the police station. They locked us up, and they let everybody go – bar me and Danny Ayoub. I don't know why they kept us, but they did. On the way back, they've got us handcuffed in the back of their little jeep and they were talking on their two-way, so I unscrewed all of the buttons on their two-way and threw them out the back and pulled all the wires off. They couldn't hear their two-way and thought it wasn't working. So they stopped, stood us up, and they handcuffed us to the roll bar and that's the way they brought us into camp. We were pretty bruised up where they punched us out. My captain said, 'How dare you put those handcuffs on that tight?! I have highly trained men here! We haven't got that many of them over here! If they have to stay out of the jungle, I haven't got men to put there in their place. How dare you?! Just keep away from my men!' So we really gave it to the American brass. My captain, Sandy MacGregor, wrote a letter to General Westmoreland [commander of US operations in Vietnam 1964–68] saying 'I'd be a bit more gentle when you're arresting my soldiers – be a bit more discreet'. Westmoreland said, 'I'd like your soldiers to be a bit more discreet when they're getting arrested'. So that was my closest call to seeing General Westmoreland!

We always fought on the fringes of the Americans because we moved together as a group and the Americans moved together as a group. When we got into a contact, they'd be probably 100 yards away and we'd be over here. It's only when the battle had finished that we had mingled, to go over and see what happened and to see the enemy, which were probably in the middle. As to being attached to the Americans – oh, I'm glad we weren't. The 173rd were a paratrooping mob but they were pretty good, the majority of them. But there were some elements in them that you wouldn't want to be caught in a gunfight with because they'd probably shoot you.

After about six months we were sent off to Vung Tau. That's the rice bowl of South Vietnam at the time. We were south of Saigon. When we cleared all the area, we had Australian headquarters come over, plus two more battalions – a total of about 5,000 men. When we got all of them settled and put a water point in, which took us about three months, they moved us up the front to Nui Dat. We had to set up Nui Dat as well so that the other battalions could come up. Virtually that's all we did – set up camp, move, clear the area, set up camp, move, set up camp, clear the area. That was for the rest of the Australian forces coming through.

The Battle of Long Tan took place on the 18th of August, '66. Two days before the Battle of Long Tan, we were out doing a clearing and we stopped to have a smoke. As I was cleaning my pistol, it discharged and I shot myself. It went in my leg and came out the other side, and I had to get Medivacked back to camp. Then they put me in a hospital in Vung Tau, which was an American hospital with American nurses. Two days later, I heard of the Battle of Long Tan. The same guys that I was out with were the guys that got caught up in the Battle of Long Tan. They had all the speakers open reporting the battle from the helicopters and the staff. The Viet Cong were trying to overrun our camp at Nui Dat. If I hadn't gotten shot, or shot myself, I'd have been in the Battle of Long Tan.

I came home, and then they sent me back over. They wanted me to join back up. I was pretty high up in my Army career at the time. And when I went back home they said, 'Cookie, we're going to send you to Malaya for two years'. I said, 'No way! I'm not going to Malaya! I'm due out in another 13 or 14 months. You've got to have two years to go over there'. Snowy Wilson – Billy Coolburra's brother as he called him – he was on the trip going back to Vietnam. So they said, 'All right, we'll sort this out. Snow, you're going to Malaya. Cookie, you're going to Vietnam again'. I said, 'I'll cop that'. I wanted to square the books because I had missed the Battle of Long Tan in August; we came home in September anyway. So it wasn't a sense of I wanted to get home early or I was scared of doing anything. That's why I went back [in 1968].

Somebody's looking after me. I don't know if there's a God or anything, but the same thing happened to me on me second tour. It was a scorpion. Before the Battle of Coral [in May 1968] I was supposed to take my section out on a listening post, an ambush. I was leaning on the sandbags and a scorpion crawled up my arm, and it bit me. I pressed it, and it bit me all the way up. I crushed it, and then they had to put me in the hospital bunker. That was around the Tet Offensive on my second tour, when they hit us with everything. They wiped my section out – wounded and killed all bar Murray Walker, my second-in-command. When I came out of the bunker the next morning, and I walked, the gun-smoke in the air was like a deep fog. You could smell the cordite and you could tell something really bad had happened. They wouldn't even let me go back to see the boys, because I didn't know what had happened to them. They threw me on a chopper and sent me back to camp. That's where I found out that my section had just about been wiped out. So it was two things: that with the Battle of Long Tan, and then Coral – a bloody scorpion saved me. I went over the hill; I went troppo. They sent me back to Australia. I ended up in Concord for about six months; that's the Army rat house in Sydney. They filled me up full with bloody tablets and Christ knows what. Yeah – it's not a very good feeling.

Not once was my race an issue. In my section, Bobby Bowtell was our corporal and our lance corporal was Ross Thorburn. Then Bob got killed in the V.C. [Viet Cong] tunnels and they made Ross up to full corporal, and they made me his lance corporal. So, I took precedence over all these other guys. They could have come from any other section as well, because they were more senior than I was. But because I knew my job, and I knew the guys, I got made up to lance corporal. Never did I have any prejudice pinned on me in the Australian Army. Not once; not from anywhere. That's why it runs so smoothly.

I only had one person writing me letters – that was my older sister Dianne. She was not able to upset me after I was over there shooting people and stuff like that. She didn't want to put any more worries on me. In the meantime, I had two kids with a woman. I wasn't married to her but I had these two kids. She was pregnant before I left, and she used to write me letters and stuff like that. But she was only young, too. While I was back home on leave six months in 1966–67, she got pregnant again. I went back over and she said, 'I'm pregnant again; you know that? You've got to get out of the Australian Army'. I was thinking about my childhood and stuff. I had a bit of money plus I was going to get DFRP [Defence Fuel Remediation Program] and stuff like that. I said, 'Yeah, I've got to get out of the Army'. So I said, 'All right. When my time's up, I'll get out'. It was the worst mistake of my life. I am devastated now that I got out. When I came home the second time from Vietnam, it felt like I had been in the bush looking for anything you can shoot and 24 hours later I was sitting in my lounge in Green Valley with two screaming kids and a missus that I didn't know whether I was in love with or not. And it was the kids that I couldn't handle. The change was so horrific; I just couldn't handle it.

When I got out of the Army, that's when the real trouble really started. And it wasn't with any people or civilians – it was with the police. The racism really hit me. I was always aggressive; when I got out of the Army, I was a very aggressive man. I had run-ins with police and stuff. They used to call me black bastard. 'What the fuck are you doing with this black bastard?' they'd say to my wife. I hated authority then. I was authority in the Army. Then, I could give the word; I'd shoot that bastard, and they'd do it. I came home and was treated like something not even human. I had fights with the police. If they couldn't charge me with anything, they'd make sure that they'd get the main charge and put the others on schedule. What I mean by that is that they'll make one big charge, and then other charges that they can't solve or anything, like armed robbery, bloody assaults, murder and stuff like that. I was a wild boy, but I never killed anybody. I hit people a lot. Don't get me wrong – I was no angel. Everything just sort of went haywire from the organised life I had in the Army to the disorganised life that I had out in civilian street. My wife never helped much because she wasn't ready for it. I wasn't ready for it. But we stayed around each other and ended up having five kids.

I got into a fight. I was probably arguing with my missus and stuff like that. I'm not quite sure how it all started. The coppers came around again to see, and this is when they started throwing the racism stuff around – 'What are you doing with the bloke anyway?' and all this sort of stuff. Then they'd take me down the police station and lock me up. Then I started being an arsehole, virtually, against the authorities. Because the first time in my life, the only person that hurt me were the coppers when they came to the primary school in Taree and took me out of the Aboriginal Taree Primary School and put me in Kinchela Boys Home. They took me to court and that, I suppose, stuck in my mind as well. These people are not to be trusted. I never trusted coppers and not even till this day. So, one thing led to another. They said that I'm a thief; I've never been a thief. They said that I was always violent.

There was some violence with my wife. I back-handed her, but nothing really killing or anything like that. I have slapped her around, and that's why the coppers kind of got involved first. I tried to get a job; I tried to get back in the Army. I even drove from here – I had a little Mini Cooper S – and I spent all my money. So, rather than drive down with my plates, I put these other plates on the Mini Cooper S, and on Broadway in Sydney I got picked up. I just came from the Army Recruiting Office, and just went in and said that I'd like to join back up, and filled out all the papers and stuff like that. These police pulled me over. They threw me up against the wall and everything, and said that I was in a car racket and everything, and said that I stole it. I showed them the papers that I owned it; it's just that I put different plates on it and I was getting it through finance. So, they said, 'Oh, you're two payments behind'. They said, 'We'll keep that car and give it back to the finance company'. They were the police in Newtown. My brother-in-law came down and he bailed me out. And he said, 'What's going on, Cookie?' I said, 'Oh, mate, I'm just falling to pieces. I just can't seem to get things working right'. Then I got a letter back from the Army saying you're medically unfit, we don't want you. All the wars were over after '72. Well, they were all over so they didn't need any NCOs or people that had experiences in many wars. So they didn't want me. So, I came home here to Raymond Terrace.

There's a big part of a lot in there that has to do with the authorities – like the police, and workers, bosses – that didn't want to hire Aboriginals. I was a builder's labourer because in the Army Engineers Corps you learn how to do all these sort of works, even know how to lay bricks. You become a demolition expert and that's what we were classed as – demolitions and mine warfare. I could blow up anything. But employers couldn't take you on because you had no certificate. The Army never gave out any certificates for what you learned. That means that you go in and learn this trade and then you piss off and do it as a civilian and get more money. So they never really gave you any certificates to say what you were. You either stayed in the Army and did it, or you didn't do it for anyone. I could drive a bulldozer, I could drive a grader, rotovator – you name it – because being in engineers, you have to learn all this stuff in case somebody gets shot.

But I found civilian life when I got out pretty hard. It had a lot to do with post-traumatic stress disorder. You go killing people over a two-year period – men, women and children – you get a bit of a complex about yourself. It's not very nice some of the thoughts that you have in your mind and stuff like that, and they can never go. They're there forever. Mate, they'd take you to the hospital – Concord Repat Hospital. They'd keep you there for about three or four months and give a bit of shock treatment. They'd shove tablets in you – lithium and Valium – that was it. Someone has a bit of a talk to you: 'Oh, you're all right now. You can go home'. I was probably in and out of there from the early '70s to mid-'80s, probably twice a year, or something like that, trying to get help. There was no one around that knew to put their finger on what was wrong with us. At least now they've learned through their mistakes with us. The only thing that they could do was say, 'Oh, give him a pension and shut him up'. So they gave us all a TPI [Totally and Permanently Incapacitated Veteran] and just wanted us to walk off into the darkness and not say any more about anything. To get my war pension I had to be diagnosed with post-traumatic stress disorder. I've been and seen specialists; I've even seen all types of people, and it all comes back to the war. I still have pretty bad nightmares. At times, I could be watching something on television – like see a movie – that night it will all start over again as flashbacks. I wouldn't be able to get it [the war] out of my mind, and then it [the war trauma] goes to sleep; it's in your subconscious. It just takes you back to where everything happened.

For instance, with Agent Orange, this is in my blood, and it's never going to leave it. I fathered five kids to my first wife, and I've got twins in this town. I had twins at 50 in this town. One of my sons – the one that I said was born second – he's got Albright's disease. If he hits his arm, it'll break because he's got chalky bones. I never wore glasses until I got old, but all of my kids used to wear glasses because there was something wrong with their eyes and stuff. I was putting it down to this Agent Orange, and they kept telling us, 'No. Agent Orange doesn't do things like that'. Mate, I saw what it did to the people in Vietnam and to their fields. The jungle would be nice and green, and about 12 C-130s would fly over, and it'd be coming down like light mist. It'd go all over you, and within three days the jungle was dead. They came in with napalm and set the whole lot on fire. When I put pressure on my arm, a bruise line comes up like I've been hit with a cat-o'-nine-tails, and that's all in my blood from the Agent Orange. I've told these people that, and they said, 'Oh, no, you've had that when you joined up'. I said, 'When I joined up in this Army, I was classed medically L1. If I had something like that, you wouldn't have taken me'.

I'd like to get back to this other part with the police and stuff. I've been locked up through violence like iron-barring people – hitting them with iron bars. They were other people, and you just can't do that sort of thing; I know that now. I was just scattered – just gone. I was never a big drinker. It was my head. I wasn't violent before I was in the Army. I couldn't be violent because I was no one's kid. I had to watch my p's and q's. Being in the Army sort of unlocked all that. I started saying, 'Shit, I'm as good as anybody else. I've led white men into battle. I'm over all this crap. It's all gone'. But it wasn't. The first fight I had, he said to me, 'They said, "Oh, there's Cookie. He's just come back from that Vietnam"'. He said, 'Oh, yes, probably a black coward'. You don't let things lie like that, so I went and knocked him clean out and showed him what sort of a violent man I was. And that sort of put a scare right through them.

When I got into trouble with the police and that, my older sister would fly down. She would come to court with me, and stuff like that, and sort of fix up money. The coppers were pretty big in those days, and if you wanted to pay them some money, maybe they'd forget about the charges and stuff like that. In the Army, if you said something, which I was used to, there was no corruption – and it worked. In the police force, they'd say, 'Ah, well'. They said, 'We're going to charge him with malicious wounding causing grievous bodily harm. But if you've got a couple grand, we can drop the charges down to malicious wounding only – give the grievous bodily harm a big miss and it could mean only a fine'. My sister said, 'Where's your boss? I want to talk to your superior'. They thought she was a dummy, and the police didn't think that I had any support. My sister, when she said that, also went and told my solicitor. My solicitor came down, and he said to me, 'You're going to walk out of this today; the charges are going to be dropped'. So, those coppers, rather than making a deal and charging me and having to bring up that they offered me a bribe, they dropped the charges. That's the sort of thing that's stuck in my craw with the police force.

I was always working when I was not in prison. I worked with a company with the name of Muse and Richards. They were a couple of young carpenters, and they used to do work all over Sydney. My brother Harry and I, we worked with them. One of the jobs we did, we built the new office blocks and that for Channel Two at Gore Hill in Sydney. But their main job was putting in bank vaults. I was never an armed robber and that, but these coppers in the earlier times tried to say that I was a murderer. They had no proof; they just strung it on me and tried get a confession about something. And what they normally did is they got you for the violence, like in bashing somebody, and they'd say 'You've done all these' – like breaking and entering or speeding and all this sort of stuff, and they haven't got a clue who did it. They put it on your rap sheet and said that they're putting it on schedule. Now, that means that they don't have to read it out in court, but the judge looks at it and says, 'Oh, he's also getting charged with all these'. They couldn't put any more than four on there because it'd get a bit worrying, but some of the judges I reckon were just as corrupt as some of the coppers.

On some occasions, I was charged and convicted. This was in the '70s. In prison, there's a lot of Aboriginals. They're like weightlifters; they had muscles, because you had nothing else to do – just do weights and stuff like that. It was the cream of the Australian Aboriginal youth back then that was locked up – a whole generation of them, and it was sickening to see. Some were there for good reasons – for murder and stuff like that – but some of them were there for paltry bloody things like stealing a car, and stuff like that. It should be only a fine or something. I didn't know the biggest majority of what they were there for. I've forgotten the biggest majority anyway. They're all in their mid-20s, early 20s. I said, 'Why can't they just grab these guys and put them in the Army? They can do it with white guys in the National Service. Why can't they do it with these blokes?' But it doesn't work that way.[10]

Prison was run by Aboriginals until the Lebanese came along. Between the Aboriginals and Lebanese, they run prisons, and the triads now as well. Up until the time that I got there, it was in the early '80s when I got out, the triads were there and the Lebanese. I was running the show because I had a lot of brains compared to the biggest majority of them. I could talk to other people, and I knew how to talk with authority. I was running them, which means you can get their buy ups, so you can get cigarettes. The prison officers back in those days were corrupt as well. If you wanted drugs brought in, you could get them brought in through the prison officers. And the bookmakers – it was like being at Randwick – they'd have a big bowl of prices and horse races up. Even the screws used to bet against the crim that was running it. Taking the bets, that money would be sent out with the police to buy stuff to bring in for certain prisoners, and I was one of them. I've always tried to climb to the top of the tree; it didn't matter what I was in. So I worked that out pretty well.

I only ever met one other Vietnam veteran in prison. He was a white, but he was a lot worse than me. He used to run around doing armed holdups. In prison I saw some very distressing things. If you showed any weakness, you were in

10   Much of David's discussion about police and prison aligns with findings of the *Royal Commission into Aboriginal Deaths in Custody*, 1991, available online from www.austlii.edu.au/au/other/IndigLRes/rciadic/, accessed 11 February 2015.

trouble yourself. My Army training prepared me, though. I often said it's like doing another six years in the Army. I was used to the solitary life – living in a cell on your own and stuff like that – I could cop that. What sort of strung me out a bit was there was no future locked behind walls. I wasn't sitting on my laurels, getting around the end of my time.

In my first time I was in there I got sent to Wilson's Island. It's a low security prison; for the last 18 months of my time I was sent there. I played two seasons of football against the Central Coast Rugby League. And I played cricket – in the summer we had a cricket team. So it was like a massive big holiday. It's on an island in the middle of the Hawkesbury River, and it was like a holiday. People used to come up past us fishing. We had no fence on the island, and it was about two miles long. We used to run around it keeping training for rugby league. I ended up there probably because I was an ex-soldier and stuff like that, and I wasn't a real pain in the arse even in the big gaol.

I went back in prison for when I iron-barred those people for robbing my house. I got five years each for the three people, but they ran it concurrently and then gave me two and a half years as a parole thing. They sent me to Silverwater; that was a minimum security prison then. The last six months of my time, I applied for a university course – Associate Diploma in Social Welfare. I got accepted, so I used to leave the prison every morning and go to the McCarthy University at Liverpool in Sydney. I'd catch a train, go the university, and then catch a train home back to the prison. I reckon it was because I was well-behaved, so that's the reason they let me out. Getting around the end of my time, I had to have some sort of an experience to get back out into civilian life. So I decided I'd do this course. The only reason I did it, I mean, is because I was getting two days a week taken off my time in prison. I did two more semesters after that, and then I just didn't go anymore. I should've. It would've been good.

I was already reformed. I knew what discipline was. I knew what it was all about before I went in. I think that's what made my time much easier in prison compared to some others. It's just the isolation of it, but then again, I was isolated in Vietnam, I was isolated in Borneo. All you saw was jungle; all you were looking at here was walls. I'm pretty self-disciplined in a lot of ways. That came with a lot of hard work, but I can take it. I often thought if I'd got captured in the war, would I be able to shut up or would I spill my guts? I think I'd have been able to shut up.

I was living in Sydney then, and it happened right up until about mid to late '80s. I was haywire back then. I came out of the Army and I wasn't trained in any sort of skills. So I was just in no man's land really. I didn't have a place to call home; home was here. I pulled myself together and I decided to come home. I rang my sister and she said, 'Yeah, come home and stay with us'. Everything panned out. Then I came home here, and got with my brother-in-law and sister. And everything just worked out. See my sister, in this town, has the biggest hardware shop north of Newcastle – Home Hardware, H & D Home Hardware. My sister and her husband own that. They employ about 20 to 30 people, and people look up to them now. Even I do because of the work that she's put into it. But people have got to the stage where the racism doesn't mean anything, because the biggest majority of the people in this town have backgrounds that are Pommies, or new Australians like Yugoslavs. So they have nothing to be racist about. They've all come from another country. So how can they be racist against the person who comes from here? That's the way they look at it now.

I've had a few fights with racist blokes around this town. This happened about 10 year ago. He said to me, 'Cookie, what's the definition of Irish cheese?' I said, 'I don't know'. He said, 'It's got a coon on top'. I said, 'Are you calling me a coon?' And he said, 'Yes'. So I head-butted him, and I split him right down the head. Three hits later I knocked him clean out. To this day, that same man won't talk to me. Yet most of the people I know associate with either one of us. Other than that, that was probably the last blue I had was 10 year ago. So, from there to this day – nothing. Before joining the Army, I never had the guts to challenge racism. Nor could I do anything about it and I had no one to turn to. When I grew up, I didn't have to worry about turning to anybody because I was it. Outside of me, I'd do the same for my sisters if they received any sort of racism and stuff like that – not a problem.

So, we five siblings all got back together because we're the only people we have in our lives. We know what it is to have family – having it taken away so early – and that's why we stick to each other so badly, even though we have the biggest arguments about things and stuff. My older sisters reckon I spend too much bleeding time in the pub when I should be working more often, and stuff like that. But, other than that, we all love each other. My brother-in-law had a mill next door to the hardware store where he used to mill all his own timber. I used to work in the mill section – me and his younger brother. Then, when he bought the farm, I went and lived on the farm. I renovated the house along with a good carpenter mate of mine, and I put in all the posts on a 50-acre block. I used to drench their cattle, send them to market. I was a real farmer. I loved it. I did it for 11 years, and then he sold it to his son. So, yeah that's all I've done. I work around Raymond Terrace; I've got some good friends, go fishing every now and again. I've got no worries, not a worry in the world. I get a TPI pension now, and they give me pretty good money. But if I ever need any, I've always got work. I'll go over the farm, do a bit of work, or do a bit of work at his business out here in Heatherbrae.

Figure 1. David Cook (right) and Captain Matta, visiting Pol Pot's grave, near Thai border

Source: Courtesy David Cook

The relationship with me and my five kids from my ex-wife has been volatile. They're all young men and women now. One son lives in Sydney; my daughter lives in Brisbane. One disabled son with chalky veins lives in Newcastle and works for Spotlight. They only gave him until he was 15 to live and he's well into his 40s now. The youngest one, he's in the Army. And my other son was in the Army in 3 Battalion – the two youngest ones in the Army. He ended up having a motorbike accident, so he got out and he's been a prison officer now for nearly 25 years. But I don't have much to do with all of them. I've got grandkids to them, but they don't come home and see dad anymore. I've also got twins in this town and they're 14 – a boy and a girl. I have a lot to do with them, but they don't live with me. I, like I said, I couldn't look after kids, so they stay with their grandparents. They bring the twins up, but if they find they want anything – any money for uniforms or whatever they want – I see them every now and again, and I give it to them. I tried to have relationships with them all. When my wife and I split up, she had two of the kids and gave the others to her sister. I had them at times come and live with me, but I just couldn't handle kids. I just couldn't.

I was just never meant to have kids because of my upbringing. They all understand that kids couldn't live with me. It is a bit because of both my childhood and my Vietnam trauma. Everything is thrown in together, but it's mainly because I've got no love in my body. I can't love anybody; I've got no feelings for anybody. I might like some people. But, even when I get a girlfriend and that, it usually only lasts a week. And then the love that they're craving for and want is just not there. So, it's damaged me in a lot of ways. It's pretty hard; I know I'd like to experience it, but I'm a little too old for it now.

My battalions have a reunion every four years. The last one I went to was in Perth for my second tour. If you're in any sort of trouble, these people will help you out. I just didn't want to tell them earlier in the piece that I was in the trouble that I was in with the police and stuff like that because they wouldn't have been all that helpful at that time anyway. After I got back I was never in touch with any of them then. It's only since we've gotten older, and I've got a stable life, that we started to get back in contact with each other. A lot of them didn't even know that I'd been in prison. They're up me about not telling them, and they could've helped and all this sort of stuff. What I didn't know at the time is that there was a network of help through the outfit guys. It was a network that I could've tapped into. But I was so proud and did not want anybody to know what happened to me, because I was their corporal of all people. I just let it wash. But maybe I should've swallowed my pride and rung one or two of them. They all had mothers and fathers that they could fall back on. I had no one, and it was vastly different. Even today some of them can probably still go and see their mother and father. I can't; my only ones are my sisters and brother. So, that's the difference of support between them and me. And they know a bit about the Stolen Generations and where we all come from and stuff, and this is why I think they are reaching out for me now. It makes it a bit touching. At the time they didn't know anything about my removal. They just thought I was just an out and about family man. They didn't even worry that I was black; they didn't even question it.

With doing the two tours in Vietnam, it's pretty hard for me to manage both battalions' reunions. I did one lot with the all-regulars and one lot with the National Service boys. All of my outfit − bar me − were National Service in my second tour. The first tour we were all regulars. It showed − the difference in training − with losing all of those guys in my second tour, compared to only losing one in my first tour. It means a lot to be trained properly, and National Service is no answer for wars because they're just not well-trained enough. But as far as reunion goes and that now, I'm going to one this Anzac Day [2010] in Tamworth. This is for the National Service boys; they're coming from all over Australia, and I've had about 10 of them ring me already to make sure that I'm going. I've got my second-in-command Murray Walker flying in from Perth and coming up here to make sure that I go to this reunion. He says, 'You come in our car or you follow us in yours. But you gotta be there because the guys are not getting any younger, and they want you to be there'. So I've gotta go.

For one reunion in Perth I went around Australia, and I got stuck in Broome because my car broke down in Katherine and I had to get it fixed. When it got fixed, I was way behind schedule and I could only make it to Broome. Well, there's a lot of Vietnam vets that travel a lot. We met up at the RSL and then we went to the cenotaph and then after that we went back to the RSL. The funniest part about it is that I had taken my books and everything with me to show the guys at the Perth reunion. When I got to Broome, and we were all in the RSL drinking, they were talking about the Battle of Long Tan and all these people and were saying, 'Yeah, well it … ' And I said, 'I was there'. They said, 'What?!' I said, 'I was in Vietnam at Nui Dat at the Battle of Long Tan'. The stories that they were telling shut up because they were nowhere near Vietnam when the Battle of Long Tan took place. You can tell that from their service on their medals. I had mine on and it's got '65 see, and I can sort of tell on the medals. And you can see '72, '68.

Eventually at the Perth reunion I realised that when some of the men finally got out of the Army after doing 20-odd years, two of them turned out to be racists. Well I didn't expect any of them to be sort of racist, but I found then those two to be racist. One was a cop who worked near a remote Aboriginal station up the top of Perth. He talked about them as if they were a piece of furniture or something. And I'm sitting there listening to him, and I pulled him up over it. This was the last time I went to the reunion in Perth. When I pulled in at his house, we went down to his local to have a few beers and stuff. And the way he talked to me about people that he used to be in charge of – like, 'I was posted here, and I was expecting it to be something like our Army posting'. But he was the boss there, and some of the things he said and did sort of struck me as being racist. It was never so prevalent – here I am, I'm dressed up with all my medals, and I'm with my second outfit in Perth, and three guys walked up and they wanted me to march with them because I served with them in the first tour. I said, 'No. I'm marching here'. But one said, 'Ah, you black c***!' No one's ever said that to me – no one! So, out of all the guys I met in the Army, there was nothing like that said in Vietnam, maybe because I had a gun. They would never say that. I said, 'Fuck off! What's this business? I'm here with my second outfit; this is where I'm staying'. I haven't talked to those men about any of this other stuff, but maybe it's about time I did. That's about the only racist thing or people that I ever found out of the 68 of us.

I'm a member of the RSL here in Raymond Terrace; I joined probably when I first came home. The thing is – they wouldn't let me into the RSL clubs. I could be a member of their club, but they wouldn't let me into their RSL. We had no RSL here. We would all drink in the bowling club affiliated with our RSL. But, I went from here to Karuah – that's only about a half-hour run down the road. They wouldn't let me into their RSL because I was Aboriginal. This was in the early '70s. And they said, 'No way! You can't come in here!' I said, 'Mate, I'm a fucking returned serviceman!' I was with a policeman, as a matter of fact. Still they said, 'You can come in; he can't'. So, we just all went up to the local hotel and drank there and came back home. But the RSL here has put all our names on the war memorial – the Vietnam vets – we're all on that war memorial down there. When they first put the names on, mine wasn't on there. I went and saw them and asked them why it wasn't there and people told me that they didn't know that I ever went to Vietnam. I told them that I was the first one to go to Vietnam from this town – twice before any of the others got sent. So they ended up putting my name there, but it's under the Second World War guys. Now I just go to the Anzac marches, through Raymond Terrace down to the cenotaph. Every four years I go to my reunion, if it's close. I am also a member of the Vietnam Veterans' Association of Australia.

Through the Department of Veterans' Affairs, when I told them that I was Indigenous, I felt that things were lacking a little bit behind the others. No one's come out and said it. I was out of the Army long before these other guys. Some of them did 20 years and stuff like that. They got out, and they got their TPIs long before I did. And yet I was fighting for it ever since I got out. Now, you ring up Veterans' Affairs and you'll have a Chinese or a Lebanese or some sort of 'nese answer the phone. So, you don't have any hassles there anymore.

I don't class myself as Indigenous. See, it was all washed out of me through the adoption; I grew up with white people. If somebody started putting shit on me about blacks, I'd take that personal with me and that's when I became violent. And I wouldn't let that happen. You don't talk to me about crap black and white. I'm as good as you, if not better. And that was my idea to prove all the way through. I didn't have to go on any movements; I was a movement on my own. Kevin Rudd's apology [to the Stolen Generations in 2008] was a bag of wind. If they were any way fair dinkum about the apology – I'm glad that it's happened because it did – but didn't Paul Keating say, 'We were the ones that stole the land. We were the ones that raped the women. We were the ones'.[11] That was only a carbon copy of that, worded differently. It means nothing; raped I was for the land that they stole. They owe us for the damage that they caused. I still don't believe that I'm a full-bloody Aboriginal. I reckon some farmer up in Ebor had their way with my mum, and my dad couldn't say a thing about it. I look so different from my brother and sisters. My name's not necessarily really

11   See Paul Keating, 'The Redfern Park Address', 10 December 1992, in *Reconciliation: Essays on Australian Reconciliation*, ed. Michelle Grattan (Melbourne: Black Inc, 2000), 60–64.

Dave Cook – it's Dave Ritchie. But then again, Ritchie isn't my only dad; he was my dad's name. Cook was my mother's name. On my birth certificate it says father: unknown, mother: Norma Cook. So that's why I always maintained if my dad had been my father, they'd have put him on my birth certificate because we were living together. The whole family was. I believe there's something astray there. I'm going out real hard to find if that's true. I've been up there once to Ebor, and there's a couple of old ladies there that I got talking to that I wanna go back and find out. If anybody's going to know, these people sound like they do because they sound like they know everything. I can drive through Taree, I can drive through Kempsey, I can go through Nambucca Heads, and they say, 'What's your name?' I'll tell them and I'll have people falling all over me and telling me, 'Oh! I'm your relative!' and all this. And here I am; I don't know them from a bar of soap. Now, usually, you know your family. It doesn't matter how distant or how far away they are, and I've lost all that.

The Stolen Generations need to be compensated so they can get on, and start bringing their family lives back together again. They're gonna need money to do it. That was the *Bringing Them Home* report, right? I never heard anything much about it, but I remember sitting in a hospital in Newcastle, and that *Bringing Them Home* report was there and I was flipping through it and reading it.[12] As far as Kevin Rudd's apology – it's all wind, sounds like he's all wind anyway. It really doesn't matter to me whether Liberal or Labor gets in. I don't think I'll see any change as far as compensation and that goes. That's the reason why I went and saw my solicitor. Regardless, I'm 65 this year [2010]. Regardless of any decision that they make, he said, 'We'll let it go for 12 months. If nothing happens in the 12 months, we'll go for it'. So, from 12 months after I seen him, if nothing happens, we're going to go to the Supreme Court or wherever.

I only ever saw my mother again twice. There was nothing. It was like meeting a stranger. This was while I was in the Army. I went up once when I was in the Army and once when I was a civilian. She's gone now; so is my dad. I never saw my dad again. We brought him here, and he died here. To tell you the truth, he didn't look like me at all. But I call him dad. I'd call anybody dad then because I was reaching out for everything.

---

12   The *Bringing Them Home* report was the national inquiry that brought the Stolen Generations to national public attention. See National Inquiry into the Separation of Aboriginal and Torres Strait Islander Children from their Families (Australia), *Bringing Them Home: Report of the National Inquiry into the Separation of Aboriginal and Torres Strait Islander Children from Their Families* (Sydney: Human Rights and Equal Opportunity Commission, 1997).

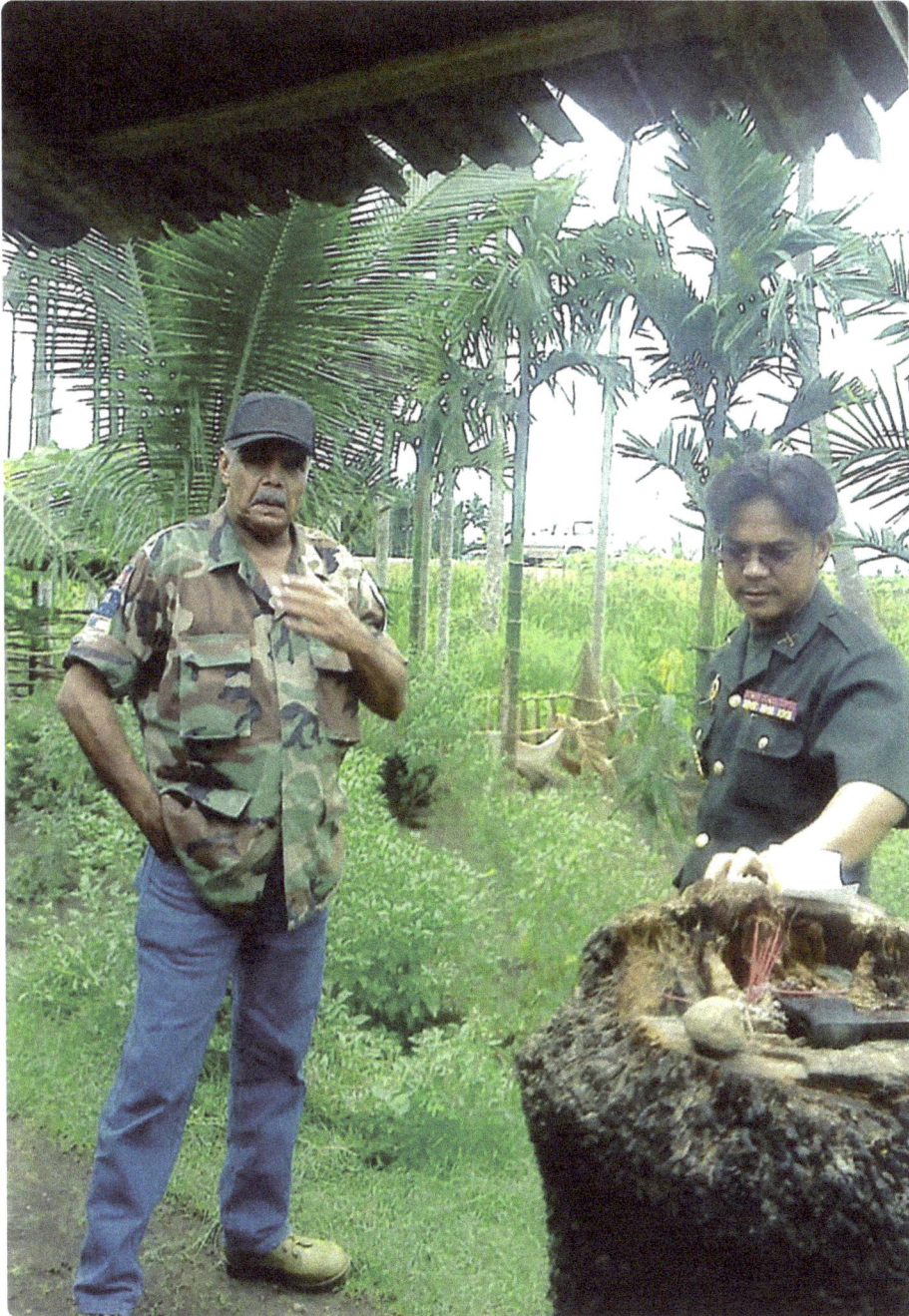

Figure 2. David Cook and Captain Vissell, Cambodia
Source: Courtesy David Cook

Thinking about it all, I'd like people to think that I was a good soldier. From the reactions that I got from my second tour to Vietnam – which were all National Service boys; they only did the two years, so we can virtually call them civilians with a uniform. From their reactions, I think I did pretty well, and I think they accepted me pretty well. I don't think I want non-Indigenous Australians to treat us Aboriginal veterans much differently, but I'd like them to give us what's due to us. If they were in the same position, how would we want them to treat us? I'd like them to be not so backward when somebody wants a bit of money to try and get their life together because they've had it stolen from under them. I reckon they should be pretty supportive of that. Indigenous Australians, on the other hand, have never really had an Army. I mean, even if you asked the guys in the Top End from around Broome and all them areas where they have the Indigenous soldiers looking after the Top End of Australia, I reckon that's a good thing. You couldn't ask for a better people to look after it because it's their homeland. That's what I'd like them to do. I think the Army is the best thing in the world. I reckon National Service should be bought back and made three years – 12 months training and two years serving the arms for everyone – black, white and blue, men and women. There's nothing so beautiful than a bit of discipline. Even with all the hassles that I had with the coppers and stuff, they couldn't believe that I was so disciplined. This is what gets me – most of the statements that were read out by the coppers were written by themselves. They thought that I was an uneducated black and they wrote it that way. I've got people back in those times and they'd say, 'You got the wrong guy. He wouldn't say stuff like that! He's more educated than that'.

4

Public Advocate

Sue Gordon[1]

Yamatji (Ngoonoroo Wadjarri) woman Sue Gordon is arguably one of the most high profile Aboriginal ex-servicewomen. She has led an incredibly full life: member of the Stolen Generations; raised at Sister Kate's Home in Queens Park, Western Australia; service in the Women's Royal Australian Army Corps (WRAAC); work in Pilbara Aboriginal communities; first Aboriginal magistrate in the Western Australian Children's Court; chair of state and national inquiries; chair of the National Indigenous Council; chair of the Northern Territory Emergency Response Taskforce; and mother. Gordon credits much of her life trajectory to the discipline instilled in her through her upbringing and her service in the WRAAC. Hers is a compelling story about military service providing new opportunities but the individual being the one to seize them.

I was born in 1943 at Meekatharra, WA, but as a result of the government policies of the day, I was removed from my mother at the age of four in 1947. I was taken from Mount James Station out of Meekatharra and brought to Perth and

---

1   This interview is available from the National Library of Australia (hereafter NLA), ORAL TRC 6260/5; reproduced with the permission of the National Library of Australia. It was recorded in Perth on 25 November 2010.

placed in a children's cottage home, later known as Sister Kate's Home.[2] I have no memories of family. I think in modern-day terminology, post-traumatic stress would have wiped any memory of a four-year-old. When I got my government file in the 1990s, it had the letters from the police officers, who were the protectors of natives. They were keeping an eye on me from the age of two: 'This light skinned child named Susie is being looked after, but should be removed', and then the Commissioner of Natives writing back saying, 'Yes, shouldn't be living with natives. Should be brought up as a white person'. Two years of letters went between police and the Commissioner of Natives and it even included the station people. The decision was made that I was to be removed and the cold-hearted letters read along the lines of: 'We should remove as quickly as possible. The mother will be upset, but they soon get over it'. They were words to that effect, but in the meantime, they were working behind the scenes to find out who my father was, so they could get maintenance out of him. They were better than the Australian Taxation Office and child support these days. They used all sorts of coercion to get him to accept that he was my father, right down to the fact that if he didn't sign the form, his name would be published in the local paper; so he signed and then began to pay maintenance.

While all that was happening, I was removed from my brother. My eldest brother, Norman [deceased November 2013], he was six at the time – he can still see it. I don't have any memory, but I was taken from Mount James, which was quite a few hours' drive from Meekatharra proper, so the police came out and took me from my mother. My brother sees this and my mother's going through whatever agony at that time was possible and I'm driven to Meekatharra. I'm handed across to a white lady called Mrs Webb from Mount Magnet and she and I are then put on the midnight train down to Meekatharra and to Perth over two days. Now, I don't have any recollection of that whatsoever. But I didn't go straight to Sister Kate's. I went to what was then called the East Perth Receiving Home. That's on Lord Street, here in Perth; the building's still there. I was there overnight, so that meant I was given to more strangers and then the next day, people from Sister Kate's came and collected me.

The funny part is some of the bigger girls who looked after me said, when I finally landed at Sister Kate's in November 1947, I couldn't speak English. I had desert blonde hair, candles hanging out of my nose, I had sandshoes on, no laces, no socks and what they called a little old gin dress. That's the derogatory term for Aboriginal women. I used to defecate in the corners of the house and I was like a little feral animal, but I was four. As I said in the *Australian Story* on television, I've got grandchildren and I cannot in a million years imagine my

2   For a history of Sister Kate's Home, see Anna Haebich, *Broken Circles: Fragmenting Indigenous Families* (Fremantle: Fremantle Arts Centre Press, 2000), 280–287; Christine Choo, 'Sister Kate's Home for "Nearly White" Children', in Doreen Mellor and Anna Haebich (eds), *Many Voices: Reflections on Experiences of Indigenous Child Separation* (Canberra: National Library of Australia, 2002), 193–207.

four-year-old, any four-year-old grandchild, going through that and coming out the other end. Obviously, post-traumatic stress set in, so I only know that now because it's in my file. We were told we were orphans, which was the practice of the day. When I was 14 there were actually people in the home who were my cousins, but you didn't know that. You grew up with all these other kids and you basically became brothers and sisters in that sense, and they're still my brothers and sisters today. I chair the organisation which is called Sister Kate's Children 1934 to 1953 Aboriginal Corporation, and we've built aged persons units for those who want to return to the only home they ever knew.

The policies and the legislation were that children whose fathers were white were to be removed, but two weeks after I was taken away, a letter was in my file. My Uncle Tony Moncrieff, who's passed away now, wrote a letter to the Commissioner asking could he have me and he'd bring me up as a white child. He would send me to school, because he was living under the White Act, the Dog Act, and they wrote back and said, 'No, she can't be living with natives'. He's had to forego any relationships, like Albert Namatjira with his family, to be under the White Act, the exemption, and yet he's told I can't be brought up with natives.[3] I took my Uncle Tony a copy of that letter in the mid-1990s, when I got my file. My late husband and I took it up to Carnarvon and he was tickled pink. He said, 'You know, I didn't write that letter'. I said, 'Who did?' He said, 'Your aunty wrote it', because he couldn't read and write. We had a big laugh about that, but I gave him a copy. I'd just come back from Meekatharra and I've got cousins and more cousins and more cousins, but you know, family's family. I think that's what makes you a person. There are people I grew up with who never found their families.

I know all my family now and it's really good. When I was 14, one of the girls found a letter in the office addressed to me and so I read the letter. There's a photo of this stockman, not that I knew what a stockman was, standing tall. He must have been in his early 20s and said he was my brother, Joe. I went down to the office and said, 'Oh, I've got this letter'. 'What do you mean, you've got this letter?' 'Oh, well, I got this letter from the office and this man says he's my brother'. One of the girls from Sister Kate's, whom I knew, Pearl, had said where I was. The letter was taken off me and ripped up and said, 'No, that's what these natives do. They'll tell you lies. You don't have a family'. So that was the trigger. Thirty years later, when a 16-year-old nephew came into the Commonwealth Employment Service where I was working in Port Hedland in the mid-1970s, said he was my nephew and I said, 'Well, I don't have any family'. Then it triggered, this letter, and I asked him if I had a brother Joe, and he said, 'My uncle Joe'.

---

3   Gordon is referring to the *Native (Citizenship Rights) Act* passed in 1944. See Tamara Hunter, 'The myth of equality: The denial of citizenship rights for Aboriginal people in Western Australia', *Studies in Western Australian History* 22 (2001): 69–82.

I now know all my family, I know who I am, I know where I'm from so I'm a complete person. I knew my mother for 11 years. It's a strange thing to say: I only knew my mother for 11 years. I never knew my father at all. I know who my father is because my mother told me before she passed away, and of course it is in my government file. She came down to me to die in Perth and she asked me not to make any contact and I won't. I know who they all are. They didn't want anything to do with me as a kid, so why bother? But my grandkids want to know the family tree, so it's all there, warts and all for them to follow up if they want to. My kids know, too; they will have the files when I die.

In Sister Kate's we were basically brought up in a little English setting. We lived in group houses, not dormitories, and we were brought up in steps and stairs. Boys and girls mixed. We went to church each day, brought up as little Anglicans. We learnt how to cook, sew and clean because we were being trained as domestics. Some kids knew that they were related, but we weren't told we were Aboriginal. We knew that we were different to the kids across the road at the school. When we got to school, we used to get the name calling – the niggers, boongs, all that sort of stuff, or arky arky little darky. But we were told to ignore them, so we developed a bit of a buffer in as much as we were all in the home, so we called ourselves the Home Kids and still do. The kids who lived outside the home were called the Outside Kids.

In the 1940s Aboriginal people weren't allowed to go to school by law, but Sister Kate just went across the road and demanded that her kids be allowed to go to school. She wanted an education for us, which we are so grateful that we were allowed to do that. In 2005, about 60 of us went to the 100th anniversary of the Queens Park Primary School, which was just across the road from Sister Kate's. I gave a speech on behalf of the Sister Kate's kids about our experiences at the school and the home. Then the other kids, Outside Kids, were talking after the speeches and to us about how jealous they were of us. We thought, 'Hello? Why are you jealous?' – because we always had someone to play with. A lot of those kids were from single child families and there were anytime up to 80 kids where we were, and there was always someone to play with. When you're playing with a big mob of kids, it's really great fun. You're playing rounders or you're going down the creek or whatever; we just took it for granted.

We didn't realise that people were envious of us. We used to whinge about the meals, but if you look at when I first went there, 1947, it was just after the war. Everybody was doing it hard. We were a charitable institution and everything was donated. We had a farm at Kenwick where the boys, as they got bigger, went and they grew all the vegetables and everything like that. We had our own cows, so we had fresh milk. We had big veggie gardens and chooks at Sister Kate's in Queens Park, plus the Kenwick one, so we weren't that badly off, but we were deprived of any contact with families.

Sister Kate (who was from a wealthy family in Bath, England, and was named Katherine Mary Clutterbuck) started the institution in 1934, but prior to that she'd been at Parkerville. She'd come out in the early 1900s from England with some waifs from the streets of London and some other Anglican sisters. They'd started Parkerville, which was in the wilderness. It's just the hills now, prime real estate, and when she turned 70, Archbishop Le Fanu told her she was too old and she should go into retirement. Being a nice nun, she didn't tell him to get stuffed. She just went with her benefactor Miss Phoebe Ruth Lefroy, from a very big farming family, who had 40 acres out at Queens Park, 10 kilometres from the central business district now. They were at Buckland Hill first; they began the home for kids, and she wrote to the Commissioner of Natives and said she'd take the lighter-skinned kids because no one wanted them. You have to look at history as well, not just the policies and the legislation of the day. The policies and the legislation were to remove the kids, but also in Aboriginal society those kids were shunned because they were white kids in their eyes. This was not in every tribal grouping, but in quite a lot. We were there and Sister Kate started the institution just to take the lighter-skinned kids, but she'd had all that experience at Parkerville and then she started to look after us. Sister Kate died in 1946 and then Miss Phoebe Ruth Lefroy continued running the place until her death in 1953. Because of the argument with the Anglican Church, she bequeathed the property to the Presbyterian Church, which went on to become the Uniting Church.

I was there in that crossover period, so in 1953, when the Presbyterians came in, they changed all the rules. There was abuse, but not when Sister Kate was in. Sister Kate did not allow men into the home; they could do the manual work in the daytime then had to leave. So there were only women looking after the kids and they were usually trusted people she'd brought from Parkerville with her. So then the type of house mothers, as they were called, changed. They became very short-term people; they came and went with complete abandon, no thought about the kids. They often came in between husbands. They had their own kids. Some of their kids abused the kids from Sister Kate's. Some of Sister Kate's kids who went out to placements, where they used to put the kids out for holidays, were abused there. Kids went out to work, even some my age and older, on farms where they were abused. Then men were allowed in the home and there was some abuse. I wasn't abused, not that I recall being abused. We were abused inasmuch at school; everyone got the cane and we used to get the strap, so physical abuse was rife, but it was rife across the country. Sexual abuse was the other one that people talk about, so there are a lot of people who went through that experience and then there was abuse among children. There's always abuse among children. There are always bully kids. We had a couple of girls who were bullies. That's as far as abuse goes in my case.

Figure 3. Sue Gordon with Miss Anderson at Sister Kate's annual fete, aged six years
Source: Courtesy Sue Gordon

There were a lot of Aboriginal people who used to come to the gates of Sister Kate's to see people because it was a bush block. There would be families who would go into the bush and the kids would run over there to see them. But because I was from Meekatharra, there were none of my family in Perth. I didn't have any contact at all, but others, the Nyoongar people of the south-west who are around Perth areas, some of their families were able to see them.

We were sent out to work in the school holidays when we got into high school. I used to go to Dalkeith, which is a very posh suburb here. They had a full-time housekeeper, who was a Sister Kate's girl. She was on her annual holiday, but she didn't go overseas or anything like that. She just went and stayed with another Sister Kate's girl because they didn't get enough money to go anywhere. I went in as the live-in childcare girl. I wasn't the cleaner, but I was there to look after the two kids while the lady of the house did her own thing, and that was quite enjoyable. The kids I was minding were totally spoilt and there were other kids in the area from St Joseph's Orphanage and some other Sister Kate's kids that were with other families doing the same as me.

As we were getting a little bit older, they used to try and put kids into homes for weekends and the holidays. That was after Sister Kate. I used to go out to a few places. I remember one place wanted to adopt me, but I didn't know what adopt meant and no one explained anything to you. I can recall the experience on Christmas Day. It was lovely to go because you were going to get a better meal than probably at home. I think we were very selfish children in that way. I went to this place and I woke up in the morning and I remembered getting on my bed a brand new Raggedy Ann doll. I was overcome with joy because everything at Sister Kate's for Christmas was broken and second-hand. We got one thing that was probably new in our little box on the end of our bed. But it was a charitable home, so in hindsight you have to look at it from that point of view. I was excited and I ran into the other girl in the house because I was going to be adopted and be her sister, not that I knew anything about all that. She had on the end of her bed the most magnificent bride doll, so in my little ten-year-old eyes, I could see that there was a difference, and on Christmas Day I demanded to go home. I was taken home, lots of tears, and I was sent to bed without any lunch and told how ungrateful I was. I didn't know what any of all of this was about; I just knew I didn't want to be there. Years later, I mentioned it to the superintendent (Mrs Minors), who said, 'But you would have had an opportunity'. I said, 'But I wouldn't have had an opportunity because I would have always been the second-hand rose'. Anyway, I had some delightful placements where I just went for a holiday.

I had a group of people called Toc H. They were formed after the First World War and the ladies of Toc H were mostly spinsters; that's a quaint old word, isn't it? They used to take me out for picnics and overnight. I used to go to South Perth – a lovely little spot. I learnt with these genteel ladies about having English high tea, and they did a lot of charitable work. Anything new I got was from these ladies – mostly knitted jumpers, twin sets – and they looked after me. The Toc H as a group, men and women, used to come out once a month to Sister Kate's and show movies in the old kindergarten. We used to call them our ladies, so I used to have them as my ladies. Somebody else would go off with another group of people. There'd be annual picnics where we'd go with the Buffalo Club to the zoo. We'd be put with a family, so in a lot of ways Sister Kate and Miss Lefroy were giving us as much taste of life as they could possibly give us. But we were still being trained to be domestics and farm hands.

I was in that crossover. Just before Miss Lefroy died, if you weren't doing well at school, you were sent out to work. So girls went out to work at 12, 13, and boys too. Once the Presbyterians came in, if you started to do okay at school you could stay. I started high school with seven kids and I think three or four of us finished. The others were sent out to work, and I still hate domestic work. There was no way was I going to be one of those. And then I was lucky. When I was in third-year high school I had a typing teacher (Mrs Scurry) who thought that there was some promise because I liked typing. It was one of those things you just take to, and she got me a scholarship to business college. So that was my out.

I went to Underwood Business College, but Sister Kate's weren't happy about that because they had to find money in a charitable institution to give me a weekly train fare into Perth and that was £1 in 1959. That was a lot of money – a whole pound. That was my weekly train fare, so I had to take my lunch and I used to meet up at lunchtime with some of the other girls who were working in the city. I did well at business college because I wanted to, and those were the days where business college guaranteed you a job. My first job where I got paid was with the Commonwealth Bureau of Census and Statistics, as they used to be called [now the Australian Bureau of Statistics]. It was a year of a census and I spent three months just typing up forms. No computers – nothing – and I'm typing up all of these things. This was 1959–60, and then when that job finished, they automatically got me another job at Skipper Bailey Motor Company, up in the top of Hay Street. It doesn't exist there now. They sold Hillmans, Humbers, Super Snipes and that's the days there were no crassy car yards; only a genteel type of customer came in. By now I was a junior stenographer, so I also had to learn how to make morning teas for the board, those little old white-haired gentlemen who came in once a month to have a board meeting. Because of my training with the Toc H ladies, I knew how to make all of that. I used to think it was a waste of time, though, cutting morning-tea cake wafer thin. But I had to do that and they trained me hard there, but that was the old school. When you went to work, you went to work. I had to get to work half an hour early to put the urn on because I also had to make the morning teas. Then the junior boy and I had to take the mail up to the post office and we had to run, because we were timed by the head lady in the office.

I enjoyed that experience, but there was something missing and I had to get out of Sister Kate's because as soon as you worked, you had to leave. You weren't encouraged to stay. There was nowhere I could stay. I had become by now a Ward of the State because my father had shot himself Christmas Day in 1951. I had to find accommodation, so I wrote to the Welfare and said could they find me accommodation without children, because I'd had enough of all these kids. I told them not to go to Sister Kate's and tell them, but they went straight to the Home, so my trust in the welfare system and social workers just went out the window. I've never had any real trust because they couldn't keep the confidentiality of a child as I was still then. So Sister Kate's said, 'We'll find you a place', and I said, 'No. I'll find something'. The pressure was on me, and by now I was 17. I went up into North Perth as it used to be called, now Northbridge, and I was in Francis Street and they had the Army barracks there and the recruiting office. I went in and it sounded all exciting. They were going to pay me and send me to Sydney. Where's Sydney, you know?

I went back home and I said I was going to join the Army and Mr Daniels, the superintendent, said, 'Well, you can't because you're not 18'. I said, 'No, when I'm 18. Then I'll have accommodation, because this has got accommodation', and he said, 'Well, there's some terrible people', and he started to tell me about bad men. I said, 'Well, you were in the Army'. God, I must have been cheeky. He huffed and puffed and he said, 'Well, we won't allow it'. Now, I don't have a birth certificate, like a lot of Aboriginal people my age. My birth was never registered anywhere but I got a letter from Sister Kate's. You can't do that these days, just get a letter. I've still got that letter that says, according their records, I was born on this date. I posted that off to the Army and then when I was 18, I went and I said, 'Now I'm not a Ward of the State anymore. I'm going to join the Army. I've been and signed the papers. But I need a letter from you to say that I am 18. That has to confirm it and if you do that, then I've got to fly to Sydney'. The day I joined the Army [19 October 1961], I joined with another Perth girl who was escaping alcoholic parents. There was another young non-Aboriginal girl who just wanted a bit of adventure, and twins, whose father was a policeman. This was the Women's Royal Australian Army Corps.[4] I'm still friends with them. All these years later and I see the twins on Anzac Day. One marches and one doesn't.

So off we went on this great adventure and Sister Kate's reluctantly took me to the airport. I'd never been on a plane. I didn't even know where Sydney was and we were all frightened. We had our worldly possessions in our suitcase and we were put on this plane to Sydney by the Army and met by the Army. Then the

---

4   The Women's Royal Australian Army Corps (WRAAC), formed in February 1951, was the successor to the Second World War's Australian Women's Army Service (AWAS). The force had a similar role as its AWAS predecessor: to employ women in non-combat capacities to free male labour. WRAAC was disbanded in 1984 as women were fully integrated in the regular forces. For a history of WRAAC, see Janette Bomford *Soldiers of the Queen: Women in the Australian Army* (South Melbourne: Oxford University Press, 2001); Lorna Ollif, *Colonel Best and her Soldiers: The Story of 33 Years of the Women's Royal Australian Army Corps* (Hornsby, NSW: Ollif Publishing Company, 1985).

yelling and jumping around started at Middle Head in Mosman, New South Wales. I didn't find it difficult because I'd been brought up in an institution and you get six weeks when you first join the Army. If they liked you or you didn't like them, you could go and no one was to suffer. I just found it rather good because the meals weren't bad, they paid me, they gave me a uniform, the girls were okay; they were just like kids from Sister Kate's. In the six weeks we were there, three or four girls went home because they couldn't handle it. We learnt how to march; we learnt how to salute the goal post because you have to practise saluting. You learnt the military history. You learnt how to spit and polish your shoes. You learnt how to do heavy domestic work. Well that wasn't anything new; I'd already done that – cleaning, cooking, those sort of things.

Then you learnt all about the facts of life. Now, I was a little virgin and here I am suddenly in this man's Army, Women's Royal Australian Army Corps it was called, and they then had to give us educational level lessons about venereal diseases. Oh warts and all – all in this one room and there's a movie screen up, and suddenly you're seeing genital STIs [sexually transmitted infections] in full colour on the screen, and everyone's going, 'Oh my God!' But we had to sit and watch that and then we had to ask questions. We had to understand these were possibilities and that if you had sexual intercourse, this was going to happen. Whoa, oh my God! It would put you off for life. They wouldn't show these in schools today. The training was designed to get you disciplined. But I already had discipline because that came from Sister Kate's, so I can't say the training was outrageous. We did march in the middle of the rain because Army always seems to want you to march in the rain, three, four or 10 miles with a great big poncho on – a ground sheet, it's called – but it never covers every bit of you. Women's Royal Australian Army Corps didn't do weapons training, so we were then going off to individual units for the next training.

The Army asks you, 'Where would you like to go?' 'What are these choices?' But you don't actually get a choice; they just send you anywhere, but it looks nice that you're asked. My mate Lyn and I, because we'd both had office backgrounds, got sent to Signals in Victoria, which was then called 403 Sig Regiment. Lyn and I went off to Signals, the twins went off to become drivers, and Gail went off to do something else. Lyn and I ended up at 403 Sig Regiment in Watsonia, but we were living at 21 WRAAC Barrack in St Kilda Road in Melbourne, and it was an old mansion, converted to barracks.

Once there we learnt about prostitutes. We learnt about lesbians. We didn't even know what they were. We were told not to wear white shoes in St Kilda Road and we couldn't work out why. We're young women and we wanted to wear white shoes with our nice summery dresses. We found out that the prostitutes used to walk up and down St Kilda Road in white shoes so the curb crawlers would know who they were – valuable lessons being learnt. We also learnt about lesbians. I had no idea about lesbians and some girls in the know, in the barracks, put you in touch very quickly: 'Make sure you don't let this one or this one get you in a room on their own, because you're green as grass'. 'And what's green as grass?' So you learnt all about those things very quickly.

We were sent off to work. Because we were going into Signals, we went to Mount Martha on the Mornington Peninsula. The Army had acres and acres of land up there. We lived in Mount Martha in this old guesthouse just for the women and we went each day with the men in Signals training because of our background in office work. We learnt to be teleprinter operators. Later we also learnt how to become cipher operators, which is 'Shhh – if I tell you, I'll have to kill you'. We then became the elite in Signals. When we went back to our unit, we worked shift work in the big tape relay centres, which were as long as this building. Today, you can put on a chip in a computer. We became special people working shifts, but then the cipher people worked in another room, which was always locked and only certain people were allowed into that room. I became a cipher operator and because we were specialists, Lyn and I were also sent to Perth in 1962 for the Empire Games to do the communications with AAP Reuters, and we also got sent up to Sydney to Dundas to do the cipher work for the boys when they were on exercise in the field. We got a fair bit of special treatment and a bit of liberty because we were cipher operators. Cipher operators are sort of cream Signal regiments. You have to be a bit special. You'd work on a shift on your own, so you'd be there bloody 12 hours on your own, but all of that training was about discipline. I say it now: 'That discipline from Sister Kate's and the discipline from the Army is what gets me now'.

One interesting thing was in Cipher and in the Signals centre. When you're doing shifts round the clock, you're getting signals from around the world. I was on duty with others when the Cuban Missile Crisis hit the fan. There are these tapes, spewing out. Now, you've seen old movies, where these tape relay machines are there and they spit this tape out. As part of our training, we had to learn to read the holes in those tapes. That's the Murray Code. You could read these tapes without any typing on them because you'd learnt that. These tapes are spewing out and they've got the code on them, which is the highest, and I think, 'Oh my God!' It was not just me; the duty shift sergeant was having a fit as well, and that meant calling higher-ranking people out to come to see all this. But we were on duty when the Cuban Missile Crisis hit the fan – John F. Kennedy and all.

They were probably highlights and being sent across for the Empire Games was another one. We came across to Perth on a troop train with all the SAS boys in second-class travel, because the Army was always second class. I'm a trained touch typist; I'm still a fast typist, first as a junior stenographer and then in the Army we went on to teleprinters. We used the teleprinters at all the venues around Perth: the velodrome, where the cycling was, and Perry Lakes, where most of the events were. We actually were seconded to AAP Reuters and we had to type up all the results. We were typing flat out. We typed up all of AAP's results and then they were just fed into the system for overseas. We also had a bit of a holiday while we were over here and then we were sent back to the eastern states on the train again.

We learnt another skill, as most Army people do. For women, if you were coming home on your own, you could come on the train first class or they would fly you home for your leave. But if you were travelling with somebody else, you travelled second class and you didn't fly; you came on the train. So Lyn and I used to plan our leave so she went on leave a week after me, so we could still be on leave here, but we came first class on the train. I suppose it's called just using and abusing the system. We had a really good time. We made so many friends. We went out together with people and you've got to remember too, it was also six o'clock closing at pubs and so we used to get signed into clubs. Someone would sign you into a club down the dives of Melbourne, which is now Southbank. It was a pretty divey country then; you've got your Crown Casino there now, but it just used to be quite seedy down in South Melbourne and there were the clubs there. During the time in the Army, you could stay in any state at the Army Club. Accommodation was quite cheap, but you also made these long-term friends, males and females, Army, Navy and Air Force.

I can still remember we used to go to a lot of parties when the Navy were in. They would send an invitation to the girls from the barracks to come down, have a party. It wasn't about sex and all of that, or drugs, because I don't know if there were many drugs around. There was alcohol. I remember going to a party on HMAS *Voyager*, the ship that was sunk by the HMAS *Melbourne*.[5] When that accident happened, I could recall going to this party and some of those boys that we would have met there would have died in that accident. When we lived in St Kilda Road, Dell, who was from Queensland, was our driver. There were Lyn and I and a couple of others who used to go out to Watsonia every day for work before we moved to Watsonia. Dell also became friends with all the mounted police in St Kilda Road. She used to get us invites to the parties out at the police stables. They had good parties out there. Then there were times, because of our top secret clearance ranking, Lyn and I used to work in Vic Barracks in the centre room there, which is now Defence Signals Directorate.

---

5   The HMAS *Melbourne* and HMAS *Voyager* collided on 10 February 1964, killing 82 sailors and leading to a royal commission.

Figure 4. Sue Gordon, Lance Corporal in WRAAC, Signals-Cipher
operator, 1963

Source: Courtesy Sue Gordon

When I was in the WRAAC there was no sexism or gender discrimination. There was not in those days because we were in designated women's type roles and promotions were set for women only. In the WRAAC you weren't being promoted in the male section and we had female officers. We were 403 Signal Regiment. There was a male colonel in charge of the whole area, but in my area of Cipher, I had a male and a female officer in charge of that. The shift sergeant was a male, so you worked with them because you were all in Signals. Even now, it's quite funny – if I march on Anzac Day the guys from Sigs always yell, 'Listen, girls. If you don't get the numbers, come and join us', because we were all signallers, so it's like a big family. Nowadays if I've got a problem – there are two groups of people and it's probably a bit sad. I will talk to somebody from Sister Kate's or somebody from the Army. I've told my own brothers and sisters and they said, 'Well, that's who you grew up with'.

I remember one particularly funny time in the Army. You've got to remember you're talking about 1961 to 1964, and there were 'reds under the bed'. I used to play basketball for a civilian club outside of the barracks. One of the girls I played basketball with was living with one of the Army boys in the barracks, who was a friend of mine and I can remember having ambitions in the Army. Although I was at the top in Cipher and I didn't want to go to another regiment, I thought I would like to get into Intelligence one day. I can still remember it, and it's not covered under the *Official Secrets Act* or anything, but I got a message that I had to go up in full uniform while I was off shift. I had to go in full uniform to the Colonel's office and there were some people from Intelligence who needed me to go before the Intelligence Corps people. It is like going before the Spanish Inquisition; it is sort of scary. But I thought, 'Ooh, they might want me to join them' – naive little person. I marched in there, because you've got to march and salute everywhere, and there are these three people sitting there and they needed to ask me some questions about people I was mixing with. It turned out that Pat, whom I was playing basketball with, was living with one of the boys. She and I played basketball, but she was a known Communist. I didn't even know what a Communist was. Intelligence put me through the third degree, asked me these questions and then told me there was nothing I could do about it; I was not to have anything more to do with her. I'm playing basketball in a team that was winning, and how do I do this? I had to stop playing basketball. I couldn't say anything. I couldn't say that I'd been told; it's very hard, but I had to manage that part of my life. So when I went back to my mate, Lyn, because we shared rooms, she said, 'What did they want?' I said, 'I got told off. I'm not allowed to play basketball. I have to pull out 'cause Pat's a Communist. What's a Communist?' That was very severe in hindsight, which is always wonderful. I'm in Cipher, which is hush-hush secret. I had a top secret clearance and so they were obviously frightened for me. I told this story at an 80th Signal Regiment dinner in Perth a few years ago and they said, 'Who was it? Who was it?' and

I said, 'Not telling you'. Anyway, it was Rory; Pat was his girlfriend. I found out years later in the Pilbara what a Communist was when old Don McLeod said he was a known Communist and they'd kept an eye on him.[6]

Figure 5. Sue Gordon, front row, second from left, captain of the netball team, Southern Command WRAAC, 1963 or 1964
Source: Courtesy Sue Gordon

I didn't have any problems in the Army. There was obviously a little bit of racism. There wasn't overt racism. There was racism in as much as I think there were some people who weren't sure why Aboriginal people (some still called us natives) were being allowed in. I used to say to people, 'I grew up in an institution with a lot of Aboriginal people who are put there from their families'. And I said, 'A lot of boys I grew up with went to war'. And I said, 'I joined the Army because I needed somewhere to go'. I didn't know much about it, but I had name calling all my life, so it was just more name calling, but I didn't have a lot. I think it was because of the nature of the work that I was doing; you weren't really in the run of the mill areas. I made a lot of firm friends and I'm still very good friends with most people I joined up with. You've got to remember that we were all 18.

---

6   Don McLeod was a member of the Communist Party of Australia who was active in Indigenous politics, especially in the Pilbara region. See Don McLeod, *How the West Was Lost: The Native Question in the Development of Western Australia* (Port Hedland, WA: Don McLeod, 1984).

We were very young people and very impressionable, and then we watched a lot of the boys go off to Vietnam. Some of them went to Borneo first with the SAS. It was no different to the boys that I'd grown up with, but I was growing up with these boys in the Army and some married within the Army. I eventually married an SAS Signaller, my first husband. Not all of them worked out. I think it's because you're working 24-7 sometimes with people; you think that's how it's going to be.

I met up with a few other Stolen Generations and other Aboriginal people in the Army. I had contact with a man that had a lot of difficulties; he was from the Northern Territory. He was accepted in the Army. One of the Aboriginal men who wasn't in my unit but was in Signals went to Vietnam and he was very popular with his fellow soldiers. He had racism because he was from the Northern Territory. One of the Aboriginal girls I served directly with, she was from South Australia. She had a lot of racism because she was pretty dark and she took offence. She only did three years, too. She got out and I don't know what happened to her after that. What I saw were just taunts. When I say taunts, I mean name calling: 'Oh, hurry up, ya boong' – things that actually hurt without thinking about it. When I look at the era, those people who were making those comments, that's how they were brought up. Their families would have acted like that, and it wouldn't have meant anything. There were lots of other Aboriginal servicemen and women, but I didn't serve directly with them.

My contacts were with the boys that I grew up with at Sister Kate's. I was the only girl from Sister Kate's who joined the Army. A lot of the boys did, because we had boys from Sister Kate's in the Second World War and in Korea. We had five in Korea; some were in Malaya and Vietnam, and now some of our grandchildren are in Afghanistan. We have a big history, a proud history at Sister Kate's, and we had this function a few years ago up at Bruce Rock with John Schnaars of Honouring Indigenous War Graves.[7] One of the Sister Kate's Korean veterans was going around to the different ones, finding out who's holding medals for someone deceased. He could get them mounted and then he was checking up who was related to whom and he said, 'Now, we're all brothers and sisters, so we're entitled to wear someone else's medals', but on the right side. When we rocked up to Bruce Rock for the function, which was part of the 'Back to the Bush – Vietnam Veterans' weekend, I think there were about half a dozen of the Sister Kate's kids, all wearing medals. Some wore their own medals and others were wearing them for one of the Sister Kate's brothers or sisters who had passed away. It was really a proud moment, because we've always called ourselves brothers and sisters. It just sort of changes the whole history of medal wearing, but it is how we view it.

---

7   See Chapter 5.

That was the Army and I did three years from 1961 to 1964. They wanted me to stay in the Army. I found it an interesting experience, but I was not ready to sign my life away. After three years I'd been promoted to a lance corporal, one stripe, and in charge of a shift and then offered another stripe to stay in, but I needed to travel. I'd got the bug and so I said, 'No, thank you'. Once I was out of the Army, after working in the office in Myer, Melbourne, for three months, I went to Queensland and worked up in Lennon's Hotel. I'd been up to Queensland with one of the girls who got out of the Army and her grandmother put me up and I got a job as a ledger machinist. The ledger machine has all these keyboards; it was this great machine that used to feed all these numbers into it and accounts. At the end of every month, you had to balance all the accounts. Skipper Bailey Motor Company had trained me to operate the machine (you can now do the same job on a laptop), so I walked into this job and I worked shifts there. I told them I would only stay for one year, and it was a very classy hotel. It was *the* hotel in Brisbane and it's a small boutique hotel now. It's not the same as it was in those days and it was a family. The manager of the hotel insisted that all the girls who worked evening shift got sent home in a taxi. It didn't matter if you were the barmaid or the ledger machinist.

I was in the office, but if you wanted to rotate through to understand the hotel, that was fine. It was part of the practice. I spent a week in the cocktail lounge, learning how to make cocktails with the girls there. Then I went into the kitchen to see how the kitchens operate and it actually paid benefits to the hotel. In the office, you would get the dockets for the functions and you would have been up in the kitchen and you then knew how everything worked up there by the time you got the dockets. It was interesting and everything ran so smoothly on the surface, but ducks disease behind. Little feet were going flat out and I recall two incidents at the hotel in 12 months.

One of the major things was I said to my boss, 'My best friend is getting married in Tasmania. I can't afford the airfare down, but I need to go because I'm going to be her bridesmaid but I will be coming back'. Now, people trusted you in those days. This was 1965, and he said, 'That's okay, Sue. We'll pay your fare'. I'd only been at the hotel for about five months. So they paid my return airfare to Tasmania and I came back and I finished the 12 months and I paid the money back. So much trust people had; they looked after the staff.

One incident happened when I was up the kitchen doing my little week. I just was observing how they were. There's the kitchen. There are all the function rooms. There are the different chefs for all the different things and then there is the lady who sits and every meal's got to go past her. So she's putting in the dockets and they're getting done. In those days, they used to put them in the little tube and – shwoop – suck them down and they'd end up in the office. I'm sitting there with Mrs Mac and there are two big function rooms nearby. I'd been to see one function room, which had the most magnificent swan sculptured out of butter, and another swan carved out of ice. There was pomp and ceremony to take food out. The little apprentice chefs in their little checked pants and white tops were coming out with the big platter with the pig on it. Mrs Mac's checking it off to send to that function room number, and the head chef is coming behind the boys. One apprentice tripped and fell. The pig went on the ground, the apprentice's bawling, the chef gives him a quick one behind the ear: 'Get up, you stupid boy! Pick the pig up!' He put the pig back up on tray. They used to have these brown paper heavy duty funnels on the bottom for piping. They used to pipe mashed potato around for decoration, so by now the pig's back on the tray, apple's back in its mouth, chef's got a bit of greenery on and he's piping more potato around it, on the pig. Then the kids walked in ceremoniously into the dining room. No one would have known what happened, except us, the observers. This pig's been on the ground. That's the goings on in a hotel. Another time I was on day shift and had arrived early one morning; we were told that there was a flood on the mezzanine floor. What happens in a flood? It happened just after midnight and up until seven in the morning, there were these big removal vans pulled up outside the front of Lennon's Hotel. Without batting an eyelid, these removalist people were coming down with dripping wet carpet, down the side of the big balcony, the staircase, just down one side, dripping on plastic, out into the vans to take it away. In the meantime, guests are coming and going and the hotel's running as if nothing's happening. But you could see it all.

After 12 months work at the hotel I came back to Perth. I owed Sister Kate's some money because before I went to join the Army, I had a Vespa scooter bike and I hadn't paid it off. I stopped off in Sydney to see Bob and Meg Simpson first, to catch up and because I had stayed with Meg when Bob went to play cricket in South Africa in 1958/59. Bob Simpson used to teach the boys from Sister Kate's how to play cricket. The institution said I had to come and cut the money out, so I went back to Sister Kate's for three months and I worked looking after little Aboriginal kids. It was the most appalling time of my life because here was me thinking I'm this woman of the world by now, and I am looking after these kids who were probably the same as I was when I was placed in Sister Kate's.

I then got a job with NASA in Carnarvon, at the tracking station. The Amalgamated Wireless of Australia was the subcontractor and they were looking for a teleprinter operator. I didn't even know where Carnarvon was, but I found out later that my uncle, all my cousins and everyone were there. I applied for this job and I went in there and I had a quasi-interview. They just said, 'When can you go to Carnarvon?' Sort of like, 'Today?' So within days, I was on the plane to go to Carnarvon. They used to take eight hours on the plane to go to Carnarvon on old DC-3s because you'd go everywhere.

I rocked up into Carnarvon in early 1966. The tracking station was doing the first of the Manned Space Flights. They'd done the Gemini and then they were doing the first of the Apollo Manned Space Flights and I was employed in the communication centre. When I first went there, my old staff sergeant was in charge and everyone else in there was ex-Army. There were ex-Air Force around the USB radar section and some other navy people were there. It was basically all ex-military, and American and English technical experts, because we all had the top secret clearances. We used to do 16-hour shifts when the spacecraft was in our area, coming across the horizon. We lived in Carnarvon at the old Port Hotel owned by later federal MP Wilson Tuckey. We were basically isolated from Carnarvon people because we worked terrible long hours. But that was our job, and it was fascinating. The space commander's talking to us, as they're going over the horizon. Again, the Army had given me that discipline and training and I just walked in that job.

When I was in Carnarvon at the tracking station, I played basketball again. I was actually playing basketball against my cousins. They knew who I was but didn't want to say anything because they were too embarrassed. Years later, I just saw one of the cousins up there and I said to her, 'You know, you mob could have said something'. 'No, no. We were too embarrassed'. That was the sort of thing that happened. I was at the tracking station working for NASA during the 1967 Referendum.[8] At the time it annoyed me what was happening in Carnarvon with the Aboriginal conditions that were there, but I had not known that I didn't have any rights, if you know what I mean. I'd been in the Army. I'd had a lot of freedoms; I wasn't restricted. I went to pubs and clubs. I didn't appreciate the fact that I wasn't supposed to be doing those things because no one actually openly told me I shouldn't as an Aboriginal woman. There were probably some veiled hints, but nothing open.

For nearly two years I worked for NASA. Then I came back to Perth and got married. My husband was in Signals in Melbourne at Watsonia in another unit, and then he was accepted into the SAS. We then got married in Melbourne and his mum was the only mother I had for 15 years, before my family found me. His mum and dad took me in basically and they paid for my wedding. That's a bit of a weird one, isn't it? We then moved to Perth as he was still in the SAS, and then he decided he was going to get out. That was with the beginning of mining in the north-west, so he got a job at Goldsworthy. He got out and I was working in the office at Western Australian Leather Goods in East Perth. I was the only girl in the office there and doing everything: ledger, machining, typing – the whole lot. Rick got this job and said we were going

8   See Bain Attwood and Andrew Markus, *The 1967 Referendum: Race, Power and the Australian Constitution* (Canberra: Aboriginal Studies Press, 2007).

to go to Port Hedland: 'Where's Port Hedland?' We went up to Port Hedland and we were with Goldsworthy Mining. I had two boys both born in Hedland, 1969 and 1971.

We went back to Melbourne a couple of times and then we went to Wickham, out of Roebourne. We even lived in Newman for a short stint. That was when I first went to Jigalong to see if the Welfare had any record of my time spent there before Sister Kate's. It was the most appalling time; the Welfare worker virtually stayed behind the wire fence and told me there were no records. I worked half days with the Ieramugadu Group in Roebourne for the local Aboriginal people and half days for the Welfare. That was my first contact with traditional Aboriginal people and that's the first time people said to me, 'Well, there's nobody who hasn't got a family'. Alice Smith [now deceased], whom I call Aunty Alice, said to me, 'You must have family'. She's the first one who said to me in the '70s, 'Your family's in Meekatharra'. I said, 'I don't have a family', and I was denying it. I'm working with these wonderful traditional people in Roebourne and learning all these beaut things about people. I was learning all the hard facts about how isolated Roebourne was, as against mining, because Wickham was a closed town then. I would go home each evening to a three-bedroom, air-conditioned house, paid a pittance rent and I could see the poverty in Roebourne, so I was seeing this. We stayed there and then we went back to Melbourne and then we were thinking about getting a divorce and then I went to Hedland. I drove to Melbourne twice with two little kids in an old Falcon from Port Hedland. All the time, when I was getting a divorce, my first husband's parents took my side: 'There's always a place here for you'. Rick had come back from Vietnam. He'd been to Borneo. He was seeing first-hand death before he was 20 and he had post-traumatic stress disorder, but none of us knew that. No one knew what post-traumatic stress was. He had malaria really bad. We were both drinking too much. If we'd known about post-traumatic stress then, if they'd have had treatment, I think in hindsight you don't know how things would have been. At that same time, I'm working with Aboriginal people and people are telling me I've got a family. So I'm finding my Aboriginality and he's going through post-traumatic stress and trying to hold down a job. You can see how bad it must have been for both of us.

We divorced and I moved to Hedland and I got a job with Commonwealth Employment Service, which was lucky because they provided accommodation as well. I was again working with traditional people and travelling out as far afield as the Great Sandy Desert and finding people who said I've got family. My family still hadn't found me and people were saying that they think I'm part of their family, and it turned out that they were. So that was good for me, but it was exceptionally good for my kids, because I had an Aboriginal lady with a big family who used to take my kids when I had to travel 600 kms a day. They were being brought up with Aboriginal brothers and sisters, so to speak.

Meanwhile, someone told my nephew [Maitland] and someone had told somebody else that there was this lady in Port Hedland who could be his aunty. I was called Lundberg, which was my first married name, but they said that they thought my maiden name was Gilla. It wasn't Gilla, but it was Giller, because the government used to change your name. They used to often split up brothers and sisters when they took them away and gave them different names, but they just varied the spelling of my name. So that's how he found me. My nephew's a cheeky little bugger. He just knew I was his aunty. I got to know my brother Joe before he died because he worked at Ethel Creek Station. I had to go out to Jigalong community, so I used to have to drive through the station. I'd sit and have a chat with him and he was also roo shooting at the time. On the way home, I'd get kangaroo tails, frozen ones, out of his van and take them home. When my family came and found me, it was not a big shock to my kids. But I went to Meekatharra with my nephew who'd found me and suddenly, in a weekend, I met my mother, my brothers and all these nieces and nephews and cousins. It was overwhelming for me. It wasn't overwhelming for my boys because they were in primary school. It was really good and I was happy after that, but it took a lot of time for my mum to talk because she thought I blamed her. I told her that I never, ever blamed her.

There were 11 brothers and sisters all up, but just recently I found out in actual fact there were 13 of us because some had died. Only I had been removed by the government. My eldest sister was the result of a rape of my mother, so she was put out to adoption. My eldest brother [Norman, now deceased] had a different Aboriginal father. Then my next brother had an Aboriginal father. Then there was me with a white father. Then all the ones who came after me had the same Aboriginal father. I found out recently that one of my sisters, who's younger than me, was actually a twin. Now, that's the first I'd ever heard of it. 'No one ever told me', and I said, 'It's not in my file'. She said, 'No. I just thought I better tell you'. I said, 'God'. Some of my siblings have died since, so there are only five of us left: just myself as the eldest and my four sisters.

My brother Joe died when I was in Roebourne. You've got to bear in mind that it's 560 kms out to Ethel Creek and it's another 200 kms down to Roebourne. I was in Roebourne and I got a phone call from the police. As soon as the police call you, there's something wrong: could I get to Hedland Airport? How long does it take? I got to Hedland Airport just in time for the flying doctor to come in with his body and his Aboriginal wife Josie. She was a mess. She couldn't do the identification, so I had to do it and I'd only known my brother a few years. I had to do it. I spent half an hour in the morgue, talking to Joe about all the things that I should have talked with him when I was a kid. It was quite sad and I was telling my sister and she said, 'Oh'. When it was time to take him to Meekatharra, I'd said to the family, 'I'll drive Brother down, 12 hours'. 'No. Get the undertaker'. I said, 'No, the undertaker's too expensive. Who's going to pay for that?' 'Oh, you work'. I said, 'No, I don't earn that much money. I'm not paying for it and you mob aren't paying', so I said, 'I'll bring Brother home'. One of my nephews [Lindsay] and I drove him home and the people were a bit funny about that, but in recent times, it's becoming more fashionable. Now there are more and more Aboriginal people who are driving their families home.

When we lost my mum she was down in Perth, and my late husband and I decided we'd drive Mum home because it was going to cost money. That's 12 hours and we had to time it just right. So we got into Meekatharra at first light so that we could take Mum straight to the morgue, but people wouldn't get in the car. I said, 'That's okay. I don't mind'. We just put something over Mum and just chatted away. I just chatted to her about being a kid. I think you've got to do things sometimes because you didn't have the opportunity before. I go to all the funerals where I can. People now know that I'm retired, and self-funded retirees can't have all these trips. I said, 'I'll come to as many funerals as I can, but I've got to remember that it's my super that I'm spending and I can't afford it'. People have this mistaken belief, even in my own family: 'But you're a magistrate'. 'Yes,' I said, 'I know and I made provisions. I've got my superannuation, but that's my pension. The government doesn't give me a pension'. 'Oh, okay'. But they still think you're rich.

The first strike in this country by Aboriginal people was the stockmen strike of 1946.[9] I had the privilege to work with those blokes who were involved in that strike and old Don McLeod, the known communist. He's from Meekatharra and at one stage he thought he was my father. I was the only public servant he would let out to the community. He used to squat on the ground and type away on his little typewriter and write letters to everybody and their dog. He sent me so much stuff and information, and he taught me a lot. He said to me one day, 'You know, Sue, there's something that I have to tell you', and I said, 'What's that, Old Man?' He said, 'I could be your father'. I said, 'What do you mean, you could be my father?' He said, in this quaint way, 'I knew your mother'. I said, 'Oh, my God'. I said, 'But you're not'. He said, 'What do you mean?' And I said, 'Because my mum told me who my father was'. He said, 'Oh', and I said, 'So you thought you'd been my father all this time?' He said, 'Yeah, I've been working up how I should tell you'. I had the privilege of knowing all of those old fellas who were part of that walk-off and then I stayed in touch with

---

9   For information about the 1946 Pilbara strike, see *How the West Was Lost*, directed by David Noakes, produced by Heather Williams and David Noakes, 72 mins, Ronin Films, 1987.

them when I came down here. They had their claim in at the Supreme Court for 1 per cent of the gross revenue under section 70 of the Western Australian Constitution. Then they sought legal advice and went to the High Court. But they lost in the High Court and on the way, two or three of the claimants had fallen by the wayside [died].

I said at a speech a few years ago: 'You know when you talk about Aboriginal people being chained up, that's how you talk about it. You say, oh, well, Aboriginal people … '. The talk was at the Police Federation. I was their keynote speaker and Andrew Forrest [mining magnate] was after me. I talked about remote policing and I said, 'In those early days, when you coppers were the protectors of natives or you just went out and rounded them up'. I said, 'You just talk about the Aboriginals or the natives were chained and they were left in the cells, chained'. And I said, 'The Aboriginal people tell the other side of the story: what it's like to be chained up with six other blokes when one wants to go to the toilet'. They just burst out laughing, and I said, 'Jacob told me that if you want to go so badly in the middle of the night, you've got to get them all up'. These coppers had a sense of humour about it, but I said, 'You're going back to those periods, back in the late 1800s and early 1900s, where police up in the north went out on patrol for six months. That was remote policing – none of these bloody radio systems, satellite phones and all of that. That was horseback, a rifle and you lived off the land for six months, and then you brought the natives back'. They were the sorts of things that those old fellas were talking about to me, so I was so lucky that I was working in the Pilbara in the late '60s. My kids had the privilege of meeting these old fellas. I used to pull them out of school and get homework sent and take them to remote communities. The Education district superintendent said to me, 'It's really a good thing what you're doing'.

I wasn't a radical, but I was a bit of a hippy in the '60s with long hippy skirts and everything else after the Army. But I was in the north of the state. An Aboriginal man once said in the east on one of his websites, quite derogatorily, 'Well where was Sue Gordon during the years of activism?' Well, I was actually working for traditional people in the Pilbara; so where was he? That was my question. I was involved in Aboriginal affairs on the ground, not in the protests interstate. I once wrote a poem about Noonkanbah.[10] I sat on the side of the road in Hedland with all the old people from the 12 Mile Reserve [later known as Tjalka Warra community] to watch the convoy go past, and we were protesting in silence on the side of the road. That particular time I was still working for the government and we just got all the oldies out at 12 Mile Reserve. We sat there on the side

10   For information about the land rights protests at Noonkanbah, see Steve Hawke and Michael Gallagher, *Noonkanbah: Whose Land, Whose Law* (Fremantle: Fremantle Arts Centre Press, 1989).

of the road and this big police inspector from Karratha came and told us to get off the road. I said, 'We're not on the road'. I used to go to meetings with him: 'Get off the road, Sue, and get the old people'. I said, 'They're not on the road, Inspector. They're on the side of the road, outside their houses, and we're here to protest in silence'. I wasn't involved on national committees then, but these were my little protests. I was working with just mostly traditional people in Roebourne and in the Pilbara generally right out to the desert communities. I had to do a lot of work, a lot of travelling with desert people, and it really brought home to me the comparisons. Even now, when I talk to the people in the eastern states and they go on and on about it, I just say, 'Look, no. You're not speaking for tribal people. You've got no right to speak for tribal people'. I have never said I could speak for traditional people either.

 In 1977, with three other Aboriginal men, two traditional and one urban, we got an Aboriginal overseas study award and we went to the USA. The two tribal guys were from Amata in central South Australia and the urban guy was from Sydney but had been working in Alice Springs. We went like little lambs to the slaughter to the US. We went mainly to the Midwest and the traditional guys liked that because it's cowboy country. I was there to study employment programs and I ended up living with the Navajos for a few months. The Navajos also took us on a road trip to the Grand Canyon and back – brilliant trip.

Back in Australia in my role I looked at employment and alcohol problems and children's issues, and then I was still in Hedland. I changed in 1983 to the position of Branch Manager of the Aboriginal Development Commission in Hedland, so I was having to go to Canberra more for meetings. I was mostly involved with traditional people. I got involved on bodies mainly with child protection in the early 1980s. I was on the welfare review in Perth. Then in 1986 I came to Perth as the Commissioner for Aboriginal Planning and the first Aboriginal person to head a government department. The Aboriginal tribal people in Hedland said, 'Well, you're going to Perth to be the big *Ngimbili* [number one]. Don't forget who you are'.

I moved to Perth simply because my eldest son was about to start university. We had no family in Perth, and also because I had managed to get a position as the Commissioner for Aboriginal Planning, making me the first Aboriginal person to head a government department in WA. I also remarried, this time to a police inspector, who retired some years later as a police superintendent.

There is one funny story about this old man who's passed away now. I'm now the big Commissioner for Aboriginal Planning in Perth, ready to chair a Heads of Government meeting. I got a phone call and my secretary had got me out. There's a phone call from Royal Perth Hospital; could I get up there? This old man's asking for me at the hospital. Because he's one of the tribal senior law men from Jigalong, I thought, 'It's got to be urgent'. So I went back into the meeting. I said, 'Look, I've got an urgent message from one of the traditional men. He's in Royal Perth. I have to go. Deputy will take over'. I rock up to Royal Perth Hospital, I get in there and I see the old man sitting on the side of the bed. I said, 'What's wrong?' He said, 'I haven't got any 'jamas'. I said, 'What?' And he said, 'I'm not wearing that'. I said, 'What are you here for, old man?' And he said, 'This eye'. And he said, 'You know that'. I said, 'Yeah, but what am I here for?' 'You've got to go and buy me 'jamas. I am not wearing that'. So I duly went off and bought him some pyjamas and some bath gear and everything. I went back, got him settled, and the nurse came and she said, 'He was stubborn'. I said, 'No, you want to tell me about stubborn'. I said to him, 'I'll come back in this evening and see how you're going', before he was going the next day for surgery. I went back to the meeting and they said, 'How is he?' I said, 'Oh, well, he's having surgery'. I didn't mention the pyjamas. I went back, and he was settled down. He said, 'I don't know how these people walk around here with their arse showing'. I used to often get messages like that. I'd have to race to the hospital and it could be something quite simple, but they just wanted somebody there whom they could trust to go and do something. It could be something simple like ringing to say where they were. I always believed in being honest with people. I never made promises, even when I was in charge of anything.

I was getting more involved in national issues. Then, when I was asked to be a magistrate, to take that on without a formal qualification, I did that. I'd been a Justice of the Peace and sat on the bench, but the Children's Court had limited jurisdiction in those days. With our limited powers we didn't deal with serious matters. We basically put the children under the care of the department – any child who was a problem child on criminal charges. If they were more serious charges, you sent them up to the Court of Petty Sessions. If they were even more serious charges, they had to go before the Supreme Court anyway. Then the Children's Court in 1989 got its own legislation and I just decided, when my youngest son was finishing his law degree, that I would do a law degree. I did it eight years part-time. He said, 'You should come while I'm there', because then he could bludge money off me. My second husband was a police superintendent, so he said, 'Oh, you'll be right'. But then he had major heart surgery through the middle of it, so I was going to pull out of the course. The boys said, 'I thought there was a rule that if you start, you've got to finish'. I had made the rule. So I did my law degree eight years part-time. Most of the kids at uni, except the mature age students, didn't know what I did for a living. You can't just say, 'I'm a magistrate'. 'But you're not supposed to be a magistrate until you have a degree'. 'It's okay; I just do it differently'.

It was a good experience. I failed some units miserably in the first year, and the Dean said to me, 'Well, we should really probably kick you out'. I said, 'No. I can come full-time'. I hadn't even worked that out yet; so anyway, I saw the president of the Children's Court. I said, 'I think I need to take all my long service leave'. I went full-time for a year and the Dean and I came to an arrangement where I would go and see him once a week, like going to the headmaster, and we became friends. I went through three deans during my years there. Then we had another arrangement where I had been so long out of the loop that I would just do practice exams and my tutors would mark them. So by the time exams came around, most of them were repeats anyway. I would go, 'Oh, I know this. I can do this'. Then when I did, I did one elective, which was Aboriginal Peoples and the Law. I can still remember the boys saying to me, 'If you fail that, you're dead in the water'. 'I don't fail. It's only an elective. Piece of cake', and I got a distinction. But I battled at uni, like a lot of mature aged students, but we had the discipline. The young ones don't have the discipline. But they've got the brains; so I thoroughly enjoyed that, but I didn't have to do it.

In the middle of that, my second husband was having major surgery and I got through that. He was in charge of Aboriginal–police relations. Can you imagine that? I was at uni when I lost him in 1998, so then the kids pushed me that I had to finish this bloody law degree. So I finished that, but then at the same time, I was then asked by the government to run an inquiry here. So I'm trying to run an inquiry, I'm trying to mourn; I'm doing all these things at the same time. I'm sitting on national bodies by now, but I'm very heavily involved in child protection and crime. Previously, in 1988–89, I had sat on the National Committee on Violence after the Hoddle and Queen Street massacres [shooting sprees in Melbourne], and that was a brilliant exercise for 12 months. I just took time out of the court when required and we travelled around Australia. But I was becoming more tied to child protection, child abuse issues. Then in the middle of all that, my children are getting married six months apart and I lost my mum and my husband. He was there for two weddings, but my mother had passed away before the second child got married, which was so disappointing, and his other grandmother couldn't come because she was too sick. They're the sort of things that happen, but I always credit Sister Kate's and the Army with the discipline. They'd get you through just about anything.

My interest in child abuse and child protection started from that period in the 1970s, in the Pilbara after a horrific rape of a two-year-old child and having to go to court. Twenty years as a magistrate, listening virtually daily to child abuse, is not a good thing, but you learn how to switch it off. Someone said to me, 'Well, how can you take children away when you used to be taken away?' I said, 'No. It's entirely different. I was taken away because of policies and legislation and because I had a white father. We remove these kids from their parents because of neglect, physical, sexual, and emotional abuse'. I said, 'And in this modern day and age, when everyone gets money, there is no need for it. The fact is some of these parents just shouldn't have children'. That's what I view it as. When I got asked to chair the Northern Territory Emergency Response Taskforce in 2007, I was treated like a pariah by some people.[11] I said, 'Well, hang on. This is about child abuse. This is about bettering Aboriginal people's conditions who have been neglected by governments of all persuasions for decades. So what do you want people to do? Let the kids continue to be abused? Do you want change in communities or do you want people to stay?' I didn't coin the words 'living museums'. Do we want to leave Aboriginal people in living museums? Aboriginal kids are still being abused, urban like the white kids and in remote areas, but there has been some change. I said, 'As long as I draw breath, I'll just keep highlighting child abuse'. People say I sound a bit stuck in the groove there, but I said, 'No, I don't care. As long as there's one child being abused, that's one child too many'.

Thinking about Reconciliation – it depends on how you view Reconciliation. There are people who want to have a warm, fuzzy feeling. I've seen so many Reconciliation plans with business, the boards that I sit on. But if it's a piece of paper, and it's sitting there and it's a lovely glossy thing they hand out to all their clients, what's the point? What are they actually doing as Reconciliation? Reconciliation is about doing something. It's not about nice, fluffy words; I don't believe in symbols and I'm well known for that. I didn't ask to be said sorry to. It should have been to my mother. She was the one whom I was taken away from. I don't have the memories; she had the memory right up until she died of over 30 years of horrific memories of your child being snatched from you. There are a lot of Aboriginal people who like symbols. I don't like symbols. It's got to be some action with it. It's intervention. I've sat on a lot of national bodies and chaired national bodies, but I'm not a radical. It's got to be practical to get me involved. I don't do symbols very well.

I had actually been invited to sit in the House of Representatives for the National Apology to the Stolen Generations [in 2008]. I was chairing the taskforce of the Northern Territory Emergency Response at the time. I'd been asked by Tiwis to go out to the Tiwi Islands, to go to the unofficial opening of their secondary college. Former Indigenous Affairs minister Mal Brough had given $10 million for a 99-year lease over their land, so they'd built this secondary college. The kids were going to it, so I went out there and I watched the apology. It didn't do anything for me because it was made very clear there was to be

11   The controversial Northern Territory Emergency Response, better known as the Intervention, has been written about extensively. For an overview of the first year of the Intervention, which Sue Gordon chaired, see *Northern Territory Emergency Response: Report of the NTER Review Board*, October 2008 (Canberra: Australian Government, 2008), available from www.nterreview.gov.au/docs/report_nter_review/default.htm.

no compensation. It was a nice, fuzzy, warm feeling, but when that was said – 'There will be no compensation' people presumed that was only the words at the time. But they found out very soon after that there's no compensation. We've seen what's happened since. Closing the gap is just three little words. CTG they call it. There are programs at the health, programs at the dentist, programs here and there, but the gap seems to be widening. The gap's not going to be closed in my lifetime. There are still a lot of people, black and white, who want the status quo to remain, because poor fella me, if I've got nothing to whinge about, don't change it. We need something to whinge about. With the Sister Kate's group, we have our annual fundraising fête every November. We work for months beforehand, most of us who are able to, making jams, pickles, everything to sell, getting donations. My oldest members are 82 or 83. They all work on the fête day selling things and having a good time, but we raise money to run our little office and we enjoy doing it. We're not sitting back waiting for a government handout. So that's the difference with some people in the community – that they're going to do things to help themselves and not sit around waiting for someone to rock up at the door, because they then own you because they own the program and they want to tell you how to run it.

I grew up with people like Polly Farmer and Ted Kilmurray – brilliant footballers. We had quite a few people who went on to do well for themselves from Sister Kate's. Some didn't do well, but the one thing is that none of us have ever discriminated against anyone else. I became a magistrate and I'm still one of the little kids in their eyes. Someone used to give me a hiding, someone used to wipe my nose; but they're all very proud for you. The biggest thing has been education. We've all pushed our children to go to school. In the Sister Kate's Children 1934 to 1953 Aboriginal Corporation that I run, there are about 140 members around Australia. We do a bimonthly newsletter and I think, amongst our kids, we've got eight lawyers and the value of education can never be pushed hard enough. My grandkids would never dare talk to me about not going to school. I've extended that to my own birth family. I say, 'Education is far too important'. It's very noticeable, but the Sister Kate's kids of my era and before that, in the main, have moved on. In their own way, they stopped being victims a long time ago because they weren't moving. It's a bit hard to explain that. If you remain a victim, you can never move on with your life. You have hang-ups and you just don't know how to get ahead. So people used to say to me, 'Oh, you're a magistrate'. I said, 'Yes, I know, but I've worked hard. I went to law school. I paid for that myself, but you don't know what's going on behind me. You've got no idea about my background. All you're seeing is me and that's your fault, because you're just seeing the face'. And I said, 'You've got to remember there are lots of other people who might not have done as well, but they didn't want to be a magistrate. They didn't want to go to law school. So they have done what they wanted to do, but the most important thing they've done is encourage their children to stay at school'. And I said, 'And you've got to look at it from all angles'. But we all carry baggage. One of the things that I find with the Sister Kate's kids, they accept what happened. While it happened, you can't change history and the more people try and dwell on, 'Oh, look at it; poor fella me', you can't change history. Nobody can change history. It's happened. You've got to accept it happened. You can't be happy with it, but you've got to now move to the next part of your life. Otherwise you'll stay bogged down forever if you remain a victim.

Figure 6. Sue Gordon, on retirement from Children's Court, 2008
Source: Courtesy Sue Gordon

You can't change history. We had five boys from Sister Kate's in Korea. They'd never seen snow. As Tom Hunt said, 'You know, we're there and we didn't get our winter gear for a month, and you've got no idea what it's like'. He said, 'You go to bed on the ground, put your ground sheet over you, because you're cold and to wake up and it's flat on your face, because it snowed through the night'. Now, the five Sister Kate's Aboriginal boys who went to Korea and came back men, when they came home, they were treated differently. They weren't allowed into the pubs and were refused service. Tom Hunt tells a funny story and it's reminiscent of a lot of them. He said he and six of his mates went into the pub when they came back, all in full uniform. They ordered beers and they were told they couldn't serve the native, which was Tom. Tom was light skinned, but he was a native. So the other blokes said, 'That's okay. Just give us six beers'. So the bloke came out, gave them six beers and they all got up and left. No one paid, nothing; just left. They just made their little stand. Yet, before they'd gone away to the war, they'd worked hard on stations, on railways, on big projects, just alongside everybody else, but they were treated differently because they were Aboriginal. If I could change things, it would be to get people to understand that Aboriginal people are just that. The book *Forever Warriors* has got Aboriginal people who are West Australians, from across the board – from the Boer War to Vietnam to East Timor.[12] Aboriginal people are still serving in all areas of defence on a regular basis and, as I said, the Sister Kate's kids have served in all those conflicts. Now grandkids are in Afghanistan and to them, it's something that they want to do. Those who joined from Sister Kate's joined because they wanted to try something else, but they all did their best. They were just like any other person.

I am a member of both Honouring Indigenous War Graves and the Women's Royal Australian Army Corps' organisation. I don't belong to the RSL. I march on Anzac Day because the Women's Royal Australian Army Corps manages to always get enough of you to march. And I attend most Honouring Indigenous War Graves ceremonies when I can. They're special days that you mark in to turn up to. I've gone through my own family; my Great-Uncle Alex went off to the First War and a lot of my relatives, as I'm finding out, were part of the slave labour list, who were just sent to stations to work for nothing as part of the war effort. I just want people to understand what history was about.

There's got to be more of the education in schools. There is some, but a lot of it's not mandatory; it's voluntary. When I went to school, we learnt about King, Country and Empire. With geography, we learnt about the pink bits on the map, which was the Commonwealth, but you learnt fairly thoroughly about the world. I'm a reader; I like to read about parts of the world and have travelled

---

12   Jan 'Kabarli' James, *Forever Warriors* (Perth: Scott Print, 2010).

to lots of parts of the world where things happened. I've been to Gallipoli and spent some time in Turkey. We need to get people to understand that Aboriginal people were part of all of that. The really horrific part, which is not common knowledge, is that Aboriginal trackers were taken to the Boer War and left behind. They weren't even brought home. So there's all these descendants of Aboriginal people running around with the Bushmen, but they were just left. Just like horses. Just left there! It's not common knowledge. Just think – they were people.

Thinking about the present-day Defence Force, I worked with Major General Dave Chalmers who was a Tank Commander. He was the coordinator of the Emergency Response in the Territory and a wonderful man – a very intelligent man who holds two Masters in strategic planning from the US. It's a different educated Army, and I did a lot of work with Norforce cadets and soldiers up there.[13] I spoke at Larrakeyah Barracks where they'd brought in 80 cadets from across northern Australia. These kids had been in cadets and loved it and they joined Norforce. I spoke to Norforce: black, white and brindle. We had Norforce who worked alongside of us with the logistics. This was the Army that everyone said we were taking in, but they were just logistics. We needed the Army to be able to use Army barges to go to those communities where there's no access.

General Chalmers and I would rock up. For instance, we went to Maningrida in Arnhem Land and he's in full uniform, right down to the feather in his slouch hat. We're having a cup of tea with these old girls who were doing the night patrol, and they said, 'Where's your tank?' He said, 'We haven't got any tanks'. And he said, 'Why?' and this old girl said, 'Well, we heard you were going to come with the soldiers and the tanks and we were going to get out there in front and stop the tanks'. He said, 'How?' She said, 'I was going to show a leg'. We just all cracked up and Dave looked at me and he said, 'It's only me and Sue. There's no Army; only me and Sue'. So they used to just laugh. But when we'd go into the communities, I said to Dave, 'The Aboriginal people like to know who you are. I will introduce myself and I'll tell them who my family is, so then they immediately can know where they join in'. (I found so many sisters and cousins in the Territory.) Then Dave would follow me and give his Army background. That's who he is. Then people could talk. He is a person who learns very quickly.

I've also had some contact previously with the former Chief of Defence, Angus Houston, because I've got a big thing about Army Cadets. I'd like more cadets out there. I said, 'I'm now the President of the Police and Citizens Youth Club, so there are cadets in there'. It's getting that discipline early into kids. I think

13   Norforce is a reserve unit operating in the Northern Territory since 1981 that employs a large percentage of local Aboriginal people.

the modern-day Army is very good. I mean the SAS is still the SAS, but what the boys do, when they go away, this modern Army – it's just horrific to think that people make these derogatory comments about military without any concept of what it's like. Since day one, there have always been armies of one sort. The Aboriginal people had an Army. Before white men, Aboriginal people had 100 per cent employment because everybody in the tribe had a job. When I said this at a talk I once gave someone laughed and I said, 'Well, the women hunted and collected stuff, the men hunted, the old people did this'. I said it was 100 per cent employment. Now we're talking about people who need a job. You can think of the funny sides of it. Sometimes, you have to have that sense of humour to make people think. But modern-day military, it's very difficult, because there are still the knockers out there. People don't have any concept of what military have to put up with. Now, it's a choice. People choose to go into it, but then you've got to respect that choice that people have made and they're doing it for their reason to join the Army, to protect the country. If we didn't have an Army, where are we going to be?

Finally, I never wanted anyone to feel sorry for me. I think it was the discipline from the Army. I realised that if something was going to happen, I had to make it happen. There was no one around me. Although I could rely on my Sister Kate's kids or my Army mates, if I wanted to move and make something happen, I had to do it. That's why I keep saying to people about discipline. If you've got that self-discipline, you make it happen. No is not a good word!

5

Commemorating Indigenous Service

John Schnaars[1]

John Schnaars has been at the forefront of efforts to recognise and commemorate Aboriginal and Torres Strait Islander military service. He is the founder of the Perth-based organisation Honouring Indigenous War Graves. The non-profit organisation arranges headstones for the gravesites of deceased Indigenous veterans. John and the other group members perform a small, moving ceremony at the gravesites to mark the placing of the headstones. John Schnaars is a Vietnam veteran himself, and what makes his story quite interesting is that he volunteered for National Service even though it was not compulsory for Aboriginal people. John's story therefore provides insights not only into the experiences of Aboriginal Vietnam veterans, but also the fights for justice for Indigenous ex-service personnel.

I was born at King Edward Hospital in Subiaco in 1946. We were living in North Perth at the time and then we left North Perth and went to a place called Kwolyin, which is up in the Wheatbelt area. We went from there to Number Five Pumping Station [Yerbillon] where Dad was a truck driver carting wood for

---

1   This interview is available from the NLA, ORAL TRC 6260/1; reproduced with the permission of the National Library of Australia. This interview was recorded in Perth on 23 November 2010.

the pumping station about 280 kms away. Then he got a job as a truck driver on the Rabbit-Proof Fence at Burracoppin when I was about five, and that's where I started my school.

One experience early in my life still sticks. There was this Aboriginal family at Burracoppin and his father had served during the Second World War. I think I was five; children used to be coming to school, but one day you're playing with them, the next they're not there anymore. One of the children asked the teacher, 'Where are the children?' She said, 'The government came and took them away to put them in a home'. He was working on the railways at the time and he served Australia and that was the thanks he got – he had his children taken away. So from that day on, that affected me, because every time I saw a vehicle coming towards that school that looked official, I was planning my escape. No one was going to take me. I was planning, checked the windows to see if they were open. I had about five or six places around Burracoppin where I knew I could hide out and no one would find me.

I had my exit strategy all worked out even at that young age. We lived on the other side of the railway lines and in the middle were the wheat silos. If we were going home for lunch during the day and I saw a vehicle at my place that I didn't know who it belonged to, I wouldn't go home for lunch. I'd just tell my sisters I'm not hungry, I'm not going home and if it was after school and we were going home and saw a car there I didn't know, I wouldn't go home. I'd play in the bush until my sisters came looking for me. It wasn't till about four years ago that I told my sister what that was all about. She used to say, 'I often used to wonder why you'd never come home and we had to come looking for you'. That more or less stayed with me right through until I left high school – the fear of these government people coming to take you away. I used to lie awake at nights worrying if these people were going to come and take us through the night. It really affected me immensely. For a bloke like John Howard to say that it only affected those that were taken away, he's got no idea what he's talking about. I know for a fact it affected other people too, and I was one of them. I'm not sure why my family wasn't targeted. A lot of people probably thought Dad was white, but he had Aboriginal blood. His skin was really fair. Mum was fairly dark-skinned so I've got no idea how we were not singled out. Dad served in the Second World War as well, same as this other bloke. I know that if anybody would have tried to take us away, there'd have been a lot of fur flying, because Mum and Dad wouldn't have let that happen. There'd have been hell to pay. All these years later, I'm still having trouble sleeping.

Mum probably more so than Dad had a strong sense of Aboriginality. Dad's mother was from an Aboriginal family. On Mum's side, our great-great-grandmother was old Grannie Nelson, Ada Foss, and then my grandmother was a very strict lady; if you stepped out of line, she put you back in line.

Our grandfather died, leaving Nanna Holland with 11 or 12 children to bring up on her own. In the whole of their working lives, not one of those uncles or aunties I could ever remember being on the dole. They all worked right through their lives because of the strict way she brought them up. When farmers around the district of Kwolyin would go on holidays, they'd get my grandmother to go and look after their sheep, cattle, chooks, and water and do their gardens because she was that reliable. They knew that if they left her to do it, it would be done. Many people had total respect for her. Mum was much the same as Nanna; if you done the right thing you were right, but if you stepped out of line … . The only time Dad would give you a cut with a bloody strap was if you done something wrong. Then, after he gave you a couple of cuts with a garden hose, you didn't do it wrong again. You made sure you woke up.

I think Mum would have been about the eldest, or second eldest. Mum worked; all the aunties all worked. A lot of the time it was kitchen hands or cooks at the hotel there in Kwolyin. But they were all taught to work when you left school. The uncles all worked as shearers, wool classers, farm hands, etc. It was after the Second World War that Mum and Dad met because Dad had already been married before the war. He had four children, then he went away and that wife shot through with somebody else. Dad's father wouldn't let her take the kids so he kept the kids at his place until Dad came home. Dad married Mum and then Mum had nine. All up they had a baker's dozen between them. With Dad's first marriage, there were three boys and a girl and then with the second marriage, my sister Marilyn was the eldest, then there was myself, my other sister, then a brother, then another sister, then a brother and another sister and then two brothers.

Dad never really spoke much about why he enlisted. He told us things that happened while he was over there. One of the things he used to relate to us were the reasons why we were born. We'd ask him, 'Why?' He was in the artillery in El Alamein; he was driving the ammunition truck and it was his birthday. This Major Day who was in charge of them, they used to call him Major Apple a Day. One of the guys told old Major Day that it was Snowie's birthday. So old Major Day said, 'Snowie, here's half a bottle of whisky for your birthday'. In the night-time Dad used to lay the tailgate down on the truck and put his swag on that, but this evening comes and he puts the tailgate down and puts his swag on it. Then he thought, 'I'll go and have a couple of drinks of this whisky with my mates in the trenches'. He done that and while they were down there, they got bombarded and the truck was blown to smithereens. So he said we owe our lives to Major Day and half a bottle of whisky. Dad served mainly over in the Middle East. He was one of the last four to be wounded at the Battle of

El Alamein. He had this big shrapnel wound across his shoulder and a bit higher up it probably would have taken his head off. He came home and that was the good thing.

In terms of racism, I don't think anybody would have been game to say anything about it to Dad. The old man, he knew how to handle himself and I don't think there would have been too many able to take him to town, that's for sure. After the war, this Jewish bloke wanted to take him to America to have a shot at the heavyweight title. That's how well he knew how to handle himself. He also did bike riding and played football. I was at Mum's youngest brother's 70th birthday and Ken Langdon and Don Langdon were there. They used to play football years ago and I think it was Ken's son who used to play for the West Coast Eagles. As soon as someone said, 'Oh, Don, this is Snowie Schnaar's son', he said, 'I remember him. I can tell you some stories about him when he was playing football'. I said, 'Oh what's one of them?' He said:

> One day it was raining a lot and it was at Bruce Rock. The umpires were from Bruce Rock, and my old man didn't like one fella too much so he knocked him arse over turkey. His head landed in this puddle of water and he put his foot on his head and just kept pushing it under. The umpire yelled out, 'Snowie, for Christ's sake take your foot off his head; you'll drown the poor bastard'.

After the war Dad belonged to the Buffalos at Merredin. I don't think he ever joined the RSL; I'm not sure.

Every Christmas we used to travel from Burracoppin to Kwolyin, which was a fair way when you had old vehicles. The whole extended family got together and they'd book the hall at Kwolyin for that Christmas night. The men would put up a Christmas tree; they'd rig someone up to be Father Christmas and all the kids would get some sort of present. That was amazing. I used to really look forward to that every Christmas and I used to look forward to my grandmother's Christmas puddings. She used to make them in old flour sacks and boil them in the copper outside. Those Christmas puddings were something to look forward to – absolutely beautiful, but nobody seems to make them anymore. We were a very close family. That's one of the things that helped me when I came back from Vietnam. A lot of blokes when they came back from Vietnam didn't get that same support and many of them committed suicide. I was lucky I had a lot of family support, which is what you need when you come back from places like that.

I started school at Burracoppin; back in them days it was called Infants. The first time in school you had one room up to year three and I think then you went into the next room until the last year you were there. In the last years at primary school in Burracoppin I used to get paid five shillings a fortnight to clean the toilets on the weekends. That was good money. You could get a lot of ice creams and go to the movies and all of that. It was a pretty shitty job but you just got in and done it and that was it; once it was done, it was done. You done it on a Saturday or a Sunday and then the teacher would pay you your five shillings on the Monday.

I remember getting into a fight with one of the farmer's kids one day. We were stuck into it and I had him down on the ground giving him a couple of swift ones to the nose. His mate ran up and he pulled out a pocket knife and he opened it up and he said, 'Here stab the black bastard with this'. I gave him a couple of extra ones and then the teacher came out and grabbed the bloody pocket knife and saved any more problems. There was a little bit of racism there, but it was just by a few that didn't have too many brains going for them. The majority of it was all good.

I went through to the last year at primary school, then went on to Merredin Senior High School. From Burracoppin you'd get a bus through to Booran, then the high school bus would pick us up at Booran and take us to Merredin for high school. I ended up leaving in second term, third year of high school. The headmaster wanted me to go on, but I stopped to go to work and help Mum and Dad with the money for the rest of the family. When I finished school in '62, I was 16 and I went up north to Mount Jackson, at the back of Bullfinch, cutting posts with the old man. That was mining area up there. Dad was cutting posts for this Tommy Brooks. The old man when he sharpened the axes, they were like you could shave with them. They were sharp and he used to go for what you call the plum axes. I was cutting posts and I was doing quite well this day when the axe glanced off a branch and I managed to cut my shin open. At first I thought it was the back of the axe that hit. I kept chopping until I felt all this wet, and I looked down and here's this bloody great gap on the bone; you could see the bone. I yelled out to the old man. He came running and when he seen what I had done loaded me into Tom's old truck. It was an old Bedford and had no brakes and was used to cart the posts out of the bush and down to the campsite. The old man's driving it and old Tommy's holding me sort of on the middle because there were no doors. The old man's really making this old truck hum down through these little tracks. They got me back to the camp and Dad had his old Humber Super Snipe out there at the time. They gave me some snuff stuff to stop me from fainting and then it was a mad dash from there to Merredin to get it all stitched up. That was the end of my post cutting days. Then I got a job with the CBH, Cooperative Bulk Handling, and ended up in charge of silos with blokes working under me.

Then Vietnam came along. I volunteered for National Service. I got a letter back saying that they didn't want me, no explanation. So I wrote them another letter then saying, 'Well this is gonna look good in the media. I'm volunteering for National Service and you're knocking me back and you're forcing others to go in that don't want to go in'. It was about two to three weeks later I got another letter saying, 'Go for your medical'. That was that. I was 20 and it was '66. Right throughout, our family have all served. My four great-uncles on Mum's side went away to the First World War and only one came home. Then my father served, four of his brothers also served in the Second World War. Two of Mum's brothers served, and then on Dad's side there were a number of uncles who served. My brother served in Malaya, so I thought it's my turn to do my bit. Myself and others were led to believe when the Viet Cong took over South Vietnam they would carry on down to Australia. We decided we'd rather fight them on their own dunghill rather than wait and fight them on home soil. We found out later that they had no intention of going any further than South Vietnam. That's why a lot of us went away. That was what it was all about. My family thought it was good when I enlisted because it was a tradition with the family.

We got on the plane here in Perth; it was a DC-3, I think. That my first ever ride in an aeroplane, which was a bit bumpy back then. We arrived at the airport near Seymour. We arrived there and it was freezing. The windows were fogged up with ice, everybody's diving into cases for jumpers and it was unreal. Over here in Perth it was beautiful and over there it was freezing. We did our 10 weeks National Service training at Pucka [Puckapunyal]. I thought it was great. The years I had in the Army, I had a really great time. I didn't really have to adjust to training because of the way I used to work and it was fairly easy really. Some people found it hard, but because I'd lived a lot away from home, working on CBH and looking after yourself and outdoors it was quite easy. Because of the way we lived our lives, to go in Army training at Puckapunyal wasn't too bad. The only thing I didn't like sometimes – especially at the first 10 weeks training – were some of the sergeants and the lieutenants; they're pretty smart arses. But that was their job I guess. I didn't really like taking the shit from them, all the same. They had to do it that way, so just get on with it. From Puckapunyal you put in for what service you wanted to go into. I put in for the Armour and I was lucky I got the first choice, so I went into the Armoured Regiment and completed training there then as a Gunner Signaller. That training was good because you met lot of different blokes all over again. That was a good life.

They were getting us ready to go over to Vietnam in January '68. They needed some gunners to go over. We only had six months left of our two years, so there were a number of us all who volunteered to go across as gunners. Before we went to Vietnam, we were doing exercises out on the Puckapunyal Range and I was driving one of the fuel trucks and you had them all loaded with jerry cans. My mate had another truck loaded with jerry cans and we were doing all this under blackout conditions. We had to fill the tanks up late at night.

This night I was pulling in alongside this tank to fill it up with fuel, and it's dark and one of the wheels dropped in a crater and hit the side of the tank. This big bloody lieutenant yelled, 'Bloody Schnaars! You bloody useless so and so!' I couldn't say nothing to him then because if I whacked him then I'd have got in the shit. We finished the exercise. It must have been about half past 10 I think that night, and Major McInerney comes over the airwaves and says, 'Right, everybody back to camp I've got an 18 gal keg all tapped ready for you to go, I've got blokes back there cooking steak and everything. Because I'm not coming to Vietnam with you, I'm putting all this on'. We get back there and he said, 'All right I'll have a chat to you boys. Wish you all a safe trip and a safe return. Tonight everybody's equal. There's no rank or anything, we're all equal'. I didn't realise until later that he was parked not far from where I was filling up the tank when I was abused by the lieutenant. I went over to him and I said, 'Major, did you mean what you said that there's no rank here tonight?' He said, 'That's right, Trooper Schnaars. There's no rank here at all tonight; everybody is equal'. My mate's standing alongside of me; he said, 'All right, Schnaarsie, go and get the bastard'. This lieutenant was a big bloke, so I went and bailed him up and I said, 'You want to call me what you called me out there tonight?' He wouldn't say boo, so I called him everything under the sun and the blokes gathered around – 'Come on, Schnaarsie, just whack the bastard anyway'. But I couldn't even get him to say boo. About 15 minutes later we heard this jeep start up and off he went back to camp. I couldn't hit the poor bastard; he would have started crying if I did. But the funny part then was years later when we were having this anniversary back in Puckapunyal. Whoever had done the seating must have remembered back then because they put me on one side of the table and him directly opposite. I was sitting down, I could see he was fiddling; he was looking everywhere but at me. I put my hand over and said, 'Okay, mate, just forget whatever happened before', and I could see he was relieved!

Before I went to Vietnam, I got a house in Seymour and invited some of my mates out. This sergeant, a friend of mine, and this corporal who I didn't know, because he [the sergeant] came with somebody else. It was about three o'clock in the afternoon and I'd just gone inside for something. Tom Skalidis, who was staying in the same place as me, his wife came racing in. 'John, John', she said. And I said, 'What?' She said, 'The sergeant and the corporal are going to start fighting out there'. I said 'No way; we'll be kicked out of this place'. I went out and I said, 'Look if you want to do your fighting, jump in your vehicles, shoot off up the road and do it up there'. Sergeant Stewart said, 'All right, Schnaarsie, no worries'. He starts putting his jacket back on and the corporal said, 'No way; you want it here, you're going to get it here'. He took a swing at him and just missed his wife's face. I just let him have one and dropped him and split his chin open. Sergeant Stewart said, 'Fucking hell, Schnaarsie! Thank Christ I listened to what you were telling me'. This guy got up and when he could talk, he was saying, 'I'll get you. I'll report you for striking a higher rank'. Sergeant said, 'Don't worry about it, Schnaarsie. I seen what happened; he's got nothing he can do'. I never heard nothing more of that either.

There were two other Aboriginal soldiers in the group that I was with. Stewie was a reg and Homer was a National Serviceman. Ol' Stewie was a funny character. He had this Holden. We'd been into Seymour and got on the piss a week before we were going to Vietnam. We had to go on the range the next morning for a last couple of days' exercise. We went into Seymour and had a few beers and then said, 'Well, better go back early and get an early night because we've got to get up early'. We were leaving Seymour and here's this big bloody Army guy hitchhiking; he asked where were we going. We said, 'Out to Pucka'. He said, 'Can I get a lift?' We said yes. We get out there – myself and Stewie in the front and another two of our mates in the back and this fella we'd picked up. We get there and pull up at the 7 RAH [hospital] opposite this car park, and said, 'There you go, mate. We'll see you later'. He said, 'Are youse pissing me off?' I said, 'No. We just gave you a lift'. He said, 'You're going to a party; aren't youse? I know what you're up to'. I said, 'No, we're going home because we want to go to bed early because we've got to get up early in the morning and go out on the range'. 'No', he said, 'You're all bullshittin''. I said, 'Look, mate, just get out'. He wouldn't, so I got out and went around and opened the door and said, 'Go on, piss off'. So then he got out, but I didn't realise he'd grabbed my mate's beach towel off the back and was walking away with it. Then Stewie yelled out, 'Schnaarsie, get that bloody towel off him! That's mine'. So I walked over and I said, 'Hey, mate, give us the bloody towel and stop your piss farting around'. He handed me the towel, and then I started to walk back. Next minute, Stewie yells out, 'Look out, Schnaarsie!' Just as he yelled out, I heard this bloke's foot on this loose blue metal and as I turned my head around he's taking a swing at me and just missed me. I just hit him in the jaw and dropped him. I was saying, 'Come on, get up you gutless bastard. Want to do some more king hitting? Get up'. By this time there's a number of people all standing around and this young girl, she's looking down and she says, 'He's not playing'. She said, 'He's got blood coming out his ears'.

So in the end, MPs [military police] arrive and while they were waiting for the ambulance they were taking accounts from everybody that had seen what happened. Then they asked me to give my name. Then they put him in the ambulance and took him away, and the MP said, 'Look, don't worry, trooper. Everyone that I've spoken to tonight said exactly the same as what your story has been, spot on, so you've got nothing to worry about'. We got back to the camp and about an hour and a half later, I said to my mate, 'I can't sleep. I've got to go the hospital and see how that dickhead is'. He drives me down there and this matron turned on me like I was to blame. I said, 'Do you know actually what happened?' And she said only what he had told her before he fainted again. I then told her what had actually taken place, then I asked her how he was. She said, 'They've taken him down to Heidelberg'. Then I said if you want to go and talk to the MPs, you'll get the story from them if you want the truth. Next day, I get a call that the major wanted to see me to hear my side of what had happened. After telling my side of what had happened I asked if he knew what was wrong with the wanker. He said, 'They just found out that he's got perforated ear drums, his jaw's fractured in three places and he's got a fractured skull when he hit the ground'. He said, 'But you've got no worries. If he takes it to court, a civilian court or something, you've got no worries because every witness story backs everything you said'. Just under a week I think after that, we finished out at Pucka, and then we went to Vietnam.

I knew some of the National Servicemen when they first joined, they didn't want to be there and yet some of those guys at the end of their two years joined up for another three years. Their whole life had been turned around when they found the mateship being in the service brought them. They really enjoyed the type of life, the type of environment. One thing I do remember when we were out was the Salvation Army, this old major. He reinforced things Dad used to tell me when he was talking about overseas. Dad said never ever go past the Salvation Army people holding the tin in their hands. Always put in some money because they're the only ones that were there on the battle line with us. When we were in Vietnam, I really realised what he meant because out there, no matter where we were, if it was a hot day, this old major come out with cold drinks. If it was a cold day, he'd come out with hot drinks and chewies and take letters back and bring mail out. He was always there, yet the other groups if you wanted to see them, you had to go to their tent where they held their church service on the Sundays. This old bloke was out there all the time and at the time he must have been in his 50s I guess. He was someone special, so I've got a really great liking for the Salvation Army people. The Salvation Army guy was also based at Nui Dat. We've got a couple of Salvation Army people as our Honouring Indigenous War Graves members now as well.

At Nui Dat was a huge mess hall where everybody had their meals. There were tables and then the passage up the middle where you'd go up the front and get tucker. They had all these tables lined up and stools. I don't know how much it must have held – a couple of hundred at least. One day tankies were in there and somebody else, and all of a sudden one bloke said something to another bloke and it was on. I'm standing back and it was just like something in the movies. There was tucker going everywhere, stools getting upended and I'm standing there watching. Next minute these two guys swung at me and I was just watching. That got me swinging back at them then and then the MPs came racing. We were banned from going to the wet mess for a fortnight after that. But it didn't stop us from getting a few beers. But that was one hell of a time, that. You do all sorts of silly things to make life a little bit easier.

I only got down there to Vung Tau twice. Once, me and this bloke went down as guard for the Salvation Army major because we wanted to get haircuts.

I did have a bit of a disagreement with a sergeant over there in Vietnam. He flogged one of the little mates while we were out one time. When I came back in, I went down into the Sergeant's mess, into the kitchen, and told the bloke, 'Tell him to get out here. I want to talk to him'. He came out and I called that bloke everything under the sun. He was a big bloke and I wanted him to take a swing, but he wouldn't. Then the duty sergeant came up and said, 'Trooper Schnaars; nothing's going to happen, so you may as well go now'. I said, 'No worries. The stink's getting too much for me here anyway'. And that's it. He didn't mind bashing a little bloke half his size, but when somebody's nearer to his size, he didn't have the guts to bloody do anything about it.

The only time I had anything to do with the Americans was we got the tanks off the jetty down there and then we went up the river on barges. The gunners had to be down inside, had the guns all ready to go, traversing the bank. I thought, if there's someone over there going to shoot something and put a hole in this barge, I would get them before they get me. This thing's going to go down horribly quick and I can't swim. When we took them off the barges at this bridge, we were put on stand-to for two hours with turret down and it was stinking hot inside the tank.

There was only one bloke that tried to be smart with me because of my race. That was when we were in Vietnam, and I put him in his place. He used to call me blackfella or blackie until one morning when I was in a really shitty mood for some reason or another. When he said it again, I reached over and grabbed him by the throat, and I said, 'Listen, arsehole, my name's John or Trooper Schnaars. That's what it's gotta be — what you call everybody else. If you say that once more, I'll ram this fist so far down your throat you'll be able to suck my thumb with your arsehole'. Every time after that, he was a very changed man. That was the only one time.

I was in Vietnam for not quite six months. If they'd let us just finish that 12 months off, we would have stayed. At the end of that time when we were over there, we volunteered to go on to finish the 12 months over there. But they said, 'If you want to do that, you've got to sign on for another three years'. So we said, 'shove it' and came home. The only time we were in Saigon was when we caught the plane back from Nui Dat. I know the baby Herc when it was coming in to pick us up, it swerved on the runway because a bit of wind was blowing and I thought, 'Bloody hell'. That scared the shit out of me a bit, as thinking is it going take off okay. But, leaving on that plane that day was probably the hardest thing I've ever had to do in my life. There were bloody lumps in my throat and a few tears in my eyes because I had mates back there that might not be coming home. That was one of the hardest things I've ever had to do in my life. On that plane back it was probably the only plane that I've ever … anyway, we drank it dry. Two hours out of Sydney we'd cleaned it out and the only thing that was left was rum. That was the end of my two years in the Army.

When we left Vietnam, we landed in Sydney at about eleven o'clock at night. There was nobody there from the Army and we had nowhere to sleep. We just had to sleep on benches. Three of us went out on the town. The next plane to WA didn't leave till ten o'clock the next day, so we had to fill in time and we got to Perth airport and there was no one from the Karrakatta there to meet us. We had to pay for taxis and everything out of our own pocket to take us out to Karrakatta. They asked us that day if any of us that lived in the country wanted travel warrants and I said yes. I caught the train that evening to go up to Merredin and I didn't return to Perth. The blokes living in Perth, they had to go back in there and report daily every morning for about a month before they were allowed to piss off altogether. They were supposed to be having bloody medicals and all that, but a lot of them were never having anything. I left and two days later I was up in Merredin driving tractors with these farmers. Yet the Army records reckoned I was down in Perth having a full medical. But I'd never been anywhere near there after I left there that day.

In Vietnam, we had the tanks up on the side of Nui Dat Hill. I jumped off the side after firing one night and twisted my knee and rammed up against the tank with my back. I hurt my lower back and knee and I was on pain killers, but I couldn't leave the tank because there was no one else to take over as gunner. None of that was put in the notes. I was later able to track down the corporal at the time, who was the RAP [Regimental Aid Post] corporal, and he ended up leaving the Army as a major. He wrote a letter saying the reason why there was nothing in his medical report about this was because he wasn't entitled to write anything in. The only person who could write stuff in was the captain or medical officer, so he said that's why there was nothing in his report. But he said, 'I can quite clearly remember treating him for it'. Then with this medical exam that I never had at the end of my service, DVA were trying to use that as what was written down to say that I had nothing wrong.

When I had to fight years later for my entitlements, they said, 'Well, your full medical doesn't say anything about this'. I said, 'That's because I've never had a medical'. They said, 'Well how come these people have signed off that you did have?' I said, 'That's bullshit'. They said, 'If you have a look at the signatures', and I said, 'They don't match up'. I had to take it to the Arbitration Appeals

Tribunal Hearing. Their DVA lawyer was in there and talking to me and the lawyer that I had from Legal Aid. I thought he was going to work with us and make it easier, but that was bullshit. He just used everything that we were talking about to try to screw us. I thought, 'You two-faced bastard'. I told him as much after that as well. In the end, we had to go back for another hearing. Barnett, who was on the bench, said to Mr Pontasorearse, 'Have you got these doctors here so that we can question them about what this man is saying – that he never had this medical?' He said, 'I'm sorry; no, I haven't'. The magistrate said, 'Well, how are we supposed to come to a conclusion what's right and what's wrong?' He said, 'You should have had them at least on a telephone hook-up so that we could question them'. The DVA lawyer said one's in Queensland, one's dead and the other one's in Tasmania. Barnett said, 'That's not good enough. This man's come here to try and prove what he's saying is correct, and you don't think it's important enough to have these doctors on telephone hook-up so that we can question them. That makes it look very suspicious to us. You've been doing this a long enough time now to know that's what should have been done'. They couldn't come up with anything else. They had to put me as winning the case. That was back in 1988.

When I came back from Vietnam, my wife and I had four kids and then she shot through. I had met my wife back here in WA. I got married the day before I left to go into the National Service. When we got married, her father and mother wouldn't come to the wedding. He reckoned I was a bodgie and a bloody blackfella and I wasn't the sort of person he wanted for his daughter. I had to get my brother-in-law to give her away and I had to make our own wedding cake. Peter was born a couple of weeks before I went away. He was born the year I left WA, 1966, before we got married. Maitland was born when I first took my wife over to Victoria in '67 and was born in Seymour. While I was in Vietnam, Graham was born in '68, and then Sharryn was born in '69.

It became like many of the marriages after Vietnam. Originally, when I came back I was drinking a lot. She obviously was thinking the grass was greener on the other side, so she shot through – in '72 I think it was – and with one of her sister's ex-boyfriends. It was about a year after that, he found out she was having it off with somebody else and he stabbed her with a screwdriver and put her in hospital up at Southern Cross. For the next two years she had nothing to do with my children at all. She never sent them Christmas cards, never sent them Christmas presents, never sent them birthday cards. I brought them up on my own then. When she shot through, I brought them up right through their school and I must have brought them up right because they're all doing well.

For two years they never heard from her or anything and then she's filing for divorce. I put in and couldn't get Legal Aid, but she got Legal Aid. I thought, well, I've got to fight it on my own, so I went to the school, got all their teacher's reports and the school nurse came round. I said, 'Don't let me know when you're coming. You just lob up whenever you feel like it and then I want a report'. So she gave me a report and I got reports from the Little Athletics that I had them involved in. I had a whole heap of papers like this because that's all I had. I went to the court and she had her lawyer and her mother and her sister, and I was there with this pack of paperwork. The magistrate sided with me that I keep full control of the children. Her lawyer then asked if she could access every second weekend and the magistrate said to me, 'Well, what do you think about that?' I said no. I said, 'For two years she's had nothing to do with them whatsoever. If she comes back and starts in their lives, it's going to stuff up everything what we're doing'. I said I'd prefer that she had nothing more to do with them until they're old enough to make up their own minds. So he granted me it. Then he said to me, 'Do you want me to put an order for her to pay maintenance?' I said, 'Well I can't really ask you to make her pay maintenance when I've asked not to let her have access to them'. He said, 'Okay, that's fine. But I'll leave this open for 12 months; if you change your mind you can have it put in place'. So that was it.

There were a lot of personal problems that I didn't realise for a long time. But after the wife had left and I had the kids on my own, I was in one room, the boys were in one room and the daughter was in another room. If I heard a noise, any sort of noise – a cockroach could run across the floor – then I'd be wide awake, and I always had a butcher's knife under my pillow. I'd go through every room in the house and make sure the kids were all right – check behind the doors, behind the lounge, in the kitchen, make sure there was no one in there. Then I'd go back to bed. That carried on for years until they left home, then my daughter had the two girls and everything started all over again. I was living about two kms away. I'd hear my youngest granddaughter singing out, 'Poppy'. It was as if it was for real and I'd get up, look around the house, walk up and down the street, walk across to their place and check the drain outside. I'd find the key, I'd let myself in, sneak into her bedroom and make sure she was breathing okay, then I'd go home. They wouldn't even know I'd been there. That just went on till they grew up. There were times you'd be worrying whether something was going to happen to them if you were away for any length of time. It was just on your mind all the time. If I came down to Perth for treatment, instead of staying down for a day or two I'd be on the first plane back because I just worried that something was going to happen to my grandkids while I was gone.

There was some veterans' support at the time, but I couldn't go there to see them for some reason. A couple of times, years later, I went there and had a chat to them. Back then I never went near them. It was pretty hard to work through. But, as I say, the main thing was that close family would give you support and that was where I was lucky. I know people who turned to drink whereas I went away from the drink. When I got to take over the kids on my own, then I was able to walk away from it, whereas others couldn't and then their family would walk away from them and the next thing, they've committed suicide. There was one bloke who committed suicide, an Aboriginal fella who had a lot of problems. He was finding it hard to get by and so his family took him to this counsellor. But the thing is, when you're counselling someone, you've got to realise if you're going too far and you've got to stop. She had probably not done too many veterans, and she just brought too much up in one hit and the next day they found him dead. He hung himself because she brought up too much at one time and he couldn't handle it. Years later, in 1986, I got help for PTSD, and it was the first time I was able to speak about it. The psychiatrist was really good, top guy, and I was able to talk to him about it. He said the only way you're going to get through this is being able to talk about it. When he saw I was having problems, he just kicked his shoes off and sat up on his desk and we started talking like two guys.

After the Army I tried playing football again, but I couldn't because of the problems with the knee. I started work again, then went back on CBH with the job that I'd left when I went in the Army. For the first couple of weeks up there, I was doing some tractor driving for a couple of the farmers I knew. After the wife left, I was bringing up the four kids on my own. I thought it was easy. I just involved myself with what they were doing; we were that close. I didn't think it was hard at all. We were right up in the bush and there weren't too many people that had TVs at that time up there. You never read anything about Aboriginal activism up in the country in the 1970s.

We came down to Perth about '78, I think it was. They were still going to school. Then I was working on that new bridge down at Fremantle, the big concrete Stirling Bridge, and I was pushing all those squares out. They were making them out at Kewdale and they were bringing them down on Brambles trucks and we'd lift them off with these big cranes and then put them on this trolley. Then I'd push them out with this Chamberlain tractor with a bucket on the front. We'd hook that onto the back of this trolley and then push them out, and there were people on the other end with the other crane who'd lift it off and then put it in place. We were on the very last one. We'd completed one side and we're just completing this other side and we had the very last one to put in place.

I was living in Gosnells, and one Friday night I said to Tom Howlett who was living in Gosnells also, 'Tom, you're sure you're going to work tomorrow morning?' He said, 'Oh yeah, I'll be there'. He got on the piss that night and never picked me up in the morning. I raced around about two blocks away to a telephone box. I rang up a taxi, raced back home; just as I got there the taxi pulled up. We're on the way down, but in the meantime the head engineer in charge of the project got sick and tired of waiting for me to turn up to push this out. So he's got this leading hand and his offsider to push it out. But they didn't hook it up properly. Just as we pull up in the taxi, they've started pushing it and the bucket had come away from the trolley. They just put the bucket down and this leading hand's standing in front of it. You're looking at 38 tons of concrete on a 13-ton trolley. The gap between the bottom of the trolley and the top of the bridge, if he had tripped, would have dragged him. His offsider was trying to put bits of reinforced steel rod under these little tiny railway wheels on the railway line. All the time it's getting a little bit quicker and so I yelled out from the taxi, 'Get the bucket and put it on the trolley and put your brakes on'. No. So I raced from the taxi to the tractor, jumped on the tractor and I'm after this thing. I caught it up half way across that bridge, and by that time it was going pretty fast. I hooked the bucket on the back of the trolley and I've got the front wheels about two feet off the ground. I've got hold of the steering wheel and I'm standing on the brakes and it's just dragging me across to the other side. Just as I was about to stop it, one of the wheels hit a piece of wood and the bucket had come off. It just slowly went and dropped over the edge. Now all the guys working inside the bridge came out, tears streaming down their faces. They wrapped their arms around me and this old fella kissed me on the cheek: 'You saved our lives! You saved our lives!' I was sitting down on the top of the bridge there and I was shaking like shit. Blokes who were working on the scaffolding under the bridge just jumped straight over; some landed in the water, some landed in the dirt.

The paymaster came out and he said, 'Oh shit, Schnaarsie, you're going to get a big bonus at the end of the year, at Christmas, 20 or 30 grand no worries'. I said, 'Bullshit'. He said, 'You've saved them bloody heaps, and you've probably saved God knows how many lives as well'. Anyway, so the Christmas party time comes, Peter Knights is there and he's thanking everybody because the project is in front of time. And he said, 'I have to thank John Schnaars for what he done that day. He stopped a major disaster, but if he'd have got here on time, it wouldn't have happened'. I said to my brother that I was really going to let fly, but my brother was able to hold me back. He said, 'No, John, don't; let it go'. So that was it. That was the thanks I got. Years later, when I first started doing this Honouring Indigenous War Graves work, we had no equipment. So I wrote a letter to the owner of the company and he ended up having the paymaster, who was actually still working there, present me with this big picture of different sections of the bridge with a little plaque on it. I've got that hanging up out at my place and they supplied us with three or four second-hand computers, chairs and tables. That's how we got started doing this work back in 2001. He said, 'I can remember the day, what had happened, very distinctly. You were definitely the hero of the day'. I thought about it after. One wrong slip like that, going over at those speeds, I'd have gone over the edge of the bridge and drowned because I can't swim. If that concrete section would have hit the end of the bridge at the speed it was going, that whole side of that section would have gone down into the river with those guys inside. Those guys would have dropped out and they would have been just crushed underneath.

In the early '80s I stuffed my knee and then I had to have two operations. Plus then I had to go back to hospital twice, had to go to physiotherapy for six weeks at a time, and I missed work. Back to hospital, have it manipulated, back to hospital for another operation on it, and finally they gave a payout. I was on that for yonks; they ended up putting me on a Disability Pension, not a veterans' pension. I ended up putting my veterans' pension in years later because I was still bringing up the kids at the same time and I couldn't get an Unmarried Mother's Pension because the kids didn't need me full-time as they were going to school. Years later I applied for the Defence Service Pension. They just changed it over and then I started fighting for the Disability Pension, which happened. It took me three-and-a-half years to finally win that case for a Disability Pension. The thing is, the governments of this country need to get photos taken. 'We'll look after you when you come back' – that's bullshit. They're nowhere to be seen when you come back and they've got these bastards writing all this crap up to try to screw you. One question will be here to ask this, then another question asks you the same question a little bit further back, but the way you look at it, it's a different way of answering it. So you answer it that way, then they've got you.

I was out of work for years, which made it easy for me because I was at home. I didn't have a washing machine, so all the kids' school clothes I had to wash by hand, plus all their sheets and doonas. I didn't have any vacuum cleaner; I had to do it with the broom. Then you had to clean their rooms every day, make their beds up, cook. It was just full-on, and then I had my leg in plaster a lot of that time as well. Then I'd walk them to school. Well, that was about two kms on this, crutches, and then come home. It kept me busy. They all went to fifth year of high school, and then they started work. They've been working ever since.

Peter's a supervisor on drilling rigs up north. Maitland started off as a croupier and now he's an inspector at the casino. He only works part-time now because he's got his own acting group. He just wrote a play that they had down at Yirra Yaakin Theatre. Then he took it up north for a fortnight to the schools. The theatre group is him and his mates; they're all Aboriginal. Graham's in his 20th year this year [2010] in the Air Force. He just came back from Timor a little while back, then he done three years earlier over in Malaya, in Butterworth. I've got a nephew who's a major in the Army. It's still going on. I've got another nephew who's in the police force. Sharryn works at the old people's home out at Armadale bringing up her two kids on her own. The old people really love her and she gets on really well with them.

I've brought them up the same way Dad and Mum brought me up: to respect your elders. If you want something, you go out and earn your money to buy it yourself; you don't take something that somebody else has worked for. If I ever stepped out of line the old man got the garden hose. You got three cracks across the arse for that and if you were slow enough, too slow, you'd get the third one; if you were quick enough he'd just miss you. But we had total respect for Dad and Mum all the way through, and the only time you'd get that is if you'd done something wrong. He wouldn't give it to you for no reason; you had to do something really wrong first, and I mean really wrong. They brought us up strict, to respect other people less fortunate than yourself, and to help your elders wherever you can help them, and that's how I brought mine up, the same way. If they stepped out of line they got a cut across the arse with a strap. They have total respect for me, and they're all doing really well.

In the 1990s I got involved in veterans' causes, which eventually led to Honouring Indigenous War Graves. There weren't really any ex-servicemen groups going up at Merredin when I lived there. There was an RSL. In the late '90s, probably, I started helping this lady with Vietnam Veterans' Federation who were based in Sydney. I started helping mid-'90s with veterans getting all evidence to present. She was an advocate and I was doing all the research for them to take to court, DVA, the arbitration appeals. Back in the 1990s, I started working on seeing if some of my cousins could get money that was owing to their father. It was a waste of time. When I found out we couldn't get them the money that was owed to them I said, 'Well, we've got to do a service for them', and that is when we started the headstones for Indigenous graves. To do the other work we had to change to Vietnam Veterans' Counselling Service and LINC [Local Indigenous Network and Communities]. This is the one we put together years ago in 2000.

I was looking into the family of Victor 'Mighty' Nelson, who was an uncle of mine. I knew that he was chasing money that he felt they owed him. He served in New Guinea in the Second World War. I went over in June to Canberra with the TPI veterans for a protest rally outside of Parliament House, and then I spoke to three heads of the Repatriation Department and put it to them that I was looking at taking them to court to try to get this back pay.[2] They told me then that you're wasting your time because they had to sign certain paperwork back then saying that after the war they couldn't claim anything virtually. I thought, 'Well, that stuffs that'. I thought, we've got to do something. We will put a headstone on the grave and do a service, and he was the very first one we did which was at Merredin on 16 September 2001. For that first one we had to raise the money. I think as that group we did about another 10 or 11. I was up at Bruce Rock in November 2004 getting out what we were doing to all the veterans up there.

---

2   The Department of Repatriation was the precursor to the Department of Veterans' Affairs.

The lady I'd been working with and this other bloke were down here going round to all the veterans who would never come to a meeting. They were telling the veterans stories to get them to sign proxy votes for a meeting in November 2004 where they put it up to have me removed as president of the LINC and this other guy take over, which is what happened.

I stayed trying to work with them until early March 2005 and I went to the last meeting with Victoria Thomas. I was getting that frustrated with them because I was wanting to do a service for Kenneth Forrest before his son died. Victoria said, 'Well, you're not coming ever back to a meeting here'. And I said, 'Well, what am I going to do?' She said, 'We'll start another group up and we'll put things in place so the same thing can't happen again'. So that was when myself and Victoria started working on putting Honouring Indigenous War Graves together, in early March 2005. We were working out of our own pockets, putting in long hours. She was really good with putting together constitutions and business plans. Chris Thomas, who does the headstones, said, 'I know how much you want to do these headstones, Schnaarsie'. So he said, 'I'll put it in place. Then when you get the funding, which I know you'll get, you can pay me'. So he put the headstone in place. We did that service on 15 May 2005 and we became incorporated on 16 May 2005. We haven't looked back since.

We've been everywhere since. We've probably got about 300 members now. Most of the people from the other group [LINC] came straight across. The other group lasted another couple of months fighting amongst themselves. They look at our group as not just talking about doing things, but talking about doing things and making them happen. We've got a tremendous amount of support. We are working with the Defence Department. Wherever they can supply catafalque parties they will, wherever they can supply buglers they will, and they work as much as they can with me. We've got a husband and wife who are retired Salvation Army captains who're now members of ours. They come to nearly every service we do and I'll get her to do the Lord's Prayer. We've got a couple of Indigenous pastors, especially one, Albert Knapp, who comes to nearly all of the services. We've got a couple of Elders. Elder Mort Hansen plays the didgeridoo, does the welcome for us. A lot of Vietnam veterans and Korean veterans and the Māori are all members of our group. They take part in everything. Then you've got the RSL people who give support wherever they can. We've got some RSL groups who now are corporate members of our group: the Port Hedland RSL, the Broome RSL. We've got shire councils who give us support and other organisations give us corporate support.

We do between 14 and 17 services a year. We always do at least one more than what we're normally paid for. Until last year most of the services were in WA because that's where we only get the funding to do it. I've got to apply for extra funding from the department to go over and do the ones east. It originally started for all the early wars, like World War I, World War II, because Victor Nelson was World War II. Then we end up doing a Korean veteran, Vietnam veterans, and we've done seven funeral services now. That all came about by doing a funeral for Cyril Fogarty up at Dalwallinu when he died. The family wanted us to do a service. So I said, 'Well, I've never done one before, but I'll give it a go'. That went really well, so I've done another six since then. Some of these families have had quite a few other members of their families that have served. That's how it virtually started, and then it's just gone on since.[3]

When I put it together I thought we've got to put this program together so that it does a whole heap of different things. You've got to be bringing communities together with a better understanding of each other. You're sometimes bringing fragmented families back together, getting them back on talking terms. As former senator and Reconciliation Australia chair Fred Chaney puts it, the service that we do are some of the best grassroots reconciliation programs he's ever been involved with. Coming from someone like Fred, that's just amazing. On one instance, I had invited him to be a guest speaker on this Sunday at Karrakatta for this old Burton. His family didn't know where he was buried until we found out, and then a lot of them for the first time were able to be there. Fred couldn't come there because he had a prior engagement. So that morning we were starting and it was just on eleven o'clock. We're about to start and then Fred walks up and he apologises to me again for not being able to be a guest speaker, and then he went to each one of these family members and shook their hands and apologised to each one of them that he couldn't stay and be a guest speaker at this special service for them. I thought, 'Well, how many people would do that?' Then he went away to his other engagement. That to me was just something very special, and that's the sort of bloke he is. That day we had the Bruce Rock Vietnam veterans' trailer, which is set up as a big barbeque, we were cooking sausages and Fred ended up spreading buns. He just got stuck in.

There have been many times where the families have come up and had tears running down their faces and wrapped their arms around you, just thanking you for the fact that they lived long enough to see it happen. There was a group of tourists up in Northampton because a couple of our members were staying there at the caravan park. They asked what was going on, so they told them. They said, 'Can we come along?' And they said, 'Yeah, of course you can. Anybody's welcome'. There were about 18 of these tourists who came along. About half to three-quarters of the way through, this young lady was trying to remember her grandfather who we were recognising that day. The last recollection she had she was about three, and she kept breaking down. It was that emotional, and when

---

3   The story of one Honouring Indigenous War Graves ceremony is told in 'The Last Post', *Message Stick*, directed by Adrian Wells, produced by the Australian Broadcasting Corporation (ABC), 2006, DVD.

I looked at these tourists at least 15 of them were wiping tears from their eyes. It was just wow. There have been many like that. The people that come along to take part, even though they may not know any of that family, they feel what they're going through at the time and it affects them as well. It's just unreal, and it's something that you can't buy with money. It's something that's raw. People say, 'Why do you put in so many hours because it's all voluntary, mate?' I say, 'Come to one of the services and you'll know why and that'll just explain better than I can'.

We went national in 2009. I was wanting to go east and try to get it into the other states. Hopefully somebody over there would start up, and then a lady by the name of Aunty Dot Peters got in touch with me and told me about her father who was buried on the Burma Railway. I said, 'Well, if we come over we can put the headstone?' She said, 'Well, Mum's grave's here. She's got nothing on'. I said, 'Right, that'll be good'. I said, 'We can put his service details on the headstone, put it there with your mother's details on', and then we ended up putting a pillar in the middle because his brother was buried in there and he served as well. Then this lady, down at Fawkner in Victoria, got in touch with me as well about her father. That's how I thought, well, we've gotta get this funding to go over and do these two requests for these two ladies. When we got that money, I got in touch with people in Adelaide to come up with a name of somebody that served so we could do one in Adelaide on our way back. We've got these other calls from these other people. That's why I'm chasing money to go back over there.

A couple of years back now we put a memorial in Broome to honour the Z Special Unit men and women.[4] This year we put a memorial in Bruce Rock to honour the Fuzzy Wuzzy Angels.[5] I was able to work with the Kokoda Track Foundation and we brought out Faole Bokoi, a Fuzzy Wuzzy from back then, plus his son Saii as his carer. They were there for the unveiling, to cut the ribbon. They had a couple of old veterans – one who had been injured and become blinded in the jungle and the Fuzzy Wuzzy helped him out of the jungle. I got a call yesterday from this daughter who said her father's still talking about it, and it's just an amazing thing.

In between services, every year we do a major raffle. That takes a lot of time making sure that it's completed and making sure that you make money. Last year we made $7,400 profit out of that. This year, it's probably just over seven.

---

4   Z Special Unit, which included Indigenous members from the Pacific, was responsible for reconnaissance and sabotage attacks behind enemy lines. See Dick Horton, *Ring of Fire: Australian Guerrilla Operations against the Japanese in World War II* (South Melbourne: Macmillan, 1983); G.B. Courtney, *Silent Feet: The History of 'Z' Special Operations, 1942–1945* (McCrae, Vic: R.J. & S.P. Austin, 1993).
5   See Riseman, *Defending Whose Country?*, chs 3 and 4; *Angels of War*, produced and directed by Gavan Daws, Hank Nelson and Andrew Pike.

That all helps with everything we're doing. With other things, I put to the highest bidder last year a .303 rifle, which we got $2,250 for. This year we did it on a plaque instead of in a box and we got $2,800 for that, and a few other things I had up for auction which we made money on. This year we'll probably come out $11,000–$12,000 in front. Last year was much the same, which is not bad, but it's a lot of work you got to do to make sure it happens.

I got permission for us to march under our own banner in the Anzac Day march a few years back; we've done it three years running now. We march through the main street of Perth, and it's amazing when they see the banner, people read it, and then the applause that comes out: 'It's about time', and they applaud us. It's just unreal. A couple of the ladies said, 'God, I didn't know whether to laugh or cry or what'. Old Albert Knapp said, 'God, John, I felt about 10 feet tall and eight feet across the shoulders. When that applause went up, God, it was unreal!' It's just amazing. The most we've had so far has been 35 marching, but this year, 2011, I dare say we'll have well over 40 marching. Where some of these other groups that are marching are getting less, we're getting more. I didn't march before Honouring Indigenous War Graves regularly, but I did every now and again. It took a while before I got permission to do it as Honouring Indigenous War Graves.

We also get together every year to do the memorial up at Kings Park in May, during Reconciliation Week. In 2007 we started it with myself and other people from DVA, from Legacy, and a couple of other groups. We also just had the book *Forever Warriors* about WA Aboriginal servicemen and women published.[6] To get the funding to get the book done took a major part of trying, and I started off dealing with three publishers. Since it came out it has been popular. I go out and talk to community groups about Honouring Indigenous War Graves: Comet Bay College down at Mandurah, the Tuart Hill College, primary schools, high schools, Rotary clubs, other organisations, veteran organisations, RSLs. We get around a bit. A lot of the times it's just myself on my own doing the talks. If possible I take a couple of other guys with us, and I'll get them up to say a bit as well. Sometimes we'll work in with the 10th Light Horseman memorial troop and they'll put together a whole heap about the 10th Light Horse and then I'll talk about the Indigenous veterans. One morning we went to the Manjimup High School, then we went and did Pemberton Primary School in the afternoon, then the next day we went and did Busselton Senior High School, and then that afternoon we did Karrinyup Primary School right down south. We covered must have been 2,000–3,000 kids in those two days. You should've seen the letters I got from all these little kids from the Karrinyup Primary School – unreal, just bloody unreal.

---

6   James, *Forever Warriors*.

I've got to fight for funding every year to do stuff where the governments of this country owe these old veterans millions of dollars. They should be just coming out and saying, 'Look, here's this much money. Do that. When you're finished, if there's anything left give it back. If there's not, so be it', without having to go hand in glove every year fighting for this every three months. Until all that gets changed, then, as far as I'm concerned that sorry was just words, and it's easy to say words; anybody can say them.

So many non-Indigenous people ring me up, stop me at the services, and talk to me about the whole thing and just how proud they are that these old Aboriginal guys have finally been recognised. The non-Indigenous people are right behind getting it out there. The fact is that the Aboriginal people served right from the Boer War. A lot of these people have got so much respect for these guys because their fathers have spoken about these guys when they've been away fighting. Some women have rung up and said, 'Look, it's just amazing that you're doing what you're doing now when this should've been done years ago'. I said, 'Well, better late than never'. I'd like the Aboriginal and Torres Strait Islander community to think about their loved ones who did serve with pride, with honour, and total respect for the families of these veterans who went away and gave everything in a time when they had no rights, in a time when they were treated like flora and fauna, at a time when they come home from serving the RSL wouldn't even look at them as diggers. Yet every time Australia got into conflicts these guys were there putting their hands up to go away, and so I'd like them to remember these guys with pride, the fact they went out there and against all of the odds and all that was against them at the time.

I recommend the ADF to any young person if they've got nothing to do. Nowadays, you get that many choices that you can do things. It's all yours – you get your pay, your tucker, your clothes, travel. They get more opportunities now than what we used to back then. In general I think we've got to have the armed forces. There are so many different things that can happen these days. It's a necessary evil you might say. I feel, if I had young guys growing up again, I'd just say to them all, 'Look, join one of the services – Army, Navy or Air Force. Enjoy your time in there, do it with pride, and just respect everybody that you're working alongside, and do your bit for Australia'. It'd be great if every country in the world didn't need to have armies, but unfortunately we got too many idiots running around some of these countries. Some of those unfortunate people in some of these countries who want peace, you've got to be able to go and try to help them. You see kids walking around with no legs because they've stepped on bloody unexploded bombs. It really hurts you when you look at it; they're innocent. These people didn't want to be like this. They've got no choice because they've got people running their agenda and they don't want peace, and yet these same people you won't see them on the front line. They get these other poor people that they brainwash.

I often worry in myself what our children, their children, and their children's children are going to be facing in years to come. It really worries you because you want to be there to protect them, but you're not going to be. The world's going to be changing, that's for sure.

6

Mentoring the Next Generation of Indigenous Service

Harry Allie[1]

Gudjala man Harry Allie served in the RAAF from 1966–89. He did not see combat, so his service reflects that of many other Indigenous (and non-Indigenous) personnel who served in peacetime between the end of the Vietnam War and the conflicts in Iraq and Afghanistan. Since leaving the Air Force, Harry has been at the forefront of movements to recognise Aboriginal and Torres Strait Islander military service. He is involved in the Coloured Digger Project in Sydney and was one of the organisers of the annual Redfern Coloured Diggers march on Anzac Day, inaugurated in 2007. In 2012, after this story was recorded in 2011, Harry was appointed as the RAAF's inaugural Elder. In this role he serves as a mentor to current Indigenous RAAF members and also helps Indigenous recruitment. Harry Allie's efforts on behalf of the Indigenous ex-service community have won him accolades from Indigenous and non-Indigenous Australians alike.

---

1   This interview was recorded in Western Sydney on 4 November 2011.

I was born on the 2 December 1942 in Charters Towers, North Queensland. My mob identifies with the Gudjala tribal people. For my first 18 years I grew up in the town, mainly because it's a pastoral area and we had a very large Aboriginal community. I was always aware of things, particularly with our people. I was very fortunate because the pastoral industry around that area meant that a lot of our people went to work on cattle stations, and even more so when a lot of them were placed under the *Aboriginal Protection Act*. Being under the Act they were only allowed into town twice a year, which was at Christmas time for four weeks, and the annual show which was around the end of June for two weeks. Then they were put back on trucks and went back to the stations. I was very fortunate my family we were never placed under the *Protection Act*, but we socialised and interacted with people that were, and we saw the many hardships they faced. That still didn't take anything away from what we had to do. We made sure that we were kept clean and we were dressed properly and ensured that we worked.

In my younger days, we were always worried that we would be taken away and always worried about strangers calling in. As a result of those worries, we were often sent down into the bush, particularly when we heard the police truck coming down the road. We even did a stint of being hid behind the mosquito nets, and then wardrobes, but it was something that we grew up with and were very aware of. As a result of that, my mother wouldn't let me go and work on stations as with all our families. I had two other brothers; they were fortunate to get jobs in the town – one with the local post office as a telegram boy and the other in the aged care facility – when they were quite young. Other than seeing the hardship that these families went through when they came into town for that period of time, we tried to have a social collective community where they could enjoy themselves before they went back to the isolation on these cattle stations.

My father started off in the pastoral industry dealing with horses. There was a period of time when they had to pay Aboriginal workers that weren't under the Act the full wages. So a lot of the pastoral places could not continue to employ them, or they reduced the amount of people, or they only kept people that were under the Act. A lot of Aboriginal workers went into the railways as fettlers, but because there were only limited positions around that local where we lived, they had to go out into areas that were much further away from home, like say 100 miles away. As a result of that, they went away Sunday night and would come back the following Friday to have the weekend at home. Because of that situation there was a lot of responsibility placed on our mothers, aunties and grandmothers.

My mother couldn't read and write because she never had the opportunity. She had strong values; they're the values that carried us through and we pass on today. My father built a house, it was just the basic house, but it was our house, what we called home. We had a bed and we had blankets and we were fed. There were times when there were ration tickets that we had to go and buy things, but again that was the idea to go and start work early to help bring more income into the household. But we got by. To enable us to compete, I firmly believe that education provides the opportunities for our young people to go forward. I found that out first-hand as I moved into the next area where I did progress to.

My family was big: on my mother's side there were 10 aunties and uncles and on my father's side there were nine of them, so we all grew up with plenty of aunties and uncles. They were a sounding board and they also looked after our interests to see that we were progressing, particularly where my brother and I were the two that worked with jobs in town, as compared to a lot of other young men who worked on stations. For the girls it was different; they worked at the local colleges. There were a large amount of colleges, so they got domestic work, but it was a job. They were pleased that they had that opportunity to have a job. There were a lot of things that people did in the community, like making their own dresses and a lot of their own tailoring. There was a lot of community involvement in those days and it was all about improving your position in life. In particular there were not a lot of black politics in it, because in those days people were just worrying about getting jobs and getting children educated so that they could move them and make a better life. I had one cousin that went to what we used to call senior, about the equivalent of Year 12 in the modern education concept. That was very uncommon to have. They were achievers and the community looked up to us to be role models, even at that early stage, because of where we were going. It was hard work working on stations, chasing cattle or riding buck jumpers at that stage and the isolation.

I've got two brothers and a sister. I am the eldest, then Valerie my sister, then there was David, and the third, Phillip. Valerie is retired after a distinguished career in education. Valerie has a lot of involvement with our communities up in the Charters Towers/Townsville area to help our community move forward. We lost David about two years ago now and some of that is from Vietnam-related service. He had an interesting story serving in the Army, and that's the way the services are. Phillip still works at the Townsville Hospital as an Indigenous Admissions Officer. That's what they have in a lot of the areas now, particularly with Townsville being the size that it is. You have a lot of people coming from remote areas and they like to relate to an Indigenous person on being admitted to hospital.

My grandfather on my father's side was Malaysian descent. Details on the wedding certificate that my grandmother had, and the paperwork that we've found on the web, says he was born in the Malacca Strait. During his time, in the late 1800s, Charters Towers was a gold rush town. He always related to being a woodcutter in those early days. From an oral story we believe my grandmother was born under a tree at Canobie Station in the Gulf [of Carpentaria]; from the records there were a lot of disease and floods in that period. The only other thing we can track is that we think a lot of the Aboriginal people were shifted from Normanton and that area, across to Yarrabah Mission. Looking at the Yarrabah records, you can see a name the same as my grandmother appears, but there are no other records. There were comments that were passed on to us that she came into Charters Towers during the gold rush, travelling down the Lind Road, through the back way from Cairns, under servitude, which they did in those days. She worked for a businessperson in one of the main streets of Charters Towers. We believe she got married very young and that was to get out of servitude, followed by marrying Charlie Allie. They then lived out at a place called Black Jack, which is about 10 kms out from Charters. As the gold petered out, the old Charlie Allie set up holding yards at the property out there. They used to bring all the horses in from the stations for World War I and they held them in the holding yards. Then they'd ship them out overseas into Egypt for Light Horse Infantry. That's the story that was passed down. We have documented a lot of the oral history and are still researching so their journey can be properly documented and passed on to the next generation.

Although my grandfathers were of different cultural backgrounds, that wasn't any debarment; because of the Aboriginal policies in place during that era if you fell into the criteria, then you were placed under the Act. On my mother's side there was my mother and my grandmother was Aboriginal. Same as my father's side – my grandmother was Aboriginal, but there's the South Sea Island heritage. My grandfather was second generation by the time he married my grandmother, but they were all put under the Act. All the Santo family were put under the Act except my mother and her eldest sister. My mother and Aunty Elsie were working at another station when they put them all under the Act, so that's how they missed out in that regard. My mother and Aunty Elsie were not placed under the Act, but the rest of the family were all under the Act. There's another brother, who was sent to Palm Island. That's how these things happened during that period, because I worked in the town, I observed first-hand a lot of the occurrences. The same as my sister remembers certain things because she's seen it from a woman's point of view. And then I've got a younger brother and he's seen things differently to what I've seen when I moved on.

I only went to second year of high school and then I left to get a job. I didn't pass what they called 'scholarship', mainly because my mother wasn't in the best of health at the time. My father worked on the railways away from home, so a lot of responsibility was on me being the eldest child. That's what happened in a lot of instances. I was fortunate to get a job with an ex-Air Force pastry cook. He opened up a pastry cook business and he employed me, so I was fortunate enough to get the opportunity to earn wages. There would have been a lot of frustration if I couldn't have got a job, and I probably would have had to look at going to work in the bush. I participated by playing football and other sporting things that went on in the town.

My mum's health came good later. Like a lot of our people she had high blood pressure and diabetes and all of those things that lead into them. Certainly, back in those days you weren't aware. You might go to a GP, but certainly in those areas they didn't have other than the stock standard things that they dealt with in their own way. Some would get a GP, but certainly not send you on to a specialist for a further opinion. If the GP felt you had to be operated, well that's where you ended up – where he said. Or you'd go to the public hospital and again, depending on what they said, then you were put in hospital. We were probably very fortunate because of the free hospital system they had in Queensland. That helped a lot. There were certain things that we noticed when my mother was admitted to hospital; whether there were other reasons for it, we don't know. Like whether the Aboriginals were always put out on what they call 'the veranda', we just took that and away we went. There was covert racism in its own way. In that era they identified people that were hard workers and trying to make a life, I guess. But like a lot of things, we tried to always move forward. We made sure that we certainly joined in with the community.

When there were unsettling issues, with mothers and children, my mother assisted families that were not travelling as well. The husbands were away and working and sometimes they'd come home and my mother would ensure that they were settled. It was always that community spirit that brought us together. Or if there was a special occasion in the community, somebody made the cake, somebody made this or the stew, but there was always something there for these get-togethers. That's community life and family life; that's what we did. You made sure that if there was a wedding dress you couldn't afford, the aunties would help get the material, and help make the dresses for the girls and often bridesmaids' dresses as well. Because it was a special moment for them, they were so proud that somebody could make them a nice dress for their special day. Today it probably might still be like that in the more regional and remote type communities, but certainly it doesn't seem to be as much in the bigger metropolitan places because people have got access to go and do their own thing. You probably don't have that same community and family life, other than your immediate relatives. We are trying to do that here in our community though. But sometimes when you've got people coming together, they've got their ideas, particularly from where they've come from. That's a fact of life and you just make sure that they are well looked after and that they are not doing it too hard.

I went to a mixed school, but again I don't know if there was racism because the way the curriculum was, we tended to be always sitting down the front. We did sit in our own area in the movies. We had two picture theatres and there were some things, but never said to us. Because we were out a lot there seemed to be a lot more in regard to dealing with the police. A lot of my people that I know had troubles with them because they extended the boundaries when they were confronted by the police, particularly if there had been alcohol involved. That was a fact of life right across Aboriginal Australia. In that regard, it's like a lot of things in all the communities; you have ones that have jobs and are hard workers and then you have some that aren't quite thinking that way as well. The same is to ensure that children are sent to school, and we always made sure that we attended school. We may not have liked to go, but we always made sure that we were there. And then like a lot of things, once you were there, well okay, let's stay here for the day. We were only too pleased to get home, but that was life. Everybody went through that.

I left school at 14 and I worked in the post office for four years, then I changed over to a telephone linesman. I particularly recall an incident, when I sat for the post office exam to be a telegram boy: I came sixth, I think it was. The postmaster rang and said, 'Oh, would you like to start as a telegram boy?' So I came in to take my position. Then a lady came into the post office and there was a lot of loud noise at the front office where the postmaster's office was located. She was quite upset by the fact that I'd been employed before her son. But the postmaster said, 'It doesn't matter who he is. He came sixth and your son came seventh'. I take my hat off to that man because he stood up for his convictions. I've got him to thank for where I am today because of his strong conviction to employ me. Because my father and all my uncles had always been hard workers, that work ethic was always there with me. It was no problem in that regard, but it certainly meant my life changed by having a permanent job. As a lot of our people used to say, 'Get a good government job, then you know where your next fortnight pay is coming from'. It's all these old clichés that come back to you and that's exactly what did happen. I'd have to pay my rent and all that, but it was also to help the household. My mother made sure that I competed with my contemporaries. My mother was an excellent ironer and you could cut your fingers on the creases of my post office uniform. I'd be good in my job, so I progressed up and people were willing to help me. There may have been a lot of things not said to my face – and probably that's what people tended to do is make reference to you in a derogatory manner but not to your face because if they did that, they knew that they could possibly be in for something that they'd have to justify saying. All through my life I've never been an aggressive person. I've tended to talk to people and to understand people so that you'd come to a common end or common agreement.

As I progressed and did more time in the post office, I felt that there were other things that I wanted to do, especially because there was a strong involvement of our people in Charters Towers serving in the wars. My two uncles served in World War II, and my aunty served in the Women's Land Army.[2] When we came into the main lounge room there was always a proud photo of them in uniform, like in a lot of households. We were always aware of their contributions, so it was easier to have a desire to improve myself and join the Defence Force when the time came. After doing something like nine years in the post office (it might have been eight years), I decided that it was now the time for a career change and went to Brisbane to be a linesman. That opened my eyes up to big city living.

To be a telephone linesman I had to go to Brisbane to do a two-year course, and then I came back from Brisbane to do what they call 'Western Service' before they allowed you to transfer into a bigger regional city position. I did three years Western Service. I went to places like Hughenden, Magnetic Island, Julia Creek, Cloncurry and Mount Isa, and there were camping parties. At the time, because of the lead up of the activities in Southeast Asia, they had to upgrade the telephone capacity, plus they were upgrading the Townsville to Mount Isa railway line. Because they were trying to haul one-mile trains, they had to make it so there was not too much descent in the railway line. That's where they deviated the railway line and we had to shift the telephone lines where the main railway line deviated. We would regularly have to cut across the main telephone lines so that we could change the direction of telephone line. We were camped in tents and there were a lot of men. Climbing around telegraph poles in the middle of nowhere, I never worried about bettering myself – other than reading the newspapers or the papers that used to be thrown out of trains when we were alongside the railway lines. To quote a particular funny incident: When we were all working alongside the railway lines, and even the fettlers used to sing out, 'Paper! Paper!' One day when I was on a train returning to work I casually said to a lady who was in the carriage, 'I wish I had a newspaper to throw out to the men on the side of the railway line'. On my comment the lady said, 'Oh! We've got to get that paper'. She then ran into the toilet saying that those poor men

---

2   See *Thanks Girls and Goodbye! The Story of the Australian Women's Land Army 1942–45*, ed. Sue Hardisty (Ringwood, Vic: Viking O'Neil, 1990).

haven't got paper, so she grabbed all the paper out of the toilets to throw out to those men standing alongside the railway line. When the train left Townsville, most passengers would buy newspapers or the latest papers to read on the train.

There was something like 1,000 or so workers, and a lot of the workforce was Aboriginal and Torres Strait Islander men. Because of the isolated locations and the long work schedules, the workers never returned home much in that period. The work schedule was they worked six days running, and on the seventh day they had a rest day; we used to play football, plus carried out maintenance of trucks, and washing, and all that. During the work days they were working 12- and 16-hour day shifts out there. There was that political thing in the way it was set up to get it done quickly – for a number of reasons. I'd had it. After three years of doing Western Service, I felt there should be something else; that's why I joined the Air Force. I became tired of looking at circling wind gusts and dust storms, so I applied to join the Air Force and I was fortunate enough to be selected. They had no vacancies for a qualified linesman as such, but there were vacancies in the logistics or supply side of things. I ended up leaving Townsville in January 1966. Whilst on holidays I went into recruiting to see if I could join the Royal Australian Air Force. I was always aware of the Air Force because they had a guarded Air Force base at Townsville. We'd always watch the planes taking off and landing. It was always a desire that I wanted to do. I was fortunate enough when I was selected; that's when the whole thing changed and I went away. In my previous job a lot of it was manual labour, but the military changed that away from the physical aspect. We never had much machinery to help us; we had old post diggers and all that, but there was still a lot of manual work involved, whereas the military took on a different concept. Particularly, there was a lot involved in training in the early days and then logistics was making sure that they had the right spares and anything to perform the role that they had to do. Certainly it was a change from doing physical work to doing a little bit more where you had to use your head and a lot more emphasis on appearance, particularly when you're dealing with the OH&S and things like that.

I wanted to join the Defence Force because of my uncles and my aunty. There was a large contingent of Aboriginal men that went away. There were even the guys that went away to World War I – it's well documented. I had no qualms about going, having seen the guys from Charters Towers and around that area and certainly seeing first-hand my two uncles, and the involvement of my aunty with the Land Army. Also, particularly with the influences of National Service, there was a big army base at Sellheim outside of Charters Towers, and also because of the Bredden Airfield. A lot of my aunties spoke about that, particularly after the Japanese bombed Townsville.

The Americans were staging a lot of their operations out of Bredden Airfield and Woodstock and all those inner airfields that weren't on the coast. There was a very large contingent of American forces, including Afro-Americans, which made their presence known in Charters Towers. I can still remember them talking about certain instances that happened while the Americans were there. I was born in '42, but they were still talking about it later on when I was older. They particularly talked about the liaison that they had with them. Because of the price of recycled metal there was a contractor who retrieved the old vehicles and machinery and scrap metal left behind by the Americans after World War II. Particularly because of their huge presence, people were aware of it and the outline of the airstrip is still there today. It appears that the Afro-American guys tended to mix a bit with our community. It appears that they were employed to do their washing and ironing, so there was a little bit of liaison in that regard as well.[3]

My brother and I joined the Air Force. I didn't want to join the Army because they used to send National Servicemen up to Charters Towers. David had tried to join the Air Force, but they did not select him, so he went down the hallway and joined the Army. That's the way things happened. Because the Army sent a lot of troops to Vietnam, David ended up there during his Army career. My family was quite pleased when I enlisted and was supportive. I spoke to them about how I was trying to better myself. If you were under 21 your family had to sign the permission form for you to enlist. You couldn't go into hotels in Queensland until you were 21, so there were a lot of things which we couldn't do. We'd taken things for granted, but you still had to get permissions for different things if you were under 21. Because the Vietnam War was starting up, my mother was a bit worried. Certainly, when my brother went over there, my family were very concerned. The Vietnam War was one of the first media reported wars because of the television. My family would get upset, particularly if there was something that got them thinking about my brother David. And there was always the thought that I could possibly end up over there too. Because the cost of phones being so dear, we always depended on getting the letters. My mother couldn't write, so she used to get my cousins to come out and write the letters for her, when I was away. I would look at the writing of the letter to work out which cousin had come out to write the letter for her. Certainly, before I got married, I'd always be looking for the postman to see if there was a letter arriving from home. That's why writing has never worried me today, because that's what we used to do in those days.

---

3   See Sean Brawley and Chris Dixon, 'Jim Crow Downunder? African American encounters with White Australia, 1942–1945', *Pacific Historical Review* 71, no. 4 (2002): 607–632; Kay Saunders and Helen Taylor, 'The reception of black servicemen in Australia during World War II: The resilience of "White Australia"', *Journal of Black Studies* 25, no. 3 (January 1995): 331–348.

From my brother serving in Vietnam, I came to respect those veterans who wished not to speak about their experiences in the early days, even about what they were doing. They might talk amongst their own guys, where they had camaraderie and togetherness, but not to a wider audience. The greatest thing David wanted to do was come back home to Sydney for his R&R. I think at the time I was at Richmond, so I went in and met him and had the weekend with him to catch up. That's how our family was. We just had a laugh. The only other thing is when they had the Welcome Home Parade in 1987, they all came together. I went in to see him, but again it was their reunion and because you weren't involved with it, you tended not to tread in their domain. You were always there to support them and that's what it was. That's what you do in the military: you support each other, the same if you served in any unit. You tend to have a rapport with those guys on those units that you served in. That's the way it was.

David went through some issues, particularly with his tour over there and also other units he served with. I think that contributed to a lot of things that he had in later life. Again, he didn't want to talk about it to us and I respect him for that. It's the same as when we get together now with guys, particularly the returned guys. They've got that mateship, that camaraderie. When we are organising these ceremonies, you look and you'd soon know where they've served. So that's what you tend to do, unless they want to talk. That's the way to keep that mateship going with them. What may be okay to you is not right with them and you respect everyone. The same issue is with some of the blokes that went to Korea and served in other conflicts (there's not too many because they are getting on, well into their 80s); you just listen to what they want to say, and say, 'Okay'. My main role is to see that there's been support; that's something that I will continue to do while I have the opportunity.

The only skills requirements for the Air Force were the IQ and the psych test that you had to go through. I would say there would be a similar thing in the Defence forces, depending on what mustering that they've got you selected for. I would say that my educational qualifications didn't help me. It went through an area and a period where there weren't many people of Aboriginal or Torres Strait Islander descent. We were noticeable on our units. There was an element where some didn't feel comfortable to identify, but again that's a personal thing. I probably didn't have any say in it because I am a little bit darker. They automatically said, 'You are Aboriginal', and you accepted that because that's the way it was. In a small unit as people got to know you it was very good. You formed a mateship and there were people that understood and grew up with you. The lack of understanding seemed to arise from people that had never seen or been involved with Aboriginal people, who were uncertain. Nobody ever came up and made a snide remark to me because there would be people there that would take it up for me. I was very fortunate in that way. If there was an odd occasion, I would question them on why they had to single me out, but again, I wasn't privy to the discussion that went on. I had section commanders that would listen to me and I made a representation to be involved in Indigenous recruitment, because I felt it would be a career that Indigenous people could go forward and have to get the self-confidence to make something of their life. They all listened to me, but because of policy it didn't go further than that.

Training at the time seemed very hard because I was homesick. The recruit course was in Adelaide; it was 10 weeks. I wasn't as homesick because you had the mateship. We were all in the same position; we were all away from home, all 32 on my recruit course. When we went to Wagga Wagga for basic trade training, you were kept busy, you were on the go. When you were with the guys you tended not to dwell; you'd formed up with mates and you did things as mates. It wasn't until I got a posting to East Sale (Victoria) that I became homesick and I just missed home. It was cold. Sale was probably one of the coldest places I've been. Again, there were good mates there that rallied around you. I was fortunate enough that I had an aunty that lived in Melbourne. I had a car and I used to go down to Melbourne to visit her which helped with the homesickness. I basically had five-and-a-half years at Sale, which is a longer period than the expected two-year term. Normally, postings last two years, so when we enquired from the Posting Personnel, we said, 'Well, why have we been here for five years, what have we done?' As a result I was posted to Amberley, Queensland.

Bev my wife was in the Air Force there; we also got married at Sale. Bev my wife was a clerk supply and I was in the supply mustering. Bev left the Air Force after we married. At that stage, servicewomen got married, they were discharged from the RAAF. In '71 when it was time for us to be posted, we went to Amberley and we had a married quarter in Leichhardt at Ipswich. Bev did things in the community. The kids were ready to go to kindergarten, so the wives banded together. I was selected to go to America for the ferry of the F111s, and Bev felt that she'd like to go home to Manjimup in the south-west corner of Western Australia about 160 kms inland from Margaret River. Bev is non-Aboriginal, so while I did my five months in America, she went home to her family to stay with them.

It was an interesting time when I went to America because the POWs were coming back from Vietnam, Watergate was on, and there was a shooting of the First Nations people at the settlement of 'Wounded Knee', so it was interesting to see.[4] This was around 1973 because when we'd go to the dining hall for our

---

4   See Paul Chaat Smith, *Like a Hurricane: The Indian Movement from Alcatraz to Wounded Knee* (New York: New Press, 1996).

meals we would notice all the US personnel were always watching the televising of the Watergate trial which was in progress. In the US, I started at McClelland Air Force Base which was outside of Sacramento. Then we had to take an aircraft, down to Edwards Air Force Base for familiarisation flights. We were down there and I was in the logistics role. When those flights were finished they sent us back to McClelland, ready for the first aircraft to fly into Australia. So I stayed there after the first ferry left to come home and then before the next one, I was ready to come home.

One of the interesting things in the States was that I was the only person that was Indigenous. On arrival in the USA I just automatically walked up the back of the bus, but I could see the whites of the Afro-American driver's eyes looking in the rear vision mirror with me going up the back of the bus. There were two mates and as soon as they saw me going up to the back of the bus, suddenly there were two mates that came and sat either side of me. In Charters Towers, in our early days of growing up, we lived on the outskirt of town and we used to always go up the back of the bus anyway, but not to the degree of what was happening in the States. They seemed to have more troubles with, and were more derogatory towards, the other nationalities. They made snide comments about those minorities, which I wouldn't have been happy about. They were referred to in a manner which certainly would have made people feel very uncomfortable. To me, a lot of them didn't fully understand where Australia was located and would make reference to and say 'Austria'. It was mainly the ones that served in the Southeast Asia area that knew more about Australia. There were quite a lot of people that had never been to Australia, so they would often talk about how we spoke so quickly. I never thought of ourselves in a different light. Generally, a lot of the Americans that we dealt with were understanding of what we were trying to do. They would take us home to have a meal and invite us into their homes and that just made our stay a bit more pleasurable. At work it's those little things that you appreciate when you are away from your home and your loved ones. Things were certainly good in that regard.

There was one time I had to go down to Burbank Airport outside Los Angeles to pick up spares for our aircraft and my biggest shock was driving out on the expressway at Los Angeles around peak hour. I had a Plymouth Ranch Wagon and there was a police highway patrol guy driving alongside of me waving a light baton indicating to me that I was not going fast enough and holding up the peak hour traffic as I was doing under 80 miles an hour. The LA [Los Angeles] freeways were very terrifying at times, especially after being used to driving in the traffic at Ipswich. It was an experience I will not forget when we were at Edwards Air Force Base. We were halfway between Los Angeles and Las Vegas so we tended to go into Las Vegas because you couldn't be down that part of the world and not go into Vegas. Working in close liaison with the Americans, we were able to see they had different opinions to Australians because they saw us as something different. In that regard it was very enlightening. Again, we were there to get a job done and as long as they were working with us to meet our priorities and targets, that's what we wanted. But certainly to understand their way of life in their home country, you know they are a lot different, but certainly in their own home country they made us very welcome and were very good to us.

Eventually I was changed over and I came back to Amberley at Ipswich. I did my role with different jobs and wherever we had to go and to provide support when they were doing exercises. I did my time in Amberley and then I got a Western Australian posting and went to Perth, to the Air Training Corps Cadets for the two years. There was a change of government policy and the Air Force had to look after the Air Training Corps Cadets. They had a different role again, but we still supported them with the facilities until they got operational. I was then posted out of Perth into the School of Air Radio [Radschool or Radio School] for six months. Before I left Amberley I had been promoted to sergeant and then I did six months at the Radio School. After that I was posted down to the RAAF Publications Unit where they dealt with all the publications for the Air Force. I did five years again, I was a sergeant in charge of the warehouse and I had a number of personnel. We had an officer and I enjoyed that role. They were very good people. For the book binders, there was a permanent posting – that was the only such posting they had in the Air Force. It was the intention that the support personnel were changed over every two or three years.

After that I was posted to Townsville and I got promoted to flight sergeant in 1980. While I was there, I was recognised for my role at the RAAF Publications and awarded a British Empire Medal. I only did 11 months up in Townsville; this short period was very hard on my wife and children. My children had three state educations in 12 months because they then posted me out of Townsville into No. 2 Stores Depot here at Regents Park in Sydney. When I came back down here, I was put into the facilities side of the Air Force where I was looking after building maintenance and facilities and quarters. I did two years and then I was promoted to warrant officer. I went over to the Regents Park side and I was in charge of 2 Site Warehouse Complex. I did 12 months, and then I was posted into the RAAF Support Unit, where I liaised with Defence contractors and supply contractors. I completed a couple of years there, and then I was posted into the RAAF Base Butterworth in Malaysia in 1985. I did two years as a warrant officer in charge of the warehouse over there. Your family were able to accompany you, so we had married quarters on Butterworth, which was located on the mainland, which is across from the Island of Penang. I did my two years up there and then I posted back to my previous position at the support unit and Air Force supply. I finished up my years in that position and then I applied for discharge in 1989.

Figure 7. Harry Allie in Malaysia
Source: Courtesy Harry Allie

Malaysia was interesting because they had three nationalities. There were three cultures, which were the Chinese, Indian and Malay. They hadn't seen many Indigenous people in the services, so they couldn't make up their mind what I was. They felt there weren't very many coloured people in Australia. So the Indians said, 'No, he is Indian', and the Malays said, 'No, he's a Bumiputura Malay', and the Chinese couldn't say much so they went along with them. I had 50 to 60 local people who were employed on the warehouse side of the operations. The local people who worked on the base were indeed great people and were greatly respected for their role. We certainly respected their cultures in every way and always remembered that we were visitors to their country. I went out of my way to have a better understanding of each of the cultures. We were invited into their homes to meet their families and did things like leaving the shoes at the front door and various other things, participated in events where invited, particularly their festivals. It was very eye-opening for my children. We played a lot of sport because that's the way the after hours working operated when we were there. The wives were involved in club activities. It was a very social type of environment up there. It made things where we all came together and we worked together, certainly to keep things moving and to support each other. That just adds to that mateship that servicemen and servicewomen have.

Sometimes a lot of civilian people don't quite understand why you want to get together with somebody you knew back in the late '60s, like 40 years later. But you have so much in common: we were single, we got married in similar time frames, and we'd seen the children born and growing up. Plus we had things that we did where we worked at different roles that we did, so it all builds up that bond and mateship. We have an East Sale reunion every two years. It's those things that people want to come to and they always take an interest in what you are doing and how you are travelling, particularly as you get into the older age. Some of us are not as fortunate as others, but that's why we always enquire on how everybody is going.

In the 23 years I served there was the odd racist thing, but as soon as they saw me they retracted. I know it was there because different people had said, but anything that happened was usually where people didn't understand and there was a generalisation. But once they got to know you and especially when you were competing on the same level, you would progress yourself forward. I was very fortunate I was promoted to warrant officer in 17 years. I was given support in every way to enable me to be promoted and I was promoted in the minimum amount of time to warrant officer in the non-commissioned ranks. I always believed that I'm no different; we are all equals and that's what equality is all about. In my case I got recognised: I got a Certificate of Outstanding Service and was nominated for a British Empire Medal, and also to be promoted in that time frame – I was supported in every way. It all goes back to my upbringing through my mother and my father to work hard. My mother would say in the early days, 'You may not be the part, but at least dress well and look the part'. That went down to the way you were dressed and the way you conducted yourself: not to be too mouthy and always take time to listen. That's something I have always taken on and it's even something that I do today when I'm dealing with people. I try to be supportive and helpful. If there is a disagreement, then I ask, 'Why?' So we can come to a common agreement. But again, there are other things that I do which is to be fully researched before you go in if anybody's saying anything to you. During my time of service I wasn't involved in Indigenous politics like the 1967 Referendum, mainly because I was serving in Sale in '67. Although, I did sometimes go to Melbourne or to church where Pastor Doug Nicholls conducted his services.[5] I made some great friends while I had the opportunity. It was indicated that I was on the reserve list for posting to Vietnam while this was going on and I didn't know when I was going to go up. I asked the guys, 'Am I going?' And they said, 'You are on the reserve list'. Depending on where you were being posted to, you we were required to do particular training before departing. However, as time went on, the government of the day brought our involvement to an end and brought home all the veterans.

---

5   See Mavis Thorpe Clarke, *Pastor Doug: The Story of Sir Douglas Nicholls, Aboriginal Leader* (Adelaide: Rigby, 1975).

We didn't have the time for activism because we were expected to be front and centre first thing in the morning. When I went to Amberley I was involved with Neville Bonner because he was trying to get recognition for Aboriginal servicemen and servicewomen, particularly on Anzac Day. He would come out because he lived at Ipswich. He got onto the base to have Indigenous people to participate, so they recognised me and they would ask me to go in and attend the ceremonies that Senator Bonner was involved with.[6]

I left the Air Force in '89 because my two children were ready to commence work or look at a university education. They hadn't grown up with grandparents on either side and we decided to settle in Sydney here to give them the best opportunity, so that's what we did. My sons were then completing schooling and looking for work; my eldest son was looking at a university education. My sons were playing top-level basketball and one was playing top-level Australian rules [football] for Sydney. We were team managers, helping them and going with them; we enjoyed that. My wife was also a good squash player and played golf. My eldest son is now a physiotherapist and my other son works for the Australian Sports Commission. He enjoys working for the Sports Commission and my son's enjoying what he's doing that with his wife and three children. We have always supported each other because that's what we do. We did all of these things by moving around the country and when the time came, we decided that we were going to stay as a family.

I worked for Plessey Australia because they were looking for ex-Defence personnel. They had a major contract which was a major step in communications for the Army. As a logistics manager, I completed 10 years with the company. We were located at Meadowbank here in Sydney. We had our own home and we had friends here outside the service as well as those that were in the service that kept in touch. Again, that's where we're happy and we have access to anything that we want; that's what life is all about.

During the process BAE Systems [British Aerospace Systems] was formed, had taken over the company at the time, and there were a number of changes that were implemented. Contracts were coming to an end and operations were being relocated to different areas. Because these changes were taking place, there were many personnel who were made redundant. After being made redundant, I was 58 years old and I took a while to get another job. I was fortunate enough to get a position with Aboriginal and Torres Strait Islander Commission [ATSIC]. At the time they wanted somebody for a short term, so my supervisor said, 'Oh, okay. We'll put you on'. Meanwhile, that went from a short contract to being there nearly nine years. I was doing policy and advocacy for ATSIC and dealing

---

6   Senator Neville Bonner was the first Aboriginal member of the Australian Commonwealth Parliament. See Angela Burger, *Neville Bonner, a Biography* (South Melbourne, Vic: Macmillan, 1979).

with supporting the elected regional council. We also had a commissioner, so I had a support role in the Sydney office. You had to be aware of the policies and programs that were being implemented in the region. When ATSIC folded, our department changed and were in the Department of Immigration, Multiculturalism and Indigenous Affairs and then we were changed again over to Department of Families Housing Community Services and Indigenous Affairs [FaHCSIA]. Again, we carried on with them and we were told that we were in the Indigenous Coordination Centre where we had community engagement with the organisations in the Sydney region. This helps me now when I am dealing with issues in the community, where you try to pass on that knowledge to the various community organisations so they can negotiate, be aware of governance, and where they can compete if there's any issue in their LGA [local government area] or community. They can apply for funding to meet those needs. It's important, and I've always believed you pass on that knowledge and you help to educate the young people so that they can carry it on and pass it on and so that we have a happy, vibrant community.

I have been actively involved with various organisations, and assist organisations which ask for my assistance, including with my land council, which I am a member of up in the Gudjula area. There are issues of Aboriginality with people. They have to confirm their Aboriginality. Then I guide people in our communities and make them aware of who they can go to. There was a little bit more with native title starting to come.[7] Again, it was identifying the families who were identified as the traditional owners and the connectivity to the land and the requirements of native title. That was a big thing where you tended to look after your mob because you were in high-profile jobs. You never got involved with the communities and the wider communities. It wasn't until later in the piece when I become a member of the local land council here, and it wasn't until I started at ATSIC that I became fully aware that the issues were Australia-wide. I saw the role that the broader commissioners and ATSIC were doing, as well as other departments such as the Department of Aboriginal Affairs and other organisations at state level. While working for them and being involved with community engagement and Indigenous Coordination Centres [ICCs], you would hear these problems. Because of your background experience, you were able to help these communities and give them options to move forward by making them aware of funding things where they could look at inequalities that may be happening in their communities. But again, there's always something and because of where I am now, I have a better understanding of the wider issues. Where we felt that government policy has been aired in

---

7   The *Native Title Act 1993* set up the National Native Title Tribunal from 1 January 1994 in response to the 1992 *Mabo* ruling. The National Native Title Tribunal is the main forum through which Indigenous Australian groups can lodge a native title claim. For more information, see www.nntt.gov.au.

the best possible way, that people have had an opportunity to comment on it, and that it's the best solution and scenario for that area or LGA, that has helped us have a positive debate.

I retired from my FaHCSIA job in July 2010. It was time to retire and I always believe in giving young people the opportunity. I was fortunate enough in the role that I was employed in to help the wider community, the region and people had access to me, I saw the changes we were moving through; ATSIC closed down and the demise that went on from there and the uncertainty. Then to see the coming on board of the National Congress of Australia's First Peoples, which is new hope to give people a word.[8] I have seen a lot of that change in history from that side, particularly Indigenous affairs, and my own history as well which I grew up with. I like to see and to guide people so they can be involved in those social areas where we are still having problems: with health, education and employment, family violence and those other problems which are causing concern. I have had the opportunities, but again, I feel we're at a stage now where there are vibrant people that can get the point across, help the debate, answer, and be representative of the people that they are in there for. I also still represent our people where I serve on a number of committees and boards and where I have been asked to participate, to give us representation. I certainly pass on information to the community and my network where I think it's relevant to help to move things forward, more so in the last 10 years.

From a North Queensland point of view, I've always been aware of what's going on up there, particularly from the Palm Island situation. That's why I always go up and try to march. My brother and I used go back to Charters Towers to march for Anzac Day whenever we were able to get up there, so that the community can see that there were two of their community people who served their country. The Coloured Diggers Project in Sydney: there was a lack of understanding when the Redfern Community wanted to have their own march and commemoration service. The community felt that they wanted to give recognition to those people who had served their country and particularly those returned veterans. The Coloured Diggers Project, Babana Aboriginal Men's Group Redfern and the NSW Aboriginal and Torres Strait Islander Veterans Services Association were instrumental in making the ceremony happen from that early period to today.

It's a different life once you leave the service. That's what you're concentrating on once you get older; you've got grandchildren and things like that, so you can be involved with other interests such as community affairs and other odd interests that really jump up with the services. I'm a little bit more involved

---

8   The National Congress of Australia's First Peoples was founded in April 2010 as a company meant to be a representative body for Indigenous Australians. As a private corporation it is not subject to the same government control as previous statutory bodies like ATSIC. For more information, see www.nationalcongress.com.au.

because of the NSW Aboriginal and Torres Strait Islanders Veterans and Services Association [ATSIVSA] and my involvement with getting recognition for our servicemen and servicewomen, and certainly working with the people in the Australian War Memorial and Department of Veterans' Affairs and Defence here in Sydney and Canberra. We have a lot of dialogue with each other to progress and move things forward. I've been able to talk to people where the outcomes have been very positive.

When we're having ceremonies or marches, there may be a thing about someone's grandfather and I can ring the Indigenous liaison officers at the Australian War Memorial; if it's something to do with veterans' things, I talk to the Indigenous officers at the Department of Veterans' Affairs; and if it's Defence or to do with recruits, Indigenous recruit course, we go to the Indigenous people in the Department of Defence. I'm still not conversant with the Aboriginal ex-service community in Victoria, but they seem to do things the same as the people in South Australia and Western Australia. I have contacts in North Queensland because it's veterans like some of the guys that know me from when we all joined up. They invited me to come on board. Just in our family alone there are quite a number of my relatives who have served in the military. There were a lot of them who had done shorter periods, but there's a few of us that have completed in excess of 20 years. We have a lot of support from the government of New South Wales in a lot of the communications that have come out. While children are being educated they, and the wider community, have an understanding that it's not all Indigenous; it's a wider thing for everybody to have an understanding. But again, it's an individual thing; if people want to come to events, they come and if they don't, then that's fine. We have a lot of involvement with the State Branch of New South Wales RSL where a lot of the things happen. They give us a lot of support, as does the DVA and some of the government agencies like Reconciliation NSW, NSW Department of Education and the Premier and Cabinet, as well as the NSW government and also the Aboriginal Catholic Education Commission here in Sydney. We have representations to have a display at the War Memorial at Hyde Park.[9] There are a lot of people there that are helping to spread the word to give them the recognition that we have been working towards. But again, with a lot of these things, you don't achieve overnight success. It's something that has to be continually worked at. That's why I've come on board to help Dave Williams [president of ATSIVSA NSW], who has always worked very hard in that regard. There are other issues, not only with previous service people, but with current serving guys as they leave the service. There are issues spreading the word, particularly with remote RSLs

---

9   Since the time of this interview, the City of Sydney commissioned an Aboriginal artist to design a sculpture to commemorate Aboriginal and Torres Strait Islander military in Hyde Park. The artwork was dedicated in March 2015.

where the whole thing is still there. But we are building that confidence and going out to support them with the Anzac Days and participating so that they have people out there in the communities and it encourages them to participate as well. It's an ongoing thing and hopefully we can get people that will support us to get more people up at face level. I wasn't involved in the founding of ATSIVSA in NSW, but Dave and the Department of Veterans' Affairs have had a big part in bringing that together. I can't speak on behalf of the other state RSLs, but certainly the partnership that we have with them here is certainly good. I speak that from the first-hand because I work with them as a chair of that ceremony we hold every year during Reconciliation Week.[10]

It's interesting to see now, 30 and 40 years later, the role and the advances that they have made to give Indigenous people an opportunity to join the services. That's why I've always been very interested in watching Defence from afar on what they are doing. Now people are aware of our culture and heritage, whereas years ago they weren't. Aboriginal people were seen as people that were lacking in so many ways, so they formed their opinions on that. But again, as we've seen, if you look at the migration over the period, the Australian attitude has been a bit that way as well. If you look at migration in its present form, the refugees are similar in that racist comments that are made are similar to any people that they didn't understand. But that's the way it is and what I try to do is encourage the younger people to be proud of who they are and to be proud of their Aboriginality – to give people self-confidence. I think if they do that then they can say, 'Well, that's why I am here to better myself'. Or they adopt their own strategy on how they can get over these things, especially dealing with the negative comments.

10   Since 2007 the Department of Veterans' Affairs has held commemorative services in the major capital cities during Reconciliation Week. See 'Indigenous cultural events and commemorative events', Department of Veterans' Affairs, online, available from www.dva.gov.au/i-am/aboriginal-andor-torres-strait-islander/indigenous-cultural-events-and-commemorative-events, accessed 11 February 2015.

Figure 8. Harry Allie today
Source: Courtesy Harry Allie

For Indigenous service they have always said that you go anywhere. Servicemen and women are role models in their communities; those are the ones that are proud of their Aboriginality or the heritage. It's much bigger because they are a closer-knit community in the Torres Strait. Most of their representatives appear to have been in the Navy because of the role that they play up in the Torres Strait. It's in those early stages, when you were trying to determine who you are, what you want to pursue, there are so many things because it's a totally different environment. If you are homesick I would like to think that in this day and age that with the IT technology that they've got – Skype or mobile phone, web things – they can keep in contact with their loved ones, their community, or even if there is a little bit of faltering, their grandmother or their mother. Or the people that they identify with as their loved ones can give them the support. Plus there's the role with Defence where they have got Indigenous units; then they can talk to them and there will be somebody to mentor them or talk to and get them through that next thing. They are no different to a lot of other recruits. There's that uncertainty of leaving, particularly if they've come from an environment that's been very close. There's good and bad. There's an opportunity for them to get home for a weekend and just get some reassurance. I would say that to get them over that first 12 months is probably the biggest hurdle – where they get into the step of their role and what's expected of them. Sometimes when they are going through trade training and recruit, they are not patted on the forehead and kissed and put into bed each night. Sometimes some of them have troubles coping with that and the mixture of putting it all together to come out, the finished product at the end of the day.

They will see that we all had similar problems, and at the end of the day it was the way we handled it. You will also get stories where people couldn't handle it. I grew up in an area where we had a strict community, we were watched and we were told by the community when we weren't doing the right thing. Then you would be reprimanded accordingly and you had to justify your behaviour. That was never a problem in my situation, or I believe in the situation of my brother. We went first and got to go the way we did and to represent our country as well as to get a job done and work with mates. That's what the military is all about: mateship. That's been proven over and over since Gallipoli to the present day. But again today there are still people that don't understand; that is why we spread the word. I believe we are moving forward, yes, but don't rest on your laurels.

7

Seaman in the First Gulf War

Neil Macdonald[1]

Australia was one of the first nations to offer its support to the United States-led coalition against Iraq after Saddam Hussein invaded Kuwait in August 1990. The Australian contribution was primarily from the Royal Australian Navy. Serving on the HMAS *Sydney* was Gumbaynggirr man Neil Macdonald. Neil's life story includes a long career in the Navy but also a strong commitment to Reconciliation, education and providing mental health support for Indigenous Australians.

My dad's Scottish; Dad and his family came out in the late 1950s, early 1960s, and Mum's Gumbaynggirr from Nambucca Heads. I'm the oldest; I have two sisters, and then I have a younger brother. Mum's mum was the matriarch of the family. I had a lot to do with my Mum's brothers and sisters. The family ended up at Alexandria in Sydney, which is just down the road from Redfern. We lived in Melbourne because Dad was an engineer, a tradesman at Cadbury Schweppes. Mum was a housewife and also she did office work for the Department of Aboriginal Affairs in Melbourne and other places too.

---

1   This interview was recorded in Canberra on 3 and 5 December 2009.

I completed Year 12, did four years in South Croydon Primary School in Melbourne and the rest at the local Catholic boarding school up at Lismore for six years. It's when I went to boarding school, that's when being Aboriginal became a major issue. When I was living in Melbourne, you never got racism. Especially when you're only up to 12 years old, no one worries about your race. When I went to boarding school up in Lismore there were a lot of people who came from Moree out in north-western New South Wales, whose views of Kooris were very completely different. They used to go, 'You're different' and 'this is what happens at Vegemite Village in Moree'. They'd put you in the same boat, but it didn't happen all the time. There were a couple of other Koori people but you learnt to keep your mouth shut and not rock the boat. We [the Koori students] all had our own things. I had sport; I did athletics and played rugby league. One person didn't like sport and the other person just liked footy and I liked athletics. And that was the way they went.

Sometimes I did rock the boat and it just used to irritate them. Some students would have a go at me about the New South Wales *Land Rights Act*. In the 1980s I think it was the *Green Paper Act* – they brought out for land rights in New South Wales. The issue that always came up was, 'Oh they're trying to claim the golf course in Moree'. Because most of the golf courses were probably on Crown land, the *Land Rights Act* basically said, and this is where I used to rock the boat, that if it's on Crown land you can't rule, you can't make a claim. If they want to make a claim they can make a claim but in the Act it says you can't, you're not going to get it. The same went with private land. So it used to piss them off if I quoted the legislation back at 'em.[2]

I joined the New South Wales public service in April or May 1987. I was in with the Roads and Transport Authority in New South Wales. In the old days it was called the Department of Motor Transport. They're the ones who issued licences and registration for cars. That lasted six months and then I went over to the Lands Department and I stayed there till October 1988. The Navy offered trades at the time and I wanted something different. I always wanted to join up and I just waited; you have to do it when the time is right. The time was right because Nick Greiner came in as premier and he was slashing the public servants. Because he froze the jobs for three to four months, I just decided then and there to leave and join the Navy. My Dad had been in the Navy before me. Dad was happy; Mum was a bit sad – she didn't want me to join up.

It was three months initial training at *Cerberus* in Victoria, down at Western Port Bay. Recruit training was pretty easy – it wasn't as difficult as boarding school. The only difference really was the fitness side of it. You still had to have

---

2   See Heidi Norman, *'What do we want?': A Political History of Aboriginal Land Rights in NSW* (Canberra: Aboriginal Studies Press, 2015).

that discipline like boarding school, which was the equivalent to what was happening in recruit school. I was in Moran division and we had co-classes. You had classes of about 20 people and in one group they lost half the class. You had a choice of optional discharge and it's abbreviated to OD, for like overdose; in one class they lost half the people. And they had one of the better instructors. They literally said it just wasn't for them.

Race didn't come into the training from the instructors. You got all their stories, we call them warries – what they've done overseas, when they're on the ship or in the naval career. They used to feed you all the information. They keep telling you 'Oh this happened to me, oh that happened' and so on. If anything ever bad happened it was the other ship or the other person. It was good; I enjoyed the recruits training, which was only three months. After that it was the technical training and that was just over nine months. That was just really basic electronics. That was pretty hard. You have to be there for nine months and most people left after six months. The training is different for every branch of the Navy. Stewards are only there for less than 12 weeks, cooks, four months. But marine mechanical was six months and then we were nine months.

I was looking at doing electrical or marine technical. You went for the basic training to get an understanding of the electrical side of things. What's AC, what's DC, what do batteries do, wires and gauges and all that so you just got a better idea. Coming up to about two-thirds of the way through, they ask you what branch category you want to go into. At the time you had the choice between being ETP [Electrical and Technical Power], as we say, electronics. Then you had the other one, which was just like being a basic electrician – electrical technical weapons system. And then you got communications and electrical technical weapons [ETW, also known as Gun Busters]. They were more into fixing up radios and all that. The branch I chose was weapons systems where we maintained the weapons systems, fired the weapons systems, or what I did was maintain it. What I went into was the naval combat data systems and at the end, later on in my career, maintained the computers and radar displays.

There were about nine or 10 of us in the class. I ended up getting on a ship in refit in Hobart. That was my first ship and I stayed on there for three to four months. I got a chance to go on *Perth* to do some sea time because I was nagging them to do some sea time. My first 'overseas' deployment was to Tasmania in early 1990; Tasmania was great. The next place was to Brisbane on the *Perth*. It was a DDG [guided missile destroyer] with about 330 people. That was the first cyclone that I went through. It was really rough and you got these belts and you would put your pillow underneath yourself. I put the belt on me so I wouldn't fall out of my rack. The next morning we would hear that a lot of people fell out of their rack on the top bunks when we got hit by these freak waves that would turn the ship over and back over.

I'd say there were about 60 people in the electrics division. That's just a rough estimate, because it's a long time ago now. You became close with the other people in the branch because you went through training at *Cerberus*. You got to meet other people by playing sport with them. Everyone in the junior ranks knew each other. As people got to know you in the higher ranks, you got to talk to them more. Being electrical we were always told our nickname's 'Greenies' because in the old days the officers used to wear their rank gold braids, green in there, which showed that they were electrical officers. And everyone says, 'Oh you Greenies, you'll go to sleep in your rack'. People think we don't do much work. Half the time if there's a fault we have to stay up and try and fix it.

It was great in the Navy. It was fantastic. Look, it's not for everyone. People honestly compare the military by watching the American bloody war movies and the bastardisation that goes on, and I say, 'Nothing like that ever happens'. They have got this extreme notion that people get bastardised in the Australian Defence Force. It's a really different thing altogether. You're under a lot of stress within the Defence Force. It's no excuse, but some people do have to let off steam. I've seen it, but at the same time there's got to be a limit. What I'm saying is that no one picks on anyone. If someone is not good at their job, no one is going to throw them off the ship into the water. They'll give them a second chance, a third chance, and the sad fact is they'll give them a fourth chance when really they shouldn't. They should be saying 'Right, we can't accept you as electronics technician, but have you decided to go to another branch, become a writer, become a stores clerk, become a cook, something else?' Some people can't make it in their trade or their branch and it might be better to transfer over to another branch. If someone wasn't good at their job, it's not about getting rid of them. There have been examples where someone hasn't been good at electronics but they've been good at the other job that they've been transferred to do. It saves the Navy money training someone else up, because they've already got the background.

On the *Perth* we went to Brisbane, came back, and then I went back to Hobart and then, about a month later, my chief called me up and he said, 'You're getting a posting on the *Sydney*, to go on the world deployment'. We went from Sydney to Fremantle; Fremantle to Seychelles; Seychelles to Alexandria, Egypt; Egypt to Istanbul, Turkey; Turkey to Gallipoli. From Gallipoli we went to Naples, Italy. And then from there we went to Tulane, France. From Tulane we went to Portsmouth, England, and we went from down there, Plymouth, Portland and then we went over to Kiel, Germany. Then we went to Sweden, Norway, back to Edinburgh and then we went over to Halifax, Norfolk, Virginia in the States. Stopped at the Panama Canal but in the US base there. San Diego, Hawai'i, Pago Pago in Samoa, West Samoa, American Samoa I should say, and then back to Sydney. That trip was six months. My nickname was Yasser. We were in the

Middle East area, Egypt, and the boys on the ship would make fun out of me by saying, 'Oh, local make good' [because of my appearance]. The major problem is, some people do go overboard, but you just treat it as a joke. You don't know their limitations. I just left it at that.

We knew from Hawai'i that we were going to go the Gulf after the invasion of Kuwait. This time it was only Navy going to war.[3] We pulled into Hawai'i overnight. We came back to Fleet Base East, Sydney, and everyone had leave and we got the ship prepared to go to war and we did work ups to prepare us for war. We sailed down via the Bight, up to Freo, and that was good because we got a lot of support. The day we left, one of the things that the sailors always have is all blue chux [wipes] and you see the waving when we were leaving Sydney Harbour. It was really good.

There are only certain things I can remember really well, but one of the main memories was when we were in the Hilton in Dubai before the invasion. A lot of us knew the girls that were on the *West Australia* because we went through training together and everyone knew each other. We were all in the Hilton and we were all drinking in our civvies and we were waiting for other people to come downstairs from their hotel rooms and meeting up with people from other ships. Behind us were all these Pommie, British businessmen, all dressed up in nice suits. The others were all talking. I had my back to them, I was listening and my mates were all sitting over there just talking. I was just having a beer being silent and what picked me up was they were talking about the war and when it was going to end and I'm going, 'Oh okay, suits all right, could be officers'. But then they were talking about how they're trying to get contracts to rebuild Kuwait. They kept going on about it and I was just listening and I was going, 'Oh my god there are people going to die and all you're talking about is trying to win contracts to rebuild Kuwait!' And that really dampened a lot, how people see it. And that's the way I see Iraq.

Once the invasion began, we stayed where we were. We spent 48 days straight out to sea and same with *Brisbane*. Our ship was protecting oil platforms, doing jobs that were prescribed to us by the Americans. For the first 24 days I was in defence watches where you're six on, six off, four on, four off, six on. I can't remember exactly, but they changed the whole defence watch system. During that time, I got a cushy job when we refuelled. When we got replenished at sea for stores and ammunition, I'd be on communications talking to the ships.

---

3   For history of Australia's involvement in the Persian Gulf War, see David Horner, *The Gulf Commitment: The Australian Defence Force's First War* (Melbourne: Melbourne University Press, 1992); David Horner, *Australia and the 'New World Order': From Peacekeeping to Peace Enforcement: 1988–1991*, The Official History of Australian Peacekeeping, Humanitarian and Post–Cold War Operations, Volume 2 (Cambridge: Cambridge University Press, 2011), 269–498.

We had been up there for a couple of months and every two weeks, we'd get the mail bags onto the ship. We were refuelling off this American ship and I was on comms and one thing I do is talk fast. Sometimes if I didn't feel like talking, and they wanted to talk, I'd always talk fast and they'd stop talking because they couldn't understand me. This particular Yank on comms asked me when we received our mail. And I said, 'Oh we get it every week'. And then he said, 'Well we've been up here for four months and we haven't got one mail bag'. Oh god did I feel small. I could not talk any further. It took me about 10 to 15 minutes to get back into conversation with him. We had to confer on replenishment at sea [RAS], or transfer of fuel. I never felt so small in my entire life.

You'd see the task force going up with the US Marines that were supposed to invade Kuwait, but they didn't. Then you'd see the old battleships and then you'd be hearing them bombing Kuwait. The skipper came down to the flight deck one day and he said, 'Did you hear that noise?' And it's just explosions. And we're saying, 'Yeah'. We thought it was artillery from land bombarding some poor bugger. The skipper was saying, 'That was the USS *Missouri* firing them big guns, doing a shore bombardment'. Oh god, hate to have been under those shells.

During the day, because of mines, the ship would go travel and be able to move, but at night all engines would be switched off and we'd float with the tide because you couldn't see the mines at night. You can't pick them up with sonar or anything. At least half the sailors lived below the waterline and where the sailors were, our hatches were shut. If we got hit by a mine, you'd probably not get out because the hatches, depending where the explosion was, have a hatch buckle so you wouldn't be able to open it. People coped at the time – but if you understand what some of the psychiatric illnesses do, you would find that some people don't worry about it, but some people would find it stressful. It's pretty bad.

I'll never forget that night before it became official that the war started (not the ground invasion). It was about 2 o'clock in the morning Persian Gulf time and I was up. This bloke came up and said, 'Yasser, Yasser, I've got some information for you'. I said, 'What, you can't tell anyone?' He said, 'The war's going to start at 2:45 in the morning'. I was on the afternoon late shift. He said, 'Don't tell anyone'. I kept it silent, right. It's coming up to midnight, it was about say 10 o'clock. I went into the 67 mil[limetre] magazine and a few people there and the XO [executive officer] was there and the XO goes, 'By the way lads, the war's going to start tomorrow morning; it's to be declared tomorrow morning'. And that was after just talking to the boys. I was walking out and the XO said, 'Yasser, don't say anything to anyone'. I went, 'Oh okay', so no problems. I walked out, went to check our space was secured before I went to sleep. I did that and

I went downstairs, and then I went to this place called the breezeway and it's where all the smokers are. I've never seen it before, but the whole breezeway was filled with smoke. It's basically kept secret by everyone but everyone else bloody knew. It was so funny that night. The skipper made an announcement and went on. I didn't listen to it much and I just fell back to sleep.

When the war ended we came in for port at Dubai and we were having fun. You had drinks and all that over and done with. And then we went back to sea and it was just a real anticlimax. And then after that it was like, okay what's going to happen next? Rumours were going through saying our time was going to be extended. Some of these rumours came from the birdies [expression for the naval aviation crew] because some of them it was their first time out to sea and they wanted to get home. They'd be spreading the rumours that we were going to be extended for another two months. And the funny thing was for all of us we wouldn't have cared.

After the Gulf War I got further training in electronics at HMAS *Nirimba*, which was near Blacktown at the time. I spent about 12 months there. Then after that I went to submarine training and me and subs didn't agree. After my first dive on the submarine they just dropped me back at Sydney Harbour the next morning. Then I went on for further training in the multi-functional display, which is the radar display. The UYK7 computer, which correlates all the data coming in and gives the range and puts the computer bits and pieces to things, says what the ranges of the aircraft are.

Electrical training was changed and that was handled dismally. In the old days you only got your apprenticeship and that was it. So you became a warrant officer and you wouldn't have any other qualifications except your apprenticeship in your particular trade. But the Keating/Hawke governments were a period of revamping the whole training scheme. TAFE qualifications were all of a sudden recognised by universities. The universities had to accept it, bad luck. So you got diplomas; by the time you were a warrant officer you got an advanced diploma, and people couldn't see that. It was shocking. That lost more people from the services than the sexual harassment because people just didn't like change. And it wasn't negative change it was a bloody brilliant change. We were setting the standards; that's what the Navy wanted to do. Some of it was bad, some of it was good. But overall it was going to help people. We were getting paid the same and at the end of the day the problem you've got is that a lot of the men didn't see that. At the same time, the hierarchy didn't know how to do things properly. It was spur of the moment. A ship is like a small town and they just didn't really know how to get it. The good thing about it was you could take your qualifications from one state TAFE to another state TAFE, whereas before, you might have to start again. The Navy decided, right we're going to do it, it's going to come in at this date, let's push it forward. You might say they were at the forefront. Before, you got a diploma, but the new system gave the non-technical trades better qualifications (apart from the cooks).

There are a lot of positives that came out of the Navy. Because we were in the Navy and we travel overseas, the Navy had a good system set up where you'll have a lieutenant, if you're a junior sailor, as your divisional officer, and then you'll have a chief, divisional chief and then your divisional petty officer. If you have problems you'd go through that rank structure. When you look at the other workforces, they don't have something as strong as that. So in certain aspects it's better than civilian workforce – it has its positives and negatives.

The Defence Force is really hard, though, especially for Kooris because you've got to have minimum of Year 10 education. If they're not Year 10 they're screwed.[4] I think at the end of the day what you've got to see is that if they join the Defence Force and they're from the outback, they'd have a lot more security than from say Bourke into Sydney, to have accommodation and food. Maslow's hierarchy of needs is the lower – you've got to have air, food, accommodation. Well, when you meet that you go to the next level and I see the Defence Force is doing that – security, jobs and so forth. Then they can self-actualise at the top and become what they want to become. It can be a good thing. They've also got to be strong themselves because sometimes they're going to cop it. Instead of punching someone they can just walk away. Or say, 'Right – I think you're wrong because of this, this and this', and leave it at that. You can't run away from it. You're going to sleep in the same block as them or on the same ship. You might end up sitting at the same bloody table on the ship and eating dinner together, or lunch or breakfast. So that's the difference. On civvy street you can just walk away from it. You might take sick leave. At the end of the day, someone may be pissing you off but you can't let your other mates around you down by chucking sick leave or something like that.

Eventually, I left the Navy when I was medically discharged. I was on a Veterans' Affairs pension, special rate pension. I've been on it since October '99. Since that time I've done voluntary work at Vietnam Veterans Federation, I've been also the Indigenous co-chair for ACT Reconciliation. I've been the secretary of the Sorry Day Committee. My belief is I may be a TPI but still I can offer myself

---

4   In 2009, the ADF commenced the Indigenous Pre-Recruitment Course (IPRC) to eligible Aboriginal and Torres Strait Islanders aged between 17 and 54. The six-week course runs across six months, combining intensive week-long residential schools with other study in between. The emphasis of the course is on improving candidates' fitness, literacy and numeracy skills so that they can meet the required Year 10 literacy, numeracy and science standards. The course does not guarantee participants a position within the ADF, but it has been successful at recruiting Aboriginal and Torres Strait Islander men and women since 2009. See 'About IPRC', Indigenous Pre Recruitment Course, online, iprc.aboriginallearningcircle.com/about-iprc, accessed 12 January 2015; 'Indigenous Pre-Recruitment Course', The Centre of Diversity Expertise: Indigenous Affairs, online, www.defence.gov.au/code/indigenous/career/adf/iprc.asp, accessed 12 January 2015.

as a volunteer to other things. My aunty set up the ACT Reconciliation down here, so she asked me to be Indigenous co-chair and I said I would around 2000. When they got my TPI for me I decided to help out on the Vietnam Veterans side. So it worked quite well.

We got grants from the government to run adult education courses. We also won the national award for adult learning education week. I forgot what year that was. During that time, we ran a lot of camps and workshops. We'd be camping out at Nymagee, or be camping at Queanbeyan, talk about Reconciliation and it was great. It was brilliant having my aunty set it up because she came from that area. It worked quite well. Later, I got asked to do Journey of Healing ACT. I was Indigenous co-chair for a while. Then I got asked to be the secretary of the National Sorry Day Committee; I'm the ACT representative for the National Sorry Day Committee, and I do secretarial work. I just kept to that; it was just all I could do. I didn't get involved in anything else.

I normally bump into Navy mates sometimes. I see them on Anzac Day, but I hardly go to Anzac Day marches anymore because the politicians always talk bullshit. They always sound like warmongers, especially after the invasion of Afghanistan [in 2001]. I remember one of my mates was still in the Navy and he just almost said word for word the Defence minister's speech at Anzac Day. He knew exactly what he was going to say, and I said, 'What, did you see it?' And he said, 'Nah I'm just hearing this crap a lot now'. My belief is it should be the Governor-General that does the speech, not the politicians. If they want to speak they can, following the Governor-General's speech.

The [Canberra] Indigenous Anzac Day service is at 6 o'clock in the morning, after the dawn service. Again, it's just the politicians who get up there and start speaking; it's just one of those crappy things. The first time the Redfern Anzac Day March was on [2007], I did read about it but I didn't know it was a continuous thing. I'd still go for a few drinks with my mates down at the RSL. We Indigenous veterans do meet up. You meet them on Anzac Day and you just have a chat. People have tried to hook us all into one group but it just doesn't seem to get there. It's really hard to and it's no one's fault.

Nowadays I don't want to be a part of any organisation that organises. I don't want to be part of the executive or committees because I'm now at uni and that's my present priority. I've done TAFE. I started spatial information, geographical information systems, mapping. I did quite well there. I then started community education, because I wanted to go into adult education and do research in it. I've since decided to do psychology. I liked doing my counselling course, which was part of community education, so I can use psychology as a building foundation to what I want to do. I haven't started psychology yet. I've done basically almost one year of community education but I can take some of that over to a Bachelor of Science in Psychology.

As you do more research you see that Australia's still got problems in its adult education field across the board. If you're retrenched we don't have a proper adequate training system. The government completely does ad hoc training, like 'Oh right, all these people are going to get retrenched, we'll give you money'. It shouldn't be like that; it should be, 'Okay you're going to get retrenched, we want you to go off to TAFE and either improve your qualifications in the field you're in or transfer. Now, we'll sponsor you; you don't have to pay school; you don't have to pay the fees; you don't have to do all that; we'll look after you there, and don't blow your money because we want to support you'. We've got to come up with a better way.

We have gone through a massive change in our adult education training, and that's what it was in the Navy. I think I've probably done about 100 separate courses. Your career is course after course after course and you've got minimum of 65 per cent pass marks, 75 when it comes to fire fighting and sometimes even 100 per cent pass marks when it comes to issues of occupational health and safety. So you're continually doing exams. In the military, if you want to go from school and thinking you're going to get out of exams, that's a load of crap. With my career now, I look at education as being an important issue with the Indigenous community. I look at education being very important within the Navy and it's influenced me to look more into adult education.

When looking at Aboriginal politics today, one problem I do have is that activism, it's a really bad terminology these days I think. I class it as a derogatory speech. It's equivalent to being called an Aboriginal leader. He's an Aboriginal leader. Aboriginal leaders are a King Billy statement, the chest plates that they used to give to Aboriginals to be the king of their tribe.[5] I'll read some of the articles by certain people who are Kooris and I just go, look mate you don't represent my issues, whether you're on the left or right. They generalise so much now and what you've got is that now all Aboriginals are the same as the Northern Territorians. Down here in Sydney or Canberra we're supposed to be the same, if you read these articles. And I don't agree with it. I want to put a paper forward on issues about how people are called Aboriginal leaders. They shouldn't be called Aboriginal leaders. In the press, if you're a white academic you'll be called an academic but if you're an Aboriginal academic, black academic, you're called Aboriginal leader or academic.

---

5   See Richard Broome, *Aboriginal Victorians: A History Since 1800* (Crows Nest, NSW: Allen & Unwin, 2005), 102–103.

This is Paulo Freire, a Brazilian famous for the book *Pedagogy of the Oppressed*.[6] It was his study on the poor farmers who have been oppressed by the big farmers. He was saying that the oppressor will continue to oppress the oppressed by saying certain things or doing certain things, and the oppressed will accept it. He says the oppressed have to take charge of their lives and get out there, and at the same time, not to put the oppressor in the oppressed spot but just say to the oppressor, 'Right we want to do what we want to do'. Aboriginals have to get up there and start making up their own terms. And if you're an Aboriginal academic it should be just academic. So that's the issue. So we as Kooris have to go out there and figure out if we have spokespeople, how they go out and represent our communities.

There are Aboriginals out there before Federation who were protecting their land against European settlement. They should be classed as heroes. If we're going to get an Aboriginal memorial, I reckon it should be broken up in two sections. The first section should be with a traditional Aboriginal with the spear and protecting his family behind him. And then the other would be to represent today's society where Aboriginal people and Torres Strait Islanders have put on uniforms of Australia. They should have the three services, represent two males and female and that's it. I feel personally that a memorial needs to represent two eras: prior to and after Federation.

As a veteran I get respect from both sides of society. When I'm at the Ngunnawal Centre at the University of Canberra, people say, 'Oh he's a veteran', and I get their respect. In white society it's the same thing. Normally, I say I'm a disabled veteran in white society, and that's it. I've never come across any angst in that issue.

---

6   Paulo Freire, *Pedagogy of the Oppressed*, trans. Myra Bergman Ramos, 30th anniversary ed. (New York: Continuum, 2000).

8

Peacekeeper and Rehabilitator

Chris Townson[1]

Torres Strait Islander soldier Chris Townson was one of approximately 1,200 Australians who served in Somalia as part of a United Nations-led peacekeeping force in 1992–93. The mission was to protect humanitarian food aid, but the work entailed confronting local militias amidst a state that was essentially lawless. Servicemen and women from Somalia, like many other peacekeeping missions, suffered post-traumatic stress disorder. Notwithstanding the new understandings about PTSD since the Vietnam era, finding ways to cope has been a challenge for veterans. Chris Townson's story tells about not only the difficulties of peacekeeping in Somalia, but also how traditional healing in the Torres Strait played a key role getting his life on track on civvy street.

I was born in Townsville on 24 September 1963. Within my family unit I have three brothers and three sisters. They were born all around the country because when we were young we travelled all around Australia, throughout Queensland, over to Western Australia and then back to Townsville. I'm the second oldest. Mum and Dad are Torres Strait Islanders. Mum was from Stephen Island, which is

---

1   This interview was recorded in Townsville on 26 September 2012.

central, and my father is from Saibai. Saibai is west, it's closest to PNG. Mum said we were like gypsies when we were younger. We were going from here to there and here and there. Mum and Dad spoke broken English, so I can understand broken English. We also spoke English with our mates and at school. My father speaks more his language when he's with his countrymen. Mum doesn't speak it as much but she can understand it. A couple of my brothers can understand what Dad says. I only can pick up a few words, but I want to learn Dad's lingo.

Mum and Dad moved to Townsville, I think in the early '60s, to start a new life down south like everyone was doing. Dad was looking for work; I think he worked in the railways and council. He stayed in the Townsville City Council for about 19 years as a truck driver. He drove the water truck, just doing whatever water trucks do: water the road, water the plants. Dad was also involved in the railway, but I'm not sure what area. During that period there were a majority of TI [Thursday Island] men who held a record for working along some part of the track. I'm not familiar which area.[2]

Mum was a housewife; she just stayed home because we had a lot of kids, so she just looked after us. She did a good job. My mother comes from a large family. She's got seven or eight members in her family. I've got uncles here and aunties here. In our childhood we'd always mix with our cousins through our aunty and uncles or we'd go fishing with our uncles. Discipline-wise Mum looked after all of us and Dad brought the money in. They ended up buying a house in Townsville in the early '80s and we're still living in the family house as of today. My brothers and sisters come and visit us when they come on holidays. Or if we've got room they can stay there. They also have their families now and a lot of kids running around.

Most of the family that I mixed with was in Townsville: my aunties, uncles, brothers, cousins. The first time I went to the Torres Strait was probably in '95, '96. I'd been overseas before I went to Torres Strait. Some people don't venture out of their state or suburb. I've been back ever since; I always go to Cape York, Seisia. My father's family live there, made up from people from Saibai. Seisia is an acronym. I remember a story that one of the islands, there was a huge cyclone and a major flood and they had to evacuate most of the community and transplanted them to Cape York. You got Bamaga; six kilometres north-west, right on the beach, that's Seisia. All of the NPA [northern peninsula area], that's

---

2   Many Torres Strait Islanders were involved in constructing railroads in both Queensland and Western Australia. See Leah Lui-Chivizhe, 'Making history: Torres Strait Islander railway workers and the 1968 Mt Newman track-laying record', *Aboriginal History* 35 (2011): 37–55.

Aboriginal land. Seisia, that little community, was given to the Torres Strait Islanders by TOs [traditional owners] of that land. But the whole NPA is now Torres Strait and Aboriginal because everyone's mixed together.[3]

I remember going to primary school. I was at West End State School in Townsville. I didn't mind that. I was a prefect when I was in grade 7. That shocked the hell out of me. I played a lot of sports; I was a jock strap. From there I went to secondary school, Pimlico State High. That was all right, grade 8 was all right, but I'd sort of had a gutful of it by then; 8, 9, 10, I did a little bit of 11, and I'd just had enough. They were all mixed races at school – Aboriginal, Torres Strait Islander, South Sea Islander, male, female. We all got on well. All my school mates, we were good buddies, but I don't see any of them around nowadays. They probably moved on somewhere else.

There was some racism, especially I remember when I was at high school. They had that African movie about Kunta Kinte – *Roots*, that's the one. And they used to call some of the fellas who couldn't stand up for themselves Chicken George. But back in those days I did boxing and if anyone tried any stupid silly business, I'd just stand up for myself and knuckle them. By me doing that they just left me alone. Back in those days you had your little gangs, your little circles. They still do nowadays. So the fellas I hanged around with, they were all boxers too. So no one would do anything stupid.

During those periods I was playing sports; I enjoyed my sports. It was [rugby] league on Saturday, Aussie Rules on Sunday and then, when Aussie Rules would go, I'd play cricket on Sundays. So I needed my sports; I enjoyed it. I did end up playing [rugby] union when I joined the Army. That's why I probably went in the military. I read a pamphlet and it said, 'Enjoy your sports? Why not come and see us? Even bring your golf clubs and you can play golf'. We saw the golf club, the golf course all right. Every time I'd run past it. I never played golf at Kapooka. It was a good ad, I liked it.

In Townsville, I completed my secondary schooling. I think I'd done grade 10 or grade 11. From there I signed up when I was 17 to join the Army. I brought all of the paperwork home to Mum, but she said, 'No way, you're not joining the Army'. So I went to TAFE for about 12 months, did an engineering construction course. I didn't like it; I'd had a gutful of school. I'm an outdoor fellow and I just had to be out and about, moving. That wasn't my line of work. I tried to get involved in it but I just couldn't understand the technical side of things, like reading plans. I was more hands-on and the military was right up my alley. I just wanted to get away and try something different. In our culture, in our family

---

3   For more information about the history and culture of Torres Strait Islanders, see Nonie Sharp, *Stars of Tagai: The Torres Strait Islanders* (Canberra: Aboriginal Studies Press, 1993).

line, they go to the railways. There were a couple of us that joined the military; I just wanted to do that. I would look at pictures and see them running out bush – holding weapons, fit, running through clouds of smoke and travelling. That's what I wanted to do.

Dad recalls that when he was only a young fella those people were being recruited for World War II. But my family had moved away from that. Within their community or village, I think some of them did try and help, but I never spoke to him much about it. But he recalls planes. My grandfather through my dad's side, I call him Athe, his name is Waraka Adidi, was a World War II veteran. He passed away a couple of years ago. I remember seeing him wear his entitlements, his medals on Anzac Day. I only spoke to him a couple of times, but I'm sure he was a sergeant in the Torres Strait Light Infantry Battalion. He actually flew down to Canberra, so they knew him because they got a Herc and flew him down there for some business. He ended up passing away with cancer. But he was a smart man; he was a well-respected man within the community. He held all those sort of high profile positions because he was a switched on person.

One of my uncles, Kelly Wacando, served in Korea. He was a big fella; because I was only small back in those days, I remember he was a big man. He always looked after us. I think from over there too it affected him. He couldn't really hold a job and he was going from here and there; he ended up passing away when he was about 45 – pretty young. They cut his leg off because he had some form of cancer. He used to drink a lot of alcohol, I remember that. He used to drink a lot. My Aunty Helen that was with him, and they were married. As far as I know she receives a widow's pension for my Uncle Kelly Wacando.

Another one of my uncles, who is younger than Uncle Kelly, is old Kulamo Wacando. He was a national serviceman. He's a bloody character. Uncle Karl was Australian welterweight title holder. He could hammer. Uncle Karl didn't go to Vietnam; he missed out. He did his time at Canungra and I think he was a drum major there. He participated in the tattoo; he said his band came second. He's a proud fella. He's a neat man – always dresses sharp and he looks after himself. He's proud of the military, as he is always talking about it.

As for me, after 12 months, come January 24, I turned 18 and I went back to the recruiting centre in Townsville. They checked all my details out and they said you're right to go. So I signed on the dotted line. It was all just a joke type thing, until I had my farewell party and I was in a Herc and I was flying out of Townsville. I was looking back out of the port window and I'm thinking, 'This is real', and I'm now heading to Sydney. My family didn't want me to go, so all sorts of excuses came out of the hat. Even whilst I was away doing my training they were writing letters and saying, 'You can leave the Army now,

I think you've had enough'. I thought, no, I'm staying. I enjoyed it. You're away, you're out of home, you're not being told what to do. I've got work, I'm getting paid. I got a bed, I got my three meals. It was good. You meet different people, you're in a different environment. It was all new. That's what I liked and I could acknowledge and take it in.

On arrival at Sydney there was myself and a couple of other Queenslanders. I was the only Indigenous boy amongst that team of men. That was in August '81. I was in Sydney for maybe two days, where we met all the other men that came from other states. We boarded the bus there at Central Station, Sydney. Then we headed off to Wagga to do our recruit training. Training was at Kapooka, Wagga Wagga. It was hard for me. I thought I had the fitness, but it's a different sort of fitness. Running around the footy oval, you can stop and have a break and let some blokes do most of the tackling and most of the running and you just walk. But there, when you go for your platoon runs, you do it as one team. They started off small, 1.2 kilometre runs. They built you up and built you up and eventually you were running 15 clickers with all your patrol order. The physical side was hard at first, but eventually I got the knack of it. But I wasn't the only bloke in that sort of situation; everyone was. Fifteen kilometres, that's a long way when you start running with a lot of gear on your back.

The other side of it was the discipline side. I think I had a little bit of that because of my sports. That kept me in line. You've got to iron your greens. When you fold your socks up, you've got to put the little smile on and pile them up. Every row of socks has got to have a smile – neat row, over your blade. Razor blades set down in a certain way, everything. Ties laid out, clothes hung with the hooks facing a certain way. I got the best locker set up. My section commander said, 'Now, I want everyone to do it like recruit Townson'. I was happy with that and I said, 'This is unreal'. It was good and I was rapt. I was one of the youngest fellas in our 24 platoon, Charlie Company. I think I was the only Indigenous fella there. I enjoyed the training; I love that sort of stuff. Towards the end I was sick of running wherever I was.

My section commander was from Townsville and in a Townsville-based battalion. He was all right, but he was abusing his position of authority. He was just coming across the wrong way when I think about it now. Part of that also was the discrimination side of things. There were a couple of little instances. Back in those days we had SLRs, self-loading rifles, that were the normal weapon all recruits had to use. I'd clean my weapon the way we were shown and we had it all laid out, and they'd come in and inspect it. They couldn't get over why one part in particular was so clean. My section commander questioned me and he drilled me and he wanted to know if I'd used steel wool on a gas plug, to buff it up and shine it up and remove any carbon. I said, 'No, Corporal'. He asked me and I just told him straight and said, 'No, I didn't do it, because I didn't do it'.

He just said all right, but he hit me from different angles. I knew the truth because I didn't do anything wrong. He wanted to charge me for something, or maybe he was doing it to everyone. Back in those days, maybe like a copper, they got to book someone once a week. Maybe he was looking for a charge, but that was one incident that sort of stuck in my mind.

Another time we were having a march out parade. He started calling me a stick name, Spook. I think it's got to do with black people: Spook, it was a nickname for that. I couldn't work out why, but I just couldn't say anything. I didn't know what to do; I just did my job. He said to me, 'Do you know why I call you that?' I said, 'No, Corporal'. He said, 'Because I've got a dog and his name is Spook, and that's why I'm calling you that name. A little black dog'. I said, 'All right'. That's always been in my mind. These are the sort of things I went through; you've got to be strong and move forward. What goes around comes around and he's probably going to get it back twice as worse, not from me but someone else. I did run into him later when I was in the battalion, because I used to do umpiring and I'd become a big fella. He saw me at the bar one day and I looked at him and he was just small. I thought I could do a lot of things to this bloke, but I didn't say anything. I just looked at him hard and he knew something was going to happen. I just walked off; I didn't hurt him. I said no, not worth it.

Back in those days, that was the culture there. I don't know what it's like there now. You always get some sort of name thrown at you. I've never thrown it at anyone. You had to be strong and that's what I found. You stand up. He was getting on top of me. But then again, I boxed. I went around the boxing thing there, and I smashed a bloke who was giving me trouble. He was older than me, but I knew how to throw my fists, left, right and left, right and he was down. After that everyone left me alone. So you got to prove yourself in that type of culture environment, that's what I've found. I learnt from that and, as I progressed through the Army, if anyone tried anything stupid then I'd just stand up for myself. In general, the fellas at Kapooka, we all got on good. I was only a younger bloke and they helped us fellas. We all spoke and I never had any dramas, except with maybe a couple of blokes, that one bloke in particular. In the ring it was all sorted out. They respected me after that. It was good.

At Kapooka, racism started but I sorted it out, and any other time I've dealt with it the way I know best. I recall one time when I did come back from Somalia later in my career. When we came back I was training the tug of war team and we had won the company tug of war. They took a photo of the team: coach, captain and the team. But when they put it in the company magazine, it had someone else's photo with the company tug of war team. I don't know what that is, what you'd call that, but that's the only sort of thing I experienced towards the end of my career. If I saw anything, I'd just stamp it out straight away. But I know other soldiers, racial discrimination happened to them bad mate. That's wrong.

After Kapooka I went to Singleton for corps training, and that was easy. I had no dramas whatsoever. I liked Singleton because it wasn't as regimental. It was easy as, and I had no problems. That was Infantry. We got taught all the extra weapons that we had to know. I just picked it up like that. I don't like weapons now because I've seen what they can do, but I liked it back then. My mind could relate to that sort of thing, whereas in the classroom doing engineering and construction stuff, no. This stuff, that's my bread and butter.

From Singo I went to 6 RAR in Brisbane, which was in about 1981. I was only there for about 12 months because I met a lady in Townsville while I was on leave. Women will send you haywire! I went AWOL a couple of times and I put in a compassionate post. I was with that lady for about 10 years. We were de factos and had one son. He stays with me now. Later I met another lady and I had another son. I'm not with her any more.

They posted me to Townsville in '82, I got to Brisbane '81, 12 months there and '82 to Townsville. I was posted to Headquarter Company, Defence Battalion, 3 Brigade. I was in Townsville for a couple of years. I was just a private back in those days. The role of the defence battalion was just playing enemy for different units within ADF brigade. Bloody cleaning, putting up tents – we were a lackeys type posting, a dog's body. That's what they call it; it's just a nickname, but I didn't mind it. I got my bearings sorted out and what I'd like to do and which way I wanted to go. When you're a young fella and have women involved, mate, it affects your train of thought. That was in '82, '83, but I had no dramas with fellas or discrimination. Even in Brisbane, everyone was good there. Because I played sports, I got on well with the fellas. If you're jock strap, you move forward and apparently you get your rank, your stripes, quicker. Because you've got the leadership skills and, you're working in a team environment, it relates if you go to war. Brisbane was good and then I went to Townsville.

In '83 we had Kangaroo 83: Katy 3. That was in Western Australia. That was a good exercise. We deployed over WA. That was hot as, but a lot of flies in Roebourne. We were there for two to six weeks. For the BMA, Brigade Maintenance Area, we would act as security party for VIPs for convoy escort. We'd look after main installations and in Karratha, like the radio station or the power station. It was a good exercise; I enjoyed that one.

In 1984 I did a couple of trips to Tully. That's the full force battle school. They used to call it back then jungle warfare. That's when I started learning about tactics, working in the jungle. I loved it. I was working with a guy called Brian Paine, who was a warrant officer class one. He taught me and he was a Vietnam vet. He was a big, big, big fella with forearms like Popeye. We spoke about when he was in Vietnam. He used to show me all the demolition side of things.

I'd watch him and he'd explain how we set things up and booby traps. I love that sort of stuff. I worked with him in setting up booby traps for the battle inoculation range. That's when soldiers go through and they have slabs of explosives going off left and right – primers going off making bangs, just trying to disorientate them, throwing whizz-bangs. But I loved the jungle since 1984.

I was posted to Papua New Guinea for one month in '85. I was still with headquarters company, but I was seconded to 2/4 RAR which is still in Lavarack Barracks. I went over as a PTI, a Physical Training Instructor, to 1 PIR [Pacific Islands Regiment]. I think it was Goroka, in Port Moresby. That was a good trip. I would basically plan and get these guys to do physical training each day. There were two of us that went over. I would either take a company or half a company for a platoon. That could be swimming in the pool, going for runs, doing circuits, or just playing football or something like that. If we weren't doing that, we'd have to throw our greens on and go out in the field with the rest of the men and we'd do all our IMT, Infantry Minor Tactics stuff, out in the field. The exercises were good, but the terrain was dangerous. There are no little tracks; this is just pure, raw jungle. People hadn't been through there. It was an eye opener, with a lot of dangerous reptiles in there, like snakes. You had to be aware of all these things that can probably take your life. I didn't realise how dangerous it was until I spoke to someone after we came back. They said the most dangerous snakes live in that area you've been. There we were just laying on the ground, just knackered from trying to walk up Ayama. If they get you in the wrong place like your eyelid, they rip it in half or rip it off. Once again, I loved the jungle.

The local Papua New Guinean soldiers couldn't work out how a coloured man (me) was in charge. I was telling them what to do and I'm this one. They couldn't believe what was happening. Once they saw that, they would come at odd hours of the night and drag me out of bed to drink beer. The first time they did it to me I said, 'All right, I'll do that'. I had a couple of beers and I said, 'I'm going home'. Then they blocked the door, and they said, 'No, you can't go'. I said, 'Rightyo'. I had one more and I said I got to go to the toilet. I went in the toilet and I jumped out the window. I went back to my room, laid on my bed. I thought no, this isn't safe. I went under my bed and I pulled the sheets down, off my bed. I was lying there and next thing I heard pitter-patter. I looked from underneath the sheets on the floor, and I could see a couple of sets of feet come in. They were looking for me to drag me back and I just stayed quiet, and they went back. But they just wanted to drink all night. I didn't want that.

Figure 9. Chris Townson in camouflage
Source: Courtesy Chris Townson

Another time we went out to the RSL. I don't know what it was, but they couldn't work out why I was hanging around with non-Indigenous people, and a couple of the PNG countrymen wanted to fight me over that. I don't know if they were civilians, if they were army or if they were police. They could be anyone. It was because I was hanging around non-Indigenous fellas. Their country is a different culture and has a different way of thinking. If it didn't look right, they'd hit you for nothing. We had to get out of that club because there were a lot of dramas. Back in those days, 1985, curfew was from 6.30 till early hours of the morning. They had the rascals back in them days. The young fellas were corrupt, and you didn't know what was going on. So I never really went out at night; I just stayed in the lines doing my work, doing my job.

That was my first trip overseas. It was an eye opener, because back in '85 it was like a third world country sort of in some parts when you saw the villages. Women didn't wear dresses; they just walked with their boobs hanging out and wearing a sort of grass skirt. It was different, but beautiful place. But it was dangerous at the same time; you just had to be careful, especially when going out in the evenings. We couldn't because come those hours, it's trouble. We'd go out to the markets during the day. Even then we went in our little groups. You've got to move around with a couple of fellas; don't go walking by yourself.

From there I got posted when I came back to 2/4 RAR. That was the actual battalion I went to PNG with. I got posted back to that company on promotion to lance corporal. One stripe, that was in '85. I saw it through till Christmas, went on leave, and in '86 (I think) I got my second stripe, so I was a full trap. I was getting into football back then, but that was union. I didn't mind that. That kept me away from the bush and then in to the sporting sort of jock strapping life. I like my footy, so I did that for '86.

In regards to local race side of things, I never had any dramas. I was just full-on into my sports and I used to pump a lot of iron. There were me and a couple of other section commanders who did weights. We'd do our training and I think because of our size everyone was scared of us. We never hurt anyone; we just enjoyed what we did and that was all good.

In '87, just before Christmas, we went to Malaysia and Butterworth. Whilst we're over there I was training for the Special Air Service Carter course. We did a lot of running because you had to do it to get in, and a lot of pack work. That was all we done for about two months, just train, train, train: swimming, running, pack work, chin ups. We did our sightseeing by day and in the evening we'd just have our full rest. We couldn't drink because we were just training all the time. That's all I remember. We came back very, very fit fellas. There were four of us, and we were all section commanders.

We came back early in the following year with the battalion and we went over and did the Carter course in Perth, WA, and that was from April for three weeks. With that course there were a lot of people who started – probably over 100 or something. Twenty-five of us completed. I was in the guys that completed, but I wasn't in the 21 that got selected for service with the regiment. They said, 'Oh mate, you're an asset to the battalion and we want you to stay'. I was crying; I said, 'Why didn't you just tell me when I was half way through or towards the end? To go through all this?' But I know what I can do now after doing all that. They break you. You gotta just dig inside and find somehow to keep going. I always think back to that and all the hard yards I've been through. What happens when you get it really hard? Do you just walk away or sit down and have a cup of tea or coffee? Think about what's happened, what's going on and then come back to it. I wasn't accepted and I wanted to get discharged then after that. I'd had enough. When I came back I put my discharge in. The RSM [regimental sergeant major] said, 'No, don't do that. Mate, you've got a good career ahead of you. It would just ruin it. Stay in for another year, I'll post you wherever you want to go. I'll get you out of the battalion. But you're an asset to the regiment. Stay with us'.

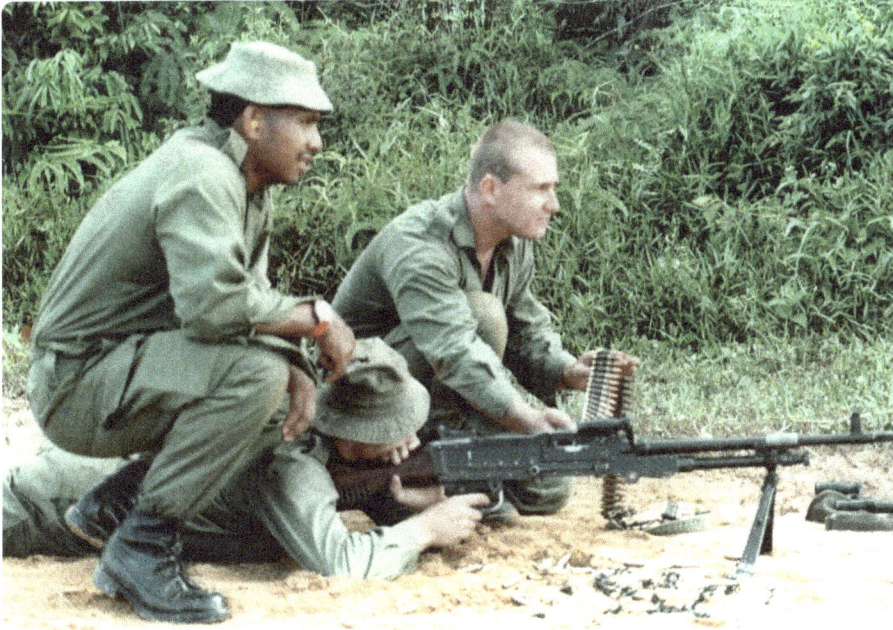

Figure 10. Chris Townson in training

Source: Courtesy Chris Townson

I didn't know what I was doing or what was going to happen. I thought I might as well just give it a bash. I said, 'Just get me out of here', because I'd had a gutful. As soon as I'd come back at Christmas '88 they sent me straight on leave. I went on leave for a long time, came back and they said, you're going to Canungra. Canungra is hinterland Gold Coast, Surfer's Paradise. I said, 'What am I going to do there?' He said, 'You're going to go 10 IRC [Ten Independent Rifle Company]'. It was pretty similar to the brigade posting I had initially. You're playing enemy in the jungle for all the different battalions or units that come in. It goes back to your basic IMT again skills. I knew that inside out, but I said okay.

I was out in the jungle nine months out of the 12 and I loved it. It sort of just relaxed me and I mellowed out. While I was there I did my subject courses for sergeant. I started in '89 in Canungra, where I did my promotion courses for sergeant. I remember sitting out bush and I had to take all my pens that I needed to study for the course. I'd be out bush and I'd carry my Esh bag and all my books were in there. I'd have candles at night and I'd be reading these books. The courses were easy, so I had no problems with them. Fitness, I just breezed through it – I was fit as. That was in '91 when I did both of my courses back-to-back.

Figure 11. Chris Townson in uniform
Source: Courtesy Chris Townson

In that year, '91, I got seconded to Larrakeyah Barracks, Darwin. I was there for I think four or five weeks, doing recruitment training for Norforce. I did that for a couple of weeks and I was acting platoon sergeant for some of it. With Norforce I remember going in to the canteen to get a can of Coke. I walked into the canteen and there were two Aboriginal boys sitting at a table. They were drinking VB; I remember green cans. I went and got my soft drink. I came back and I said, 'Can I join you fellas?' And they said, 'Yes, Corporal, don't care'. I put it down. I just sat there talking about things. The windows were open and I looked out and you could see the clouds, they were dark, and the wind was blowing and coming through the window. I smelled it and I said it's going to rain soon. They looked at each other and said oh, and I put my soft drink down. I went and got chips, and whilst I was there it started coming down. When I came back the two beers were there, but the two fellas were gone. I'm thinking these fellas must think I've got magic or something. But anyway, that's the good thing about the military: my senses. And just your other sense, you can sense things, your gut feeling – intuition or whatever you call it. I've found I can use that more now, especially coming back from Africa. Those are the senses I relied on back then and they got me through a lot of strife.

For this intake of Norforce that we were training as Army Reserve they were non-Indigenous. They must have been doing it just for that group of people. We taught them drill, taught them discipline, how to operate out in the field, taught them navigation, all the basic stuff about the ration pack, how to walk in the heat (and a lot of people had issues with that), conserving your water.

When that course completed I got back to Canungra and they flew me with a couple of other guys to Vanuatu to train the army and police. It was a team of us and we had to train the army and the police in their subject courses for promotion. So some of it was drill, or the other part was the IMT, Infantry Minor Tactics: the navigation and contacts out in the field. We were there for one month. We arrived at Port Vila, jumped in a smaller plane and that took us to Espiritu Santo. That was the island; it wasn't as large as Port Vila but there weren't many people there because it was just a lot of jungle. That's where we went in and we set up our little camps. We set up ranges, so they could do their shooting. For navigation we had our field kitchen set. The people who trained, they were experienced in the jungle because that's where they lived. That's where they were born, that's where they walked all their life. For example, in the navigation phase, these people are very pedantic. We'd work out a nav data sheet and that individual had to go from A to B. A would be the corner of a fence line in a paddock. The example would be that individual would park his butt in the corner of that fence line with the bearing set on his compass. He would start from there. That's the type of people.

They were good people. They were easy to get on with, always joking. But within their culture too is that spiritual side of things. For example, the snake is classed in most Indigenous cultures in the Pacific Islands, and within Australia, as a demon. With that demon, we were patrolling through the jungle again, single file. I had two scouts and myself, the section commander. There was a navigation phase. They walked along a goat track and they stopped. They turned around and looked at me and I said, 'Keep going; move on'. They said, 'No'. I said, 'Why?' They said, 'There's a big snake there'. I said, 'Rightyo. Get out the way'.

I moved forward, had a look, and said, 'I can't see no snake'. These fellas have got very good eyes. They look through the jungle and see what's where. I couldn't see it, so they told me to move forward and put my left hand out. I did that, and I was wearing weight gloves to protect my hand. I opened my left hand out and I could slowly see the snake's head move. It was probably about the same size as my fist, a diamond-shaped python. It had come out from the vegetation. At the same time I pulled my machete out. The snake came out, it was getting closer to my left hand, and I struck the snake just behind the head. The snake's head came off, still hanging by a bit of skin. With my left hand I grabbed the snake, just below the cut and I pulled it. And all the men behind me, the Ni-Vanuatu (Ni means native, from Vanuatu), they all stepped back a couple of paces. I said, 'It's all right men. The snake is dead now'. But they saw that as a bad omen. It's bad to kill something like that. I pulled the snake, and I didn't realise how big it was. The snake came out and it started wrapping around my arm. It just kept going and going and I thought, 'Uh oh, I'd better get some help'. And I turned around and these guys had just dropped their packs and they ran in the opposite direction.

At this stage the snake started going around my neck. I was calling out for help. I dropped my machete and I was trying to reef this snake off. It was pretty big, pretty long. One of the Ni-Vanuatu soldiers came back and we unfolded the snake. At this stage I had a bit of blood on me from this thing, as it was pissing out everywhere. I threw the snake and said, 'Where's all the soldiers?' And he said, 'They're gone, Corporal. They were scared, so they ran'. I said, 'Get 'em back here now'. So eventually he did gather all the men. We moved on, not far, setting up our hoochies [basic sleeping shelter]. And I spoke to 'em and they said, 'No, that's a bad sign by you killing that snake'. I said to them, 'I apologise. I didn't know. I'm sorry'. Then they said we should go back tonight. I said it's too late now; it's dark. You can't move through that jungle at night because the vegetation is too dangerous. I said at first light when we wake up, we head back. And they were all worried and I said, 'Okay put your hoochies up'. I had about 10 men, so two men per hoochie, five hoochies. We'll stay tonight, go back tomorrow.

That night it was windy as and I was lying in my beautiful, comfortable hammock because it kept me off the ground. The canopy was thick, so it got dark in the afternoon because the sunlight couldn't come through. The guys had a feed and everyone was down resting. I don't know, it was just windy as and because of the canopy blowing, it was sort of shaking my hammock. I was sort of dozing off, but there was just something that wasn't right. Throughout the night I could hear scuffling like pigs or something running around my hoochie. I just tossed and turned all night and I said something's wrong here. I had my bayonet with me and that was in my sleeping bag, just in case.

I woke up in the early hours of the morning. It was still dark. I put my boots on and made my coffee. I said, 'I'll go check the men'. I put my torch on and I went to the first hoochie. There should be two fellas. No one's there. I went to the second. No one. Third, no one. Fourth – where the hell are they? He said, 'They've taken off'. I went to a fifth and all the 10 men were in the one hoochie. I sort of screamed too because when I put the torch on all these eyeballs were looking up at me. I said, 'What is going on here?' He said, 'No, Corporal, they come last night. They came here last night'. I said, 'Who, what? What's going on?' They have little people there. They came because of that killing of the snake; they came to see what was happening and who was here and why did this happen. They were running around; they said they were checking me out, running around my hoochie, trying to work out who I was. They said, 'They just wanted to know who you were and why did this happen'. And I said, 'All right, did you explain to them?' He said, 'Yeah we explained to them, but they're not happy'. I said, 'Rightyo, have breakfast, have a shave, cam up, clean your boots, clean your weapons. We're leaving'. So we did all that and we moved out. Whether that's true I don't know, but I couldn't sleep that night because something wasn't right. I just couldn't; I sensed something. I didn't know what it was. Maybe that's real; I don't know. They are spirits, but they are small people. I've heard of that saying, the small people, in some parts of communities, say up north. In Bamaga they have small people running around – spirits. So that's my understanding and that was in Vanuatu.

Towards the end of '91 I got posted to 1 RAR in Lavarack Barracks in Townsville – 1st Battalion, Australian Regiment. The next thing I know, we were told to come back to Lavarack, get all our gear ready. We were sailing in HMAS *Jervis Bay* to Mogadishu. I don't know how many days we'd been sailing, but we departed here 24 December 1992.[4] On arrival at Mogadishu, it was an eye opener. You see it in the movies, big buildings, good-sized buildings with big holes in 'em from anti-armour weapons or missiles. It was just unreal. You look

4   In the original interview Townson said 24 January, but this was in error as the *Jervis Bay* left Australia in December 1992.

at things and think, 'Am I really here?' That first shot rung as we were coming off *Jervis Bay*. Everyone just hit the deck – we're here and this is real. From there we went to the Mogadishu airport. We didn't go anywhere else – directly to the airport and we flew to Baidoa. Our battalion was based just outside of Baidoa. It was a secure position. It was 1st Battalion, Royal Australian Regiment in there and other non-infantry units. You had the medical, you had the dental, you had the postal, all those type of different units. It was a secure place.[5]

We had relieved Americans and the French in Baidoa, but as far as I know I think it was just the Australians that were there looking after that community. We saw the Americans not much; I saw the French Foreign Legion over there but no interaction. It was mainly Aussie diggers in our battalion group, working together. We'd get deployed out and provide security for other communities or villages so that they'd get their food. With providing security you'd be surprised how many people the villages hold. You've only got a platoon, which is about 30 men, and you have about a couple of hundred people. When they storm and rush to get – when they see the food, that's what we'd deliver. We'd go with the NGOs, so whether it be Goal or Care Australia. We provided security, getting them in an orderly sort of fashion to come through and give them an amount of food.

Baidoa was another city within Somalia. Alpha Company was the first one there. We commenced our regular patrols at irregular hours. We'd patrol by day or by night and we'd just rotate within the company team. We were there all the time; they got to see the Aussie Diggers and they knew we weren't messing around. Americans were always in their humvees, cruising around. Aussies, we were on foot every day. All the soldiers did well because the heat there was hot as. We had access to as much water as we needed because you needed that to keep operating. When we did conduct the patrols, we had access to GPS. Back in those days these were big metal boxes hanging off your chest. That was just extra weight, including all your live ammo, your six grenades, if you had to carry 'em, your 66 [gun]. I didn't carry all that, but I had all the grenades and the ammunition. With your flak jacket on – that's got a steel plate and that – your Kevlar helmet, it's a fair bit of weight, then you've got that big thing hanging off your chest – the GPS. That was handy because you knew where you were when you were working off your map also. By night we would walk that trace. Then by day I would go over the same area again to see where we'd gone.

That first night we were patrolling. It was just undulating, rough, smelly ground. These people did number one and number two anywhere. I'm thinking, just be careful where you sit. We were just walking up and down and we'd sat

---

5   For a history of the Somalia campaign, see Bob Breen, *A Little Bit of Hope: Australian Force – Somalia* (Crows Nest, NSW: Allen & Unwin, 1998); Peter Londey, *Other People's Wars: A History of Australian Peacekeeping* (Crows Nest, NSW: Allen & Unwin, 2004), 179–193.

down and had a break: sitting down, just listening, looking, taking intel in. We understood a little bit of their lingo. I don't know the other stuff, I should have brought our little lingo books for Somalia. One guy in particular was very good at speaking it. He was like my linguist if we needed to speak to someone. We would just listen and look and see if we could see anything out of the ordinary: any weapons, people walking around with weapons. We were sitting there and I'm thinking this place stinks. So we had a little break and we moved on. When we got back it was as hot as and we've got to do our debriefs with intel and tell them what's happened and where we've been and what we saw happening. I could still smell that smell. I said, 'Man, something was bad, rotten, dead'. When you're hot and sweaty all you do is unpack your sleeping bag. It gets pretty cool there at night and you just dry off and the next day we went on the same route. But coming back over the little things, we realised they were shallow graves. What had happened was that this ground, they just shoved a body and they just threw rocks over the body, and they didn't cover everything. You might have an arm coming out or a leg; the locals just weep. They're just rotten, they're dead. We were sitting on these things. We'd probably been soiled with dead people. That's the smell. I'll never forget that smell; it was bad. When we found out about that we got rid of our clothes.

We came across people blown up. It may have been famine or it may have been we want your food, give it to us now. They wanted their cut. That was the sort of thing that was happening. The bodies were in makeshift graves, but they sorted all that out. The longer we were there, we showed them the right way to do things. Then they came around. With the constant patrols things were improving as time went on. If you look at their policing, they didn't have any form of policing set up. They used to but it just got overridden by the bad people, by the bandits. They called them Skinnies: Somali Skinnies. Because of that there was no policing. When we were there they set up a prison correctional service centre. They started bringing in and catching all these bad guys. We were helping them bring them in and they would just process them through their system. It was the policing side of things.

Their community, in regards to shops for food, for clothing, even to get water, was overrun by bandits. They'd moved out because we came in and that was starting to get back to normal. Things were building up. They even had bakeries that started to run, people starting to make bread. They had markets come back in. You'd walk, patrol through the township and big markets, and you'd have big camel heads in there. That was their food. It was unreal to see something like that, but that was their feed. They'd have camel, or the fresh bread, and when you smelled that over there, it was beautiful. I've eaten some and I hope I haven't caught anything off it, but it's nice bread. All that stuff was up and running and they were moving forward within that community because the bad people moved on. They fled because of our constant presence of Australian military – Army. By them taking it back you got the bad guys waiting there. When we left they came back and started their business again. We were all the same across the board with locals. We waved to them, smiled to them. If we had spare rations, we gave them chocolates. So they knew the Aussie soldier-mate, who were the good people, helping them move forward, and they liked us. Everyone was always waving and you could see the change in the community and because of us being there all the time. People were getting married, they had weddings and they'd drive down the road doing their cultural thing in regards to weddings. Everyone was happy.

It was also non-stop action for us. It was good and it was just go, go, go, go. I wanted to be there longer because I liked it. You do peacetime army, mate, for so long and then when you get the taste of it, it's why you keep going. All of that training kicks in, and with that training, one incident: I can't give a date or time or name of village, I know it was daytime. We were coming in; I was lead vehicle, mounted APC, Armoured Personnel Carrier. We were coming in, probably a couple of kms short of the village they put an anti-armour round on one of the wheel ruts. I don't know, but it may have gone off if we hit it. The driver didn't realise until the last minute and had to shimmy the track so we could come off. By that stage, when I realised what happened, I thought, 'I can't warn the boys because they're already sitting down. I'm standing here so I'll probably just get blown out one way and land somewhere over there. I don't know what's going to happen with these fellas'. Somehow we missed it. We stopped and told all the other vehicles to stop, mark it and move around and keep going. They probably had it as an early warning to let them know we were coming. But you can hear us in this type of vehicle. It was something similar to an IED [improvised explosive device] but not to the standard over in Afghanistan. But the thing was, I don't know, it may have gone off, it may not have, we don't know. It's a rusty old thing, but I didn't want to touch it. We went around it and kept going.

As we approached the village one of the bad guys took off from left to right. He was heading towards a copse of camel thorn – that's vegetation and it's dangerous. It's not good and it's similar to lantana here in Australia in the jungle. It grows high, you've got a shaft with a trunk, and it just interweaves and mangles and grows up and out and thorns are like that. They'll go through you, no dramas. He was heading towards that, so we said, 'Boss, we're going to go right'. We went right; the other two vehicles went in and cleared the village for possible bandits. Only one bloke appeared to run from left to right, so I was standing, looking the other guys down, ready to come out, deploy. He'd gone in and we hit the vegetation. I was watching him, and he was going left every time we'd surface. He'd come up in a different area, but he was making a pattern, zig-zagging. I said to the driver, 'Keep going; keep going'. I said, 'Now, go left; he's going to come up there'. We cut him down and then I slowed down, I got the guys ready to deploy, because you have got to get the ramp down. We slowed down and we were looking.

And then he popped up, point blank in front of the APC with an AK-47 — a brand new one. He was dressed in nice clothes. Because I was watching him, these are things I remember: nice shirt, nice lap lap, like a calico, with bright colours. He was facing the opposite direction from the way we were travelling with his weapon. I was the only bloke up. I said, 'Mate, put the ramp down'. I didn't know what had happened. I'm thinking, the reason he didn't drop it is because we were point blank range, and it would have just been mass confusion if these guys would have deployed. The ramp couldn't drop down because of vegetation. I just said, 'Mate, this bloke's reversed it; he's surprised us. He's now got the initiative'. So I jumped out and got up, stood on top, to the right of this bloke, and it's like we had Steyrs with the scopes on. I said to him, 'Put the weapon down. Stop, weapon down. Stop, weapon down'. I just had to regain the initiative because this bloke caught us. I was lining him up, the sun was behind us. He rotated around till he was facing me with his weapon. I had him lined up. I pressed the weapon to auto. I was going to spray him straight up the centre. It was just me and this guy and I was talking to him and I said, 'Drop the weapon! Drop the weapon!' I was just leaning in to it and I was saying, taking the trigger pressure: squeezing it, squeezing it, squeezing it. He turned and he looked at me and he smiled. When he smiled there was gold in his teeth. And the sun went bang and he came straight back to me. I was looking at the gold, and in the meantime I was squeezing because I was waiting. I said 'drop the weapon' because I knew I was going to spray him straight up and down.

Then he looked at me and the weapon came forward and I said, 'Fuck! Why isn't my weapon going off?' Everything started going in slow motion. I said, 'This can't be right'. Then he just let it go. I think I was well within my rights to kill him. But I knew within myself, because of my training, I could have taken him out. But I couldn't shoot him in the back. Other people could have, maybe. But not me. I allowed him by giving him too much — standing there with a weapon, diagonally across, and then coming across slightly. I should have taken him out, but I thought no, I can take him any time, I'm just waiting, waiting. He did drop it and the weapon was falling but it was like taking forever. It just came down. I just thought what the hell is going on here? The weapon went down, then I've sort of got a blank from then. I think I went forward and I took him down. I remember my 2IC coming out and securing him with cuffs, basically, and we cleared the area. I took this bloke out, but I didn't kill him. I could have, but … I gave him the benefit of the doubt. Anyway, so we secured him. I didn't realise I'd done this until only a couple of years ago. I didn't realise what I had done because everything was just too much, too quick. I could have got killed because of that. I think the training just kicked in, like I said, initiative.

We missed the enemy a couple of times. We came across fresh dead bodies, just been killed and we were in pursuit. We did a lot of reconnaissance on a village, and we were sort of dangerously close to those potential bad people. If anything went wrong, I thought we've got to then kill. I said to my gunner, 'If anyone sleeps, anyone snores, because we are so close, I want you to gag him'. So what happened? I snored. He's a big fella. His hand just came over and gagged me. I didn't realise what happened and I went to strike him and he pinned me. He said, 'Towno, you said if anyone snores, gag you'. I said, 'All right mate; let me go. I won't do anything'. Those bad people were there but by day you didn't know. They could be walking past you, waving to you. By night, they could be there out causing bloody damage or doing wrong things.

We did do an ambush once while we were waiting for someone. Bad guys used this track. They didn't end up coming, but we were waiting there. You're just waiting for someone to come through and they're bad and you're going to kill them. I can't remember, just that main one is that bloke. It sort of sticks out in my mind because it was full-on. Every day, all day, it was different, whether you were bloody doing escorts, or you're going out on a patrol, or doing some other duty or task.

Then we had the R&R period. We went to Kenya for that one. That was good and we needed that because everyone was just burnt out and knackered. Everyone just drank themselves every day, blind as. That's when we had an incident when a couple of fellas went AWOL. They did end up handing themselves in later down the track. I went and represented one bloke in the AWOL case he had. On arriving back at Baidoa, our platoon sergeant at the time said, 'Chris, mate, if you want, you can represent soldier A in his court martial at Mogadishu in relation to the AWOL'. I said, 'Rightyo'. I thought about it, and I said, 'Mate, this is the bloke who has been on patrols with me. He's laid in ambushes with me. He's done everything that's asked of him leading up to this stupid thing that he's done'. I thought about it hard and I thought about it good and I thought about it long. And I said, 'No, I'm going to go and I'll just want to represent him and say what I can. I know he's done the wrong thing. Mate, I don't know why he done it. But for me, I want to go forward'. When I think back and look at it, I was that bloke that was sort of in his position all the time, with all these things that have happened to me. No one's ever come forward and helped me in regards to the racism or picking on me. I understand what he was thinking, but I knew he'd done the wrong thing. I felt within myself that I wanted to go forward and bloody say something to try and help him out. I just gave my character witness statement and they whisked me out. As far as I know in regards to entitlements that we had over there for the medal side of things, they didn't receive it I think. I just wanted to give my side on how he operated with me whilst out in the field. I don't know why he did it, the silly bugger.

Another Indigenous guy was in Africa with us, and we were the only two Torres Strait Islander boys in there. His name is Ken. He's still in the Army now as a company sergeant-major. I remember one day we were on a patrol at a VCP, vehicle checkpoint. We'd just come to that checkpoint and we were going to occupy it with his APC, armoured personnel carrier. He saw me and I saw him and he said, 'Hey, how are ya? Good, good. So you come through everything'. He said, 'Come in, bulla'. That means brother. He opened up his APC, and he had a nice hot can of Pepsi for me, or Coke. It feels cold over there, regardless of how hot it is! He had a packet of peanuts. I said, 'Mate, this is luxury'. It was good sitting there. We just connected for that little bit of time together and he departed and went on his way. The next day I had to go my way. Through the '80s I remember five of us Torres Strait Islanders in the Army. There were also a couple of PNG boys there and a couple of Fijian boys.

We went to Somalia in '92, 24 December. We were over there for '93 and we came back in March '93 after three or four months. We just went there, did what we did for that specific time and came back. But when I did get back to Australia, that's when I hit the piss. The PTSD – I couldn't adjust when I got back. It was too slow; I was just used to go, go, go, go, go. I started seeing it in other soldiers. One of them was an Indigenous soldier who was in my company. I couldn't work out why he was going like that. He was getting in trouble and he was drinking too much. Then it happened to me and I started going through the same business. I was due to be made up, to get my third stripe. The RSM should have known this would have happened. They should have taken the appropriate steps to refer them to other areas to sort it out, but they didn't. They were just military morons and they dealt with it like this, this, this. This is what's going to happen, you're going to get busted. You're going to go here. You're going to get busted, you move here. Busted means remove your rank. That's what happened to me. Because of alcohol, you're not thinking straight. You want to bash people. You're violent because of the PTSD, which I didn't realise I had at the time. I'm lucky I didn't kill anyone because it was in me. Your drive is you just keep going. You can't sleep; you just want to keep going like you're on something, but you're not. It activates extra stuff to mix in your adrenaline. You just want to go and take on anyone, everyone.

I was at 1 RAR, Lavarack Barracks when in '93 it started building and I started drinking slowly. It just got worse and worse. In October '94 I left; I'd just had enough. Things weren't going right. I was just messing up bad; I didn't know why or what was wrong with me. People in places, positions, should have known from past experience. They were just big he-men and didn't want to go down that line and help people. I just said, 'No, I'm discharged; I've had enough'. I was TPI [totally and permanently incapacitated] then because of my PTSD.

After I left the Army I joined corrections on the 10 October 1994, in the Townsville prison service. I did my training at Wakehall, Brisbane, and from there I stayed with the corrections till 2003. I started off as just an officer on the ground looking after a unit, or a block, which accommodates 20 men. Their offences range, but they were Indigenous, non-Indigenous, all sorts of cultures are there. We looked after them, doing all the administration stuff and making sure everything's running good. We made sure they attended programs to rehabilitate, like counselling and all that sort of stuff. I did that for a couple of years. Then I went over to the security/surveillance side, operating security cameras and doing high security escorts. From there I went away and did my firearm instructor course, chemical agent instructor course and armour instructor course. I did my hostage negotiator course. I was sort of travelling everywhere then, doing all sorts of crazy. I needed that because I was still hungry, after coming back from Africa. For nine years I was full-on busy. I burnt myself out. Then I went TPI in 2003. I just left because I couldn't do any more. I was burnt out.

Whilst I was with corrections I was an above average officer. I did everything and everyone was happy. I attended a couple of Coroner's Inquests for deaths in custody. I enjoyed that sort of stuff. In the end it just knackered me and I was drinking heaps. Whilst I was working in corrections, I was booked for DUI twice. There are a lot of ex-military people working in corrections and one of the guys said to me, 'You'd better go see this fella here'. He put me on to another bloke, a doctor. I didn't know what was wrong with me. I didn't know I had PTSD all this time since Africa until I joined these fellas in going AWOL. I was still doing my job but I was just drinking too much. One thing led to another then I spoke to the right psychiatrist. They did all the paperwork up and sent it away and they said, 'This is what you are now. This card here is what you're going to get'. That's a gold card for medication. They put me on all sorts of stuff, but I didn't like it because I couldn't do my job. I thought no, I'll just keep going. I did keep going. I did as much as I could until I went to Brisbane once and attended a chemical agent advanced course. I just thought, mate, I blew it. I didn't end up coming back. I stayed in Brisbane and just drank. I lost the plot. I didn't go to work anymore. It was all over. I didn't even worry about going back to work. I didn't worry about anything. I went to the doctor. I said, 'I can't work anymore. I'm going to kill someone. I don't trust myself because I have access to everything for my job'. I said, 'It's going to get out of control here'. He said, 'No, we'll have to put you off'.

I went straight up the Torres Strait to sort myself out. I had to go back to my culture and learn and start again. I had to just see things, smell things, look at things, listen, walk on the sand in bare feet, go in saltwater. We're saltwater people and that makes me strong, makes me understand. I was just being around my father's people and my mum's people, and that was it. I grew my afro, grew a beard. I was a different man. I think it was 2004 when I went there, or '05. I went to Seisia. I thought, 'I got to try and cure myself. I don't want to take medicine'. I tried a little bit and I just couldn't do much. I didn't like that business. I still want to be able to think and see and understand what I'm doing. My brain thought, I want to go up land and do it. I've got to go there and reconnect. I don't like taking medication. I'd rather do it naturally. If I'm sick now, I'll eat noni fruit. I tried all that traditional medicine. It grows up there on the land; my father showed me this stuff. I take it in and listen. I know saltwater's good for me and that's my culture. I would go down the rock pool and dip my body in there a couple of times, relax, come out. I told my boys that: 'That's a medicine, mate. Because my blood's in you, you're gonna go in there'.

Once I felt better, I could think clearer, and I did come back to the mainland. When I say mainland, to Townsville and back up north. I knew in myself I felt good. My two boys look after me. I've got to have someone to look after me. I don't know, maybe from being overseas too I just look at things differently to the way I used to look at things. You see all the bad things and you come back here and people complain over the smallest things. I say, 'Mate, you don't know until you've been there and seen things'. Once that was right and I was mixing with the people up there, and I could see they had issues there, I wanted to try and help. I was coming back on track again but I was thinking, 'I need to help these people. What can I do?' The issue with them was transport. I wanted to start up a little bus service to help people commute from up at Seisia to Cairns. I tried that, but that didn't work out. I was thinking, 'Everything's bloody failing around here'. That's when this project came up: Pipeline to Prosperity they call it. They needed someone to look after it. I just needed work somewhere and there's work there but not much and it didn't pay well. A bloke that came up with this idea wanted someone to look after it and the people they were bringing in had been in gaol. They'd been incarcerated. He wanted someone with a correction background and discipline background to make sure these people would run straight. I thought, 'All right, I can oversee it for you. It's only 12 months work'. This was in 2009.

I came to oversee this project. We didn't think we'd get this far. I was basically showing the Townsville City Council that black people can do this sort of stuff. I had to recruit people, I had to train people, I had to place people and oversee and maintain the pipeline and the vegetation. The ex-prisoners did that, but council was watching us. They were worried at first, but we did the right thing. They said, 'Rightyo, that's good. In 2009, that's good. We'll let you do it again 2010 but you picked certain people out. You only can have a small team. You're going to do it again'. So we did it again in 2010.

They were observing us and they liked what they saw. They said there's a potential opportunity for BARK – Brothers Act of Random Kindness. Townsville City Council came into partnership so we could maintain the pipeline. Come the end of 2010, I had a big meeting. The media was there, the guy who came up with this idea was there. I was there with the men I'd selected to maintain it. They signed an MOU, Memorandum of Understanding, for BARK to have a three-year contract to maintain the pipeline. In doing that they also gave us other positions within council to fill. I selected the men, got them in placements and the main thing with this is the mentoring which I do basically every couple of days. It's good but I can feel myself starting to burn out again. People keep asking me, 'How do you do it, Chris?' I just refer back to all the training I've done in the past. BARK helps long-term unemployed Indigenous men gain employment. Those men may have been incarcerated, come out, be on parole. These are guys who are lost and they need that assistance, sense of direction. That's what we're all about. I bring them in, I mentor them. Once again, it's that training, placement and the ongoing mentoring support, direction and guidance. We just talk straight up and down. There's no either this way or that way. This is what you must do in order to get permanent work, and good outcomes are that we have got people work permanently. We present these outcomes to council for them to say, 'Your investment is working. If you continue, we'll continue getting more people off the streets and into permanent work'.

With council, we have positions in Townsville Water, which is the pipeline crew. We have positions in construction and maintenance. That could be a concreting crew, asphalt crew and a line marking crew. We also have in council parks and services and we just recently put someone in Townsville waste, so that's another position. We also have a contract with North Queensland Small Business Centre. We have Indigenous men maintain that complex. We have an Indigenous female cleaner, she maintains the toilets there. We're just waiting for other things that are in the pipeline. Hopefully we can place people. Another major one is Jazeem Barracks through refurbishment, on the Strand. Hopefully we can place some people there. I told them I'm not a CEO and I don't worry about that business. I just want to be a bloke on the ground who helps people. With the mentoring there are some good people that help me, like the CEO of North Queensland Small Business Centre and Social Ventures Australia, they're based in Brisbane. They're the main sort of mentors for me. I still do other jobs within this organisation. When I don't have people to do the jobs I go clean the toilet. I cut the palm leaves. I collect all the rubbish. It's all character building. I don't care; I've done it all before and I'll do it again. I don't worry about rank. I do it because of my passion to help people that have got these problems. If not I wouldn't be here now and building this organisation.

Every March we take on whatever vacancies we have for the positions. If there are 11 operators, we take on 11 new participants and they're for 12 months. In saying that, I tell them at the induction, 'In order for you to stay here you must attend mandatory mentoring'. The main problem for the council is sickies: too many sickies and you can't stay. Everyone abides by those rules. They sign the contract; they attend the mandatory mentoring. It really works out well. They want work and they get it. This is the second year, 2012 and 2013 is the last year. Hopefully the directors of the board for BARK will look at presenting to council some form of presentation so we can get an extension on the contract.[6] It's a good thing that's happening and they need it. We're slowly making our name, our imprint on Townsville for the Indigenous people. At this point in time I'm the only one there, doing all the dancing and singing and yelling. I'm going to get someone else to help. Since 2009, it's good to see when you see the boys walking around town. They're dressed respectably, in good clothes.

I do attend Aboriginal or Torres Strait Islander community meetings when they have issues within the community. In regards to Indigenous problems, I just go in and listen in and sit down and see what's happening. You just keep your finger on the pulse. But the only organisation is BARK. And I give 110 per cent of my time to that. I was involved with NAIDOC and that was a couple of years ago when I was working with corrections. I can't recall the year, but it was with an organisation called Magani in Townsville. They were overseeing NAIDOC Week. I was in the committee, just helping to set up. I hadn't done anything like that before and there is a lot involved. When I was working with corrections I was involved with recruitment and retention of Indigenous staff. I ended up designing a poster, which was state-wide for recruitment and retention of people. It was just some high glossy PR shots on the poster and they went out for recruitment purposes.

When I initially left the Army I didn't go to any Anzac Days for a number of years. I didn't want to do anything and I just stuck to myself. I don't know how long ago now, but I've been attending every Anzac Day. I just go with my Uncle Karl Wocando. Sometimes we may not go to the Ingham one and we'll go to Innisfail or come to Townsville, or we'll go to Mount Isa. Uncle Karl likes to go to different places and just chat to people, to share their stories. I remember one time at Mount Isa, by the end of that night we were booked on a plane to go to Mornington Island the next day to recruit some people to join the Army Reserve. In the end I said to the office, just think about it realistically. We won't wake up in time to catch any plane, if we can book a plane. It was a good little story and Uncle Karl was all motivated and he was teed up, ready to go. He said, 'We got to go home and pack our suitcases. We're going to Mornington

---

6   See BARK's website on brothersactofrandomkindness.wordpress.com.

Island tomorrow'. We like those sort of occasions, and Remembrance Day. Just recently we attended a lot of nasho [national servicemen] functions. I attend with Uncle Karl. We're all spruced up: black suits, ties, and high-gloss boots or shoes. I think everyone loves them when they see us. We look like the men in black. He likes that sort of stuff and so do I because I support him.

I'm a member of this Townsville RSL. I was a member of the Ingham RSL but that's expired. I'm a member of most clubs now. I like going out and just sitting down and relaxing. The hours I work are long and when I get time off, I just sit down and relax. I'll just sit in the backyard and water the palms. I have flashbacks of Malaysia. I think there is a Peacekeeping Association because I've heard of it.[7] I know there's a Somalia group organisation;[8] I've heard of them because my ex-diggers have contacted me, but I'm just too busy. I've got all the details, but I like going and seeing all my ex-soldiers. I've tried to contact some but they're either too busy and I understand it's school holidays so they might be away. When I get a chance I just like to go and see them face to face. Every time we see each other we're getting older. I'm even older than them. I just try and keep active and on my toes.

There have to be more Indigenous, whether it be male or female servicemen, that need acknowledgement and recognition. That has to come forward, come out by them acknowledging that. I'm sure we'd be on par and non-Indigenous people would recognise that and pay their respects. It is just a matter of going out and seeking and finding out and people coming forward, like with me. If the history of our service were to come out, I'm pretty sure, the way things are going now, they would respect you and acknowledge it. I think they're doing it now, acknowledging it in the Anzac Day ceremonies and Remembrance Day ceremonies. I've been to Bamaga on a couple of Anzac Days, where they do especially acknowledge the past Indigenous soldiers and the present ones that are currently serving. I'm sure they'd be doing that in other communities. It's the way things are going now in society, acknowledging regardless of whether it's black or white. It's a big activity, Anzac Day and Remembrance Day. Everyone's celebrating – uncle, father, brother, sister, mum – all of those people who have been in. Some of the soldiers that I've seen around, they are very respectful of you attending Anzac Day.

I enjoy what I do. It all comes back to what I've done in the past and that's helped me. It's been an up and down journey, but that's life. Everyone has it – as long as you learn from it and you move on.

---

7   See Australian Peacekeeper & Peacemaker Veterans Association, www.peacekeepers.asn.au.
8   The Australian and New Zealand Somali Veterans Association formed in 2013, after this interview. See www.anzsva.org.

9

Peacekeeping in the Asia-Pacific

Steven Maloney[1]

The 1990s were a time of transition for the Australian Defence Force. Australia was taking a more active role in peacekeeping missions, exemplified in 1999 when Australia took the lead in organising International Force for East Timor (INTERFET). Steven Maloney was one of the 4,318 Australian service personnel who participated in INTERFET, as well as in a Service Assisted Evacuation (SAE) mission in Cambodia in 1997. Steven's experiences show an Australian Army in transition towards forward defence in the Asia-Pacific. His story also reveals the challenges Aboriginal servicemen have had to navigate both within the ADF and upon the return to civilian life at the turn of the new millennium.[2]

I was born in 1976 at the Mater Hospital in Brisbane. It was a good childhood. We lived mostly in the eastern suburbs of Brisbane. Sometimes we spent a lot of time on North Stradbroke Island and lived there from time to time. I have a mixed family – my father is Australian but his heritage is both Irish and German, and my mother is similar although with a British-Aboriginal heritage. My Indigenous side comes from North Stradbroke Island, the Qandamooka and

---

1   This interview was recorded in Brisbane on 24 September 2012.
2   All military information is released pursuant to Australian Military Regulation 770.

Noonuccal people. I have two brothers – one older and one younger and quite a lot of cousins, aunts and uncles on both sides of the family. My father was an earthmover and he had a number of companies over the years and made quite a lot of money on different occasions. My mother was a housewife.

During primary school, years 1 to 7, I got on with my family quite well. We moved around quite a lot. There were dozens of houses because my father was in earthworks, so we moved where the work was. I couldn't say I attended only one school because it was a lot of schools, and I couldn't say I did too well at school but my parents always made sure that I went. My father started work when he was only 13 years old, so he never placed much emphasis on academics, rather work experience and a steady pay check. I started primary school a year early because I was born in February, so that meant I could jump up a grade and begin when I was five.

In terms of the education itself, I'd probably say there were times I wasn't treated equally. One of the places I did feel as though I was treated equally was when I was at primary school on North Stradbroke Island, where there was quite a large proportion of Indigenous to non-Indigenous students. Plus it was my ancestral home and where my mother grew up, and also my Indigenous grandmother. It wasn't a mainstream school; it was a community school, so that was the place I felt the most comfortable.

As an island, North Stradbroke is not accessible unless people want to get a ferry across. I lived in a place called Amity Point and there would be a local bus and it would pick students up to take them to school at Dunwich State School. You wouldn't have full grades; you would have a teacher who would teach a number of grades and they'd also be teaching at a number of different levels. There were fewer people in that environment and it was definitely more community oriented. It wasn't like a mainstream primary school in Brisbane; you're on an island, so it was a tight-knit community with the local Indigenous residents and my relatives offering constant support. I can remember coming home from school hungry and would ask my mother for some food. She would reply, 'Go down the street and catch a couple of bream'. And 10 minutes later, I would be back with two fresh, pan-size bream, straight from the ocean. She would cook them both up, one for me, and one for Mum.

For high school I went to Balmoral State High School most of the time – I think all of the time, from Year 8 to 12. I repeated Year 11, and I repeated Year 12, so I had three sets of school friends that I knew and still have today. I think attitudes were different back then for my parents – one was Indigenous and one was white. I'm not saying they weren't accepted by the Australian community, but they were looked at differently to start with. The teachers didn't seem to consider the Aboriginal children in the same way they would other students.

They were seen to be perhaps a lost cause; it didn't matter whether they passed at school or not, however, it was only a mild indifference. If you said something in class, well then it's just class, turn your head back to the teacher now and 'Let's get on with teaching the good eggs'. I could say that I was ostracised on different occasions. I was punished a little bit harder than the others; if I did something small it would be a case of getting detention or even the cane. Corporal punishment was still permitted in both primary and high school in the '80s. In my early primary school days it would also be that you couldn't go on school excursions. I personally felt that it wasn't so much the punishment for not doing my homework, as it was more ostracisation from society and 'It's better for you not to be on this field trip because it's for us white Australians'. There were different nationalities at school so I can't say it happened to all nationalities, and I can't say it happened to all Indigenous students. But I think Indigenous males especially were looked at as something that's not a success story, with a happily ever after ending; it's usually not worth the time or the effort for a teacher to put energy into an Indigenous student. The worst things at school would have been the name calling, the titles, the Indigenous kids getting into fights all the time, the Indigenous kids wagging school and getting into trouble with the teachers. Objectively it was mild, but that was my childhood experience. Did I feel as though I was treated differently? Yes, of course; without a doubt. I attended school formally until about grade 10 and then I started getting part-time jobs, like working in smallgoods factories or labouring with my father, though surprisingly I did enrol through to the end of Year 12. I didn't receive anything for it after Year 10 because I didn't get good enough grades in Year 11 and 12 – only a record of attendance and an exit statement.

I got charged with stealing when I was 13. We used to wag school and it's obviously a long time ago. I'd like to think I'm a good person these days, but just as a child, we used to break into unlocked cars to steal money and some of the other kids used to even steal cars. We sometimes stole push-bikes; we used to get into a lot of fisticuffs and brawls in the schoolyard. I can even remember, only one time, in high school the principal and a few teachers came around to a friend's house when we wagged school in Year 9 and some of my sillier friends were caught sniffing petrol. I had friends who died during high school as well, Indigenous friends; they'd hire a room out for the night in an expensive hotel or something like that, and then they'd all go up and party all night, and a school friend died that way through an overdose. He fell unconscious in a bedroom of the Hilton and never recovered. At the time, some school friends got up to so much mischief that they did go to boys-town gaol. Others dropped out of high school and others stayed in. It wasn't a positive experience for me personally. I'm not going to say that I am resentful, but I always felt the other kids got a bit of a head start with education. It wasn't a good value system to entrench in yourself so young. I'd like to think my parents were concerned about my welfare, but didn't know how to address the complexities of identity and my apathy towards my studies.

I think one of the things that changed me the most was when I was in high school. It wasn't so much the racism in the playground but one of my Indigenous uncles. He lived on North Stradbroke Island when I was about 15 and in Year 10. He was murdered outside the Point Lookout Hotel on North Stradbroke Island, where he used to smoke a little bit of weed when he drank beer at the pub. He went down to a car to buy some more pot and a guy with his dog pulled out a shotgun and shot him in the head. I don't know why he did it, but it was ugly because it was something in which race had a big role to play. I heard the guy got less than five years gaol, and it was a bit upsetting for my family in the fact we all felt that justice wasn't done – that you could kill an Aboriginal with a shotgun and be out in a few short years. If it was anyone else, I'm sure the court would have weighed their life more dearly. I used to fight a lot after that at school because I was quite angry at life. I also had Indigenous uncles who served time in prison; one uncle did time in Long Bay in the '70s, and one did time in Boggo Road in the '80s, and they were all pretty tough guys in their younger days. One uncle even got gangrene in his leg from sleeping in the park too often and it needed to be cut off. That was my upbringing, so that's what I remember from high school.

I was particularly close to my Indigenous uncles and cousins; my two brothers are lighter skinned than myself, so I felt more of a connection with my Indigenous heritage. They got into a lot of mischief themselves. I'd call it mischief, but some of it was not a good example for me to follow. I guess on my father's side of the family, my uncles and aunts grew up through an Irish influence because of my grandfather, who was Irish-Australian. He served in World War II as a driver and my father even said he drove General MacArthur on one or two occasions. I don't think they had it any easier than the Indigenous side. Our two families were mostly connected through North Stradbroke Island, and the two families have a very close connection. For instance, my mother and her sister married my father and his brother. There were other relationships between the uncles and the aunties of each family as well. Then the grandparents – my great-uncle on my dad's side was with my grandmother on my mother's side after my grandfather died. It was just the day, but on North Stradbroke Island and Cleveland Point in the '50s and '60s, that's kind of how the extended family operated. The two families had a lot of catching up on weekends with a lot of food and beer drinking. There was also a lot of playing cards, bingo and different social activities like feasting on seafood conducted by my elders, during my school years.

I remember seeing pictures of my parents married in Cleveland and you can see my father's parents on one side and my mother's parents on the other, and you can tell it's a different day and a different age. It was just a simple marriage ceremony at the local Anglican Church. I couldn't say they weren't frowned upon, those mixed inter-racial marriages. I wouldn't say that they were totally ostracised because of it either, but certainly there was something I think was always unspoken. If you had heaps of Indigenous kids running around the yard and you have the Indigenous mother and the white father in the house, they're all tarred with the same brush. We perhaps weren't treated the same as an all-white family would have been treated at the time.

I think being an Aboriginal played an important role in my childhood. You are different, so you're treated differently and you have Indigenous relatives who live a different lifestyle. It may not be that it's a traditional lifestyle with hunting kangaroos or throwing spears, but they definitely had different values from the other side of the family. When I was a lot younger and still at high school, I still managed to go on different school trips that consolidated my Indigenous identity, such as four nights at Carnarvon Gorge in Year 9 with the other Indigenous kids at Balmoral. The school had a number of programs catered specifically for Indigenous students, like tutorial and community associations. My Indigenous identity was mostly reinforced by my friends at the time. Some of my Indigenous friends in high school and even primary school have since been in adult prisons in their later years; some of them have also been successes – not so much at making a million dollars, but having a good stable family life with a job through an apprenticeship or something like that. It's a mixed bag, but I guess Indigenous students usually didn't aspire to academic success in the '80s or early '90s. It was something where you usually wagged school and you went and stole something, or went and got up to some mischief and got into a fight. But it was always the negative side of things with Indigenous students; for me, it wasn't the positive things at high school I remember, like a Year 12 graduation ceremony which the other students received.

When I was about 14 or 15, I joined the Army Cadets. I did have members of the family who served in the military. My dad served in the Army for three years from 1967 to 1970. I have uncles who served in the Army; I also had an aunty who was enlisted at the time. I probably got my first idea about what the Army was when I was 13, but didn't register for the cadets until I was a year or two older. About a week after I turned 17, I joined the Army Reserve. During the last years of high school, it was a matter of getting different part-time jobs and also working in the Reserves. I was always looking at joining the Regular Army, but I didn't have a high enough education. I only had a Sound in Year 10 English, and I took the path where I went to the Reserves first because

I thought it was a little bit easier to get into.[3] Then I could transfer straight into the Regular Army from the Reserves. When I was 19 I joined the Regular Army and stayed in until I was 24, and then I discharged and came to the University of Queensland not long after that.

I think my primary motivation to enter the armed forces was when I was 13. There was an Indigenous aunty and she made it all the way to Warrant Officer Class 2. She was in my corps, RA Sigs, and that was my saving grace. As much as you had your uncles who were a bit wayward, you also had an aunty who took to the good side of things and who'd been in the Army since she was young herself. She might have joined around '85. I remember she was posted up to Darwin at one point, so we both drove together from Brisbane to Darwin when I was a young kid. Other times she would visit and bring home Army friends. When I was 13 and I was living at Tingalpa, she brought home a boyfriend one day. He was a commando and he sat down with me and really told me about the Army. He said, 'This is what we do … and this is where you want to get into, once you're in the Army, and this is what I did the other day with Leopard tanks'. It stirred something in me; I was only 13 at the time, but I definitely wanted to say, 'Well, I want to join up'. I think that's where the spark took place. I would go and buy my own books on generals and other great military leaders when I was between 13 and 17 years old and say to myself, 'Wow, this is what this guy did'. I remember buying General Schwarzkopf's book, *It Doesn't Take a Hero*.[4] I went straight down to the store when it was first published and came home and read the whole thing in a few weeks. I used to also buy all the *Army Magazine*s, the ones they give to the Army guys for free but you can still buy them in newsagents. I was still only in my early to mid-teens and saying to myself, 'That's where I want to be in life'. So my aunty was a good influence.

On the other side of the family there was another Warrant Officer Class 2; he was my great-uncle. Both male grandparents served in the Army; one was in World War II and I believe the other was in both World Wars. I don't remember because he died when I was very young, but I know he had service medals. My grandmother on my dad's side also served with the Australian women's Air Force [WAAAF] during World War II. As for my Indigenous grandmother, she was an Elder on the Brisbane Council of Elders. So one Indigenous grandmother was an Elder, one grandmother was in the WAAAF, and the other two grandfathers served in the Army during the World Wars.

---

3   In the Queensland education system a Sound Achievement is about the equivalent of a C.

4   H. Norman Schwarzkopf with Peter Petre, *It Doesn't Take a Hero: The Autobiography of General H. Norman Schwarzkopf* (New York: Bantam Books, 1992).

Army Cadets was my first formal experience of the military and used to be a part of Balmoral State High School. When you are in your early teens and in the cadets, you'd do parades and do after school training with a compass or they'd give lessons. The guy who was looking after it was a cadet lieutenant, but he was in the Regular Army for a long time. He went to Vietnam and was a qualified marksman, so everyone looked up to him. You would have your different ranks for the cadets as well, but it wasn't something you could ever use outside of the school grounds. We would go to the rifle range every now and then, and we'd fire .22s and other small arms. We'd be taught how to shoot in groupings and basic fieldcraft. I'd say it was one level up from boy scouts – boy scouts with guns.

The Reserves was the next obvious progression from cadets. I was calling up a recruiting officer even before I was 17 to try and get into the Reserves and they'd say, 'No, you've got to wait until you're 17'. I'd say, 'No, I got told 16 and a half', and they'd say, 'That's only if you want to be an apprentice'. I would finish by saying, 'No, I want to be in signals; I want to be where this guy was, so I'll wait'. I officially enlisted one month after I turned 17. I don't think my family could have stopped me; I was joining up whether they liked it or not. I remember Dad took me into Kelvin Grove to do an interview and I was saying on the way, 'I want to be a radio operator'. There was a warrant officer who started the interview process who was obviously a Vietnam vet, and I remember he was sitting at the other side of the table from me and my dad. My father kept answering all his questions and he was going, 'No, no, I want to hear from him. He's only 17; I want to know whether he's capable of being a soldier'.

For the Reserves, we still had to do the full testing as if you were joining the Regular Army. You were given an Army number and you have that for life. That's where I got my initial Army number, from the Reserves after I took my first Oath of Allegiance to the Queen of Australia. This was '93, so there were still quite a lot of Vietnam vets around at the time. We used SLRs [self-loading rifles] during that period, did our recruit training at Wacol, and then another course to complete your Initial Employment Training [IET] with communications. That second course would be more oriented towards your trade. My job was a radio operator, and after those two courses were completed we could go into areas around Brisbane and do exercises for a weekend. Sometimes we would do two-week camps. It was signals and radios, so we would drive a vehicle with a trailer, set it up, put the camouflage mesh over it, and then do radio shifts. It was a signals-based unit, so you'd be looking at higher communications networks with different types of equipment, to encrypt it and to protect the information. It was different from an infantry man with a radio on his back;

we would have radios in cars with much larger antennas and be required to maintain communications with headquarters. We were corps signallers, and regimental signallers were a lot different at the time.

Reserves was only part-time, so I was still labouring a lot in the summer and I went to high school as well, having repeated Year 11. I only just received my Year 10 school certificate, which I didn't really deserve because the principal said, 'We always give that out because you'll understand later. A Sound Achievement in Year 10 English, that's what you'll need to get into the Army, isn't it?' If I didn't have that junior certificate, I wouldn't even have got in the Reserves. I can't say that I earned it, perhaps I did, but then again it was something that got me a start in life so I don't care anymore. I'm happy and appreciative towards the principal for doing that regardless.

Between '93 and '95, you could do quite a lot in the Reserves. If you wanted to do more you could do more; if you wanted to do less you could do less. I think it served my purpose in knowing that I was going to join the Regular Army, and it basically acted as a stepping stone until I was 19 and could serve overseas. I did have some tough sergeants when I was in the Reserves. My first drill sergeant had been to Vietnam and I was told by a corporal in the mess one day that he'd been on patrol in Vietnam, and a mortar had gone off near his head and blew the back of his skull off. I don't know if it was true or if he was only scaring me, but he said he had a titanium plate on the back of his head. I respected the sergeant a lot more after that.

I don't remember any other Aboriginal or Torres Strait Islander personnel who served with me in the Reserves. I did get the odd joke or two, but I guess it was no different to what everyone else copped. I could look after myself a bit better back then, so they didn't give me as much stick as some of the other soldiers of different nationalities or ethnic backgrounds. I definitely remember times when I got fed up. One guy, I followed him out of the base in my car one Tuesday night from Kelvin Grove and I caught up with him at the traffic lights and said to him through the window, 'Mate, I've had enough – stop riding me or I'm going to belt you'. When we were outside the military environment he didn't feel so tough without his friends and said, 'Fair enough'. On the odd occasion in camp I definitely got some Aboriginal stigma attached. But there was good stigma as well; they would think you might be a better scout or naturally better at fieldcraft. It wasn't always negative stigma in the military; I'd say the positive stigma outweighed the negative in that you were much better at some things than others, and they were much better at some things than you.

When I transferred from the Reserves to the Regular Army in '95, I remember having to do the recruit course and my Initial Employment Training all over again. The recruit course was only two weeks in the Reserves and IETs was two weeks as well, but in the Regular Army it was 13 weeks at Kapooka and then nine months at the School of Signals. I stayed about a year in Melbourne just getting onto the next level and to my new unit. I served in the Regular Army from when I was 19, in August '95, to May 2000. The corporals were pretty tough at Kapooka. I copped it there a bit. I also got into one or two fights with the other soldiers in Wagga Wagga.

The corporals would sometimes play games with me. I could probably say three times where they played games. I know it was only because I was an Aboriginal soldier. A corporal came in one time when our platoon had a rifle inspection with the CSM [company sergeant major]. He said, 'Can I see your rifle barrel, Recruit Maloney? I just want to inspect it before the CSM gets in'. I was cleaning some other things at the time with another recruit, but gave him my barrel and turned around to keep cleaning while he checked whether it was clean enough for the formal inspection. He gave my barrel back to me and said, 'This is okay; put your weapon back together'. He checked my friend's barrel and then went around to the other side of the room and left. I said to my mate after he left the room, 'Sorry, this isn't my barrel; it's your barrel' and we both swapped. When the company sergeant major came in a few minutes later with the corporal to check all our weapons and that the room was clean, he checked my barrel and weapon and said, 'This is all clean', but when he looked down my friend's barrel, there was a whole heap of dirt inside. It turned out when the corporal checked my barrel, he thought it was mine. When I wasn't watching, he turned around and chucked a big handful of dirt down inside. So when the CSM saw this, he wanted to charge my mate. The thing the corporal didn't realise was when he went around to fetch the CSM for the inspection, was that we both swapped our barrels right before CSM stepped inside. We were cleaning our weapons for like an hour before this, so both weapons were immaculate and in perfect inspection order. When the CSM was yelling and saying he wanted to charge my friend, the corporal was just standing there red-faced because he thought it was going to happen to me. The other guy got hammered.

Another time we went on four days leave from Kapooka, and you've got to lock your locker before you go. It's the one thing that everyone remembers to do before they leave the room. Everyone locks their cupboard door and everyone double checks and triple checks. If you don't lock your locker for four days and you go away, you are going to be in big trouble when you get back. I went out on holidays, I came back, and we looked up through the window from the outside and there was this locker undone. We were saying to each other, 'That guy is so dead meat'. I went into the room and realised it was mine. Obviously, these are just cheap locks and if you mess around with them, they can be opened quite easily. Not to mention, the corporals had a spare copy of the key just in case someone loses theirs. I opened my locker and there was a framed picture of my corporal standing on the parade ground with his finger pointing towards him. If you got the picture in your locker, it meant you had to see the corporal immediately and then get extra duties. It was silly things like that. You're just saying to yourself, 'Why are you stirring me up?' Another time, the same corporal put me as the recruit platoon leader and he did it on the basis that he wanted the other guys to hate me because an Aboriginal was in charge of the platoon. He soon realised the other guys weren't going to belt me, and were just as scared as I was. It backfired on him again, so he put me in that position for a day, and then said, 'Don't worry about it then'. I'm thinking, 'You've put these other recruits in this position for two weeks or three weeks at a time, and you've put me in for only one day'. It was quite mean-spirited and I would say there was definitely a racial aspect there. It was perhaps only one corporal who gave me excessive grief. There were other corporals as well; don't get me wrong they weren't all the same. There were some good guys there too, like the lieutenant. He got me into the job that I wanted. I wouldn't say that my section commander took a disliking to me, but he said to me one day, 'I didn't get it easy at Kapooka and I'm not going to give it to you easy either'. However, it wasn't so much that he was less hard on the others in my mind; I think I felt I was a bit of a softer target for a bully. But, that was Kapooka … .

After Kapooka I went to Melbourne into the Royal Australian School of Signals. My trade was OISR. It was an Operator of Information Systems and Radios. This was my trade so you had to learn how to use radios and different equipment on a more advanced level than the Reserves, and you had to learn how to send and protect information to go to even higher headquarters in Canberra and other places around the world. You needed to know how to set up antennas and do your job which was to communicate messages. I spent 12 months there because there wasn't a position open in OISR for the first three months before the course started. I was in Signals in the Reserves, and it was always my intention to get into RA Sigs [Regular Army Signals] because of what my commando uncle had told me about the corps. He said it was a good utility corps, and that means you could be employed in a lot of different areas. I understand today in the Army you select your corps and you select your trade, then you get drafted. They don't just walk up and down the lines and tap you on the shoulder, like they used to in Kapooka, and say, 'Armoured, Infantry, Artillery, Engineers, Catering … '. That's pretty much how they did it. If your corps wasn't open at the time, well then you wouldn't get it; you'd have to go to Infantry or Engineers. At the time there were no positions open in Signals and I said to the lieutenant, 'I had my heart set on Signals. I've done my best here in recruit training and the Army Reserves to get into that corps, and I'd like to think that I wasn't the worst soldier to ever pass from Kapooka. If you could see when the next course is and get me on it, this would be a good thing, for me at least'. And he said, 'Yeah. I'll do that'. He did that and kept his word, so I stayed in hold-overs for three months at Watsonia before they started the course. I went to Melbourne straight from 1 RTB [1st Recruit Training Battalion] and did general duties for a while, and then I did two four-and-a-half month courses. At the end of it all, I was trade qualified so I got sent to my first field-force unit.

Figure 12. Steven Maloney Army photograph
Source: Courtesy Steven Maloney

My unit was in Perth; it was a Signals unit and it was very surprising that I actually got sent there for my first posting. They were looking for soldiers who hadn't been exposed to eastern states units. I guess they were looking for a clean slate from where they could train people up who had the potential to be what they required. There was only me on my course who got sent to that particular unit in Perth and it helped that an Aboriginal sergeant was the person to choose my posting. It's definitely a real eye-opener going there. It was like going from being a kid to a very hard reality. These guys were the best at what they did and you were only this young, dumb kid who didn't have any exposure to the professional Army. You were thrown in with the best of the best, and these were your idols from a really young age. You fly from Melbourne to Perth and as soon as you march into the barracks you're asking yourself, 'What am I in for?' I was so young; I may have only just turned 20 and was one of the youngest guys there, if not the youngest. A lot of the guys were middle-aged or even older. If you went to any other unit in Australia, around 20 would be the norm; from perhaps ages 19 to 24. However, in this specific unit, it was late 20s to mid-30s. That was day one of the Army for me. Everything else was only a lead-up to this moment, and you get there and you know you're in a special place; you can feel you're not in Kansas anymore. It was professionally tough. I was in a privileged position, in a high profile and very professional unit. You had to really step up to the plate and say to yourself, 'If you're going to be here, make sure you do your responsibilities they give you and make sure you're mature enough to handle what's being done by the unit'. It was the frontier of the Army and all my training and military experience led me here.

There are definitely some good stories and memories. There was a lot of esprit de corps in my unit; it was something in which you were proud to get up every day for. We had a base that was on the beach; we were young, in our prime, and everything was exciting. You would try and outdo your friends at every opportunity, whether it be doing silly stuff when drinking, being out on an exercise or a course, picking up the girls and always trying to put one over your mates. The physical training was very hard. I remember one story comes to mind. We were on exercise in a place called Lancelin, and me and my friend were in a four-wheel drive with a trailer. Somehow we were driving across a huge sand dune and the trailer just catches on fire. There was an investigation after it, but what they said was that some of the gas bottles had been overfilled. There's a safety release valve at the top, but because it was hot that day and the bottles were undercover, the gas expanded in the gas bottles. LP gas is heavier than air, so the gas went through this safety valve and dropped straight to the bottom of the covered trailer. A spark set it off, and we had these magnesium batteries inside. Magnesium burns pretty hot, but [laughs] when we got to the middle of this dune [laughs] the fire – I could see the trailer caught on fire. But we were apprehensive about unhooking the trailer by hand because we had things that could explode inside, not only gas bottles.

We stopped the car in the middle of this dune and all of this sand was around us. My friend turned the car off when he saw the fire and we both started running away and the car's just sitting there with this trailer ablaze. We got about 100 metres in front of it and my friend said, 'Mate, we've got to go back; we've got to go back for the car. You've got to unhook the trailer because the whole thing will catch on fire'. By that time the whole trailer was now on fire and we were waiting for gas bottles to explode and for these magnesium batteries to blow up. The mate says, 'All right, let's run back; I'll jump straight into the car, and drive it off. But then you have to go around to the back and unhook the trailer first'. He said, 'Just keep your head down', and I said, 'Okay, but we've got to do it quickly because if it gets any hotter these things are going to start exploding'. We run back to the car and he jumps inside, he puts it in gear and I jump under the trailer and unhook it. Just then the magnesium batteries started shooting up into the air and they were pinging off, and they shot about 50 metres all around like red and orange fireworks. I was holding my head down. These cells were shooting in different directions and I could hear the trailer baking and cracking, and then you could hear small explosions inside. I was protected from the side by the metal siding, but when I unhooked the car he drove it straight off. I remember running after the car along the sand dune laughing. After we got away safely, everything really started blowing up and we called in a safety helicopter that came shortly after. It was flying around this trailer that's on fire, circling overhead and you could see your friends on board looking down and waving their finger at us. We were all laughing so hard when we were calling the helicopter; we didn't know how to do it without laughing because we were almost crying, saying, 'We've lost tens of thousands of dollars' worth of equipment and it's all exploding – how the hell did this just happen?' The melted trailer was always put out the front of our headquarters for a long time, only to remind us by saying this is not something you should do. That was a really funny story for me and my friend.

Signals was a lot more sensitive because it dealt with information. My unit was definitely an important unit in the Australian Army and my role was to support the regiment in a Signals capacity. So whatever role the regiment played, there would be Signals support required. It was an operational unit in the sense that headquarters would be functional 24 hours a day, seven days a week. The unit was a very professional unit and a place where a lot of emotion was conveyed. They expected higher levels of emotion to be created within the unit, and to teach soldiers how to properly deal with it – the emotion of getting the job done right, going the extra step, knowing where the unit was being deployed and what they were going to be asked to do. When you're exposed to that type of intensity, it's hard to get rid of it or shake it off. It's not only the adrenalin of training; it's the nature of what the unit was about. I had a good friend who killed himself in the unit a few months after I arrived. He finished work one day and was still in his uniform; he walked down to the showers and put a toggle rope around his neck and just knelt down. I remember the MPs carrying out his body in the morning and were just outside my room downstairs – he had been hanging all night. He didn't deserve to die like that.

When I first got to the regiment, there was a sergeant there; he'd done a few years in the WA police force before he came across to the military. He was from Fiji, I think. He took me down to his office one day and said to me, 'If there are any problems with anyone giving you stick because you're an Aboriginal, just come down and see me'. There were only three dark-skinned guys in the regiment at the time. There was another Aboriginal corporal, there was the Fijian sergeant, and then there was me and perhaps a few others here and there. They were pretty much the only coloured guys that I knew or saw there at the time.

I'd like to think there wasn't racism, but I believe that's wishful thinking. It's not that it was malicious, but it was something that was entrenched in the psyche of the military itself – more like institutional racism. You are an Aboriginal and in the Army, so you do sense it from time to time when you're asked to do an unpleasant duty that you feel as though you were targeted to do. I think there were times in which some of the corporals deliberately targeted me, but it's only those silly, childish games again. I remember when I got into my unit in '96, it wasn't so much that I was young – it's that I was a young Aboriginal. I was feeling pretty good about myself and they thought they'd cut me down to size a bit. I was in a particular area and a corporal's walked in and he said, 'Your brother's on the phone in the other office'. I said, 'Well, how did he get patched through to this area?' He said, 'I don't know, he must have called the lines and they patched it through'. I said, 'Okay'. So I walked in to the other room and you're supposed to answer the phone formally, but I just said, as you would to your brother, 'Hello'. There was this corporal on the other end and he just revved the shit out of me over the phone and said, 'Come down to my office', and then he revved me again. I said to myself, 'You pricks set me up for that'.

I also remember there was a rugby tour to go to England, and I was playing league in Perth at the time. These corporals got together and said, 'You're not trying out for the team'. I said, 'Well, why not? I'm here in the unit. I'm entitled to go across there if I make the selection'. They said, 'No', and a corporal came up and said, 'If you try out for the team, I'll give you one'. I said, 'Well, what can I say to that?' On the day of the tryout I sat on the sidelines wanting to play, but they wouldn't even let me try out. I think there were aspects of racism, not just inexperience in the junior NCO ranks, with the other corporals not wanting to accept a young Aboriginal to be part of a football team to go to England.

I found that especially in Perth. I wouldn't say it's a racist city, but if there are a few white soldiers going out on the town, then you as an Aboriginal soldier would sometimes act to their detriment when they are trying to pick up the ladies. Generally, the white girls in Perth didn't like talking to Aboriginals. Perhaps it's something entrenched from high school and it didn't matter if you're in the Army or serving your country, they just don't like it. You would sometimes be ostracised from your friends when you go out together because they wanted to talk to some girls. I remember one time in a nightclub, I was talking to a girl and she came back from her friends after buying a drink and was a bit upset. I said, 'What's the matter?' And she said, 'My friends just asked me what I'm doing talking to you'. I don't believe that I was overly targeted; the other guys did get their fair share of one-sidedness in different ways, however, that was just the Army and the attitude of the '90s. I hope things have changed in the twenty-first century.

In terms of operational service, I served in Cambodia for a short mission, and I served in East Timor for a tour. Both of those countries had suffered genocide and, at the time of me serving, were basically destroyed and razed. Phnom Penh was on fire in a lot of places as well when I went in country. I was a lot younger when I went to Phnom Penh than when I went to Dili, but they were both very destructive and unhealthy environments. They were both on fire and many buildings had bullet holes or RPG [rocket-propelled grenade] damage, especially Pochentong Airport. Surprisingly, there were good things you could take away from the experience. I suppose the two things I remember most regarding my overseas service were on two separate occasions: one was in Phnom Penh when we were evacuating Australian citizens on the very last aircraft, leaving late at night. I was standing in uniform on the back ramp of the C-130 Hercules and this civilian lady walked quickly up the ramp, and she was the last Australian we were evacuating, and she said to me, 'Thank you'. And I thought it was a good thing at the time – she was pretty thankful!

The other time was later in East Timor. I was at the heliport and I was going somewhere, but there were two young East Timorese girls who were in our compound who used to wash our clothes. As I was walking along, they were behind me and were singing. They were still only very young, probably about 15 years old, and I thought, 'You can sing all you want; you're safe and protected here in this compound'. I think that's a good thing to take away from environments that are really destructive and unhealthy: the fact you're either protecting Australian citizens or two young girls from whatever they might have to face if your mission wasn't there.

It was '97 when I was in Cambodia; it was called a Service Assisted Evacuation. Our team flew from Perth to Cocos Islands and then trained at RAAF Butterworth in Penang for a few weeks. We were required to go to the Australian Embassy in Phnom Penh and, without getting into too much detail, there were military personnel in the embassy, and there were RAAF personnel and Air Defence Guards who stayed at Pochentong Airport. I remember there were all different countries and nationalities who were evacuating their own respective citizens. It wasn't a brigadier, but I think it was the equivalent in the Air Force who was responsible for the overall process. There were a lot of international civilians involved too and the Australian military was asked to provide support for the duration of the SAE.[5]

I was in East Timor from day one of INTERFET, only a week after I finished my 10-week Subject 1 for Corporal at the Land Warfare Centre in Victoria. It was different being there on the first day. It wasn't pleasant; it was something in which these people lived through what was called a 'scorched earth policy'. So militia and the TNI [Indonesian National Armed Forces] pretty much destroyed a lot of infrastructure before withdrawing and it was also cleaning up after 20 years of genocide. It wasn't something enjoyable and, knowing the unit I was in, we would have a different type of role to play than other units. There were many other units conducting mainstream roles patrolling or doing certain things and I can't speak for them personally. Our unit was based at the heliport so we would be first to respond to any incidents. We were called 'Response Force' and the role was carried out effectively and professionally – the squadron was actually awarded a Meritorious Unit Citation for their contributions to INTERFET and East Timor during my tour.

This is day one; it's kind of like after the scene of the crime. You could always smell the fires in the air – that nasal smell where you've got that heavy stench. It's hot, humid, and sticky, and there's always an orange haze, the thickness of the smoke in your lungs and that dense air you're breathing in all the time. Also, to top it off, no fresh rations for the first two weeks – only freeze-dried ration packs. I served in a number of areas and there were different multinational peacekeepers who were there as well. It wasn't only Australian forces; there were individual nations doing other things to rebuild the country. But going from one area to another you would notice the difference with locals when they're in the mountains as opposed to the cities, whether they were young or old; what their personal experiences were over the last 20 years. Some had only just come back from West Timor, so they didn't see as much as the people who stayed throughout the entire genocide. I also remember being sick for a few days when I got dysentery from drinking bad water.

5   On Australia's operation in Cambodia, see David Horner and John Connor, *The Good International Citizen: Australian Peacekeeping in Asia, Africa and Europe, 1991–1993*, Official History of Peacekeeping, Humanitarian and Post–Cold War Operations, Vol. 3 (Cambridge: Cambridge University Press, 2014); Londey, *Other People's Wars*, 165–177.

Everyone who served with INTERFET experienced something different. I personally thought the local East Timorese people were nice; they were humble and decent. The TNI soldiers and pro-Indonesian militia were not so nice; they were getting kicked out of the country so they were unhappy about what was happening. They'd had all of the power for so long and then suddenly they had no power at all and became ordinary human beings, and they didn't like that one bit. So they did things from time to time just to feel they still had power over people, like killing monkeys with a knife or pointing their weapons at peacekeepers or other Timorese civilians, but it wasn't really effective against a professional army. It was an overwhelming and decisive victory in terms of the militia not being able to match what INTERFET had brought, with their Chapter VII mandate from the UN Security Council as well as the resources and professionalism of all of the people who served in East Timor. It is considered a successful campaign; it's something that people identify with as how a UN-sanctioned peace enforcement operation should be conducted. INTERFET was responsible for securing East Timor after the independence vote. There were things that happened there during INTERFET: there were contacts, there were deaths and there were mass graves.[6]

I shook General Cosgrove's hand in East Timor once, and I saw him a number of times in Dili. I've also read what he's written in his autobiography about the country many years later.[7] I had to do assignments on this as well, in subjects like the 'Politics of Peace Building'. We would do case studies of East Timor in class and, going back a second time in 2003 as a student at UQ [University of Queensland], I met people whom I didn't realise I'd actually met the first time with INTERFET. I even met a Nobel Peace Prize winner, José Ramos-Horta, and had a photograph with him on the beach in Dili. The East Timorese people would also fill me in on certain things that happened during INTERFET and I would get a better picture from all of this only years afterwards. I think the East Timorese are good people and were trying to rebuild after total destruction – when a country has been totally razed to the ground and destroyed, and then trying to rebuild on those ashes. They were humble people to start with because they lost everything and knew they had a lot of rebuilding and hard work ahead. But our work was also trying to lift their spirits through a hearts and minds campaign, trying to increase their morale and say, 'On these ashes, you guys are going to build your new country. You now have the opportunity to build the country the way that you want to build it. You're going to decide your own destiny from this moment forward'. There were also a lot of internally displaced people. Up and down the roads there were thousands of families

---

6   See Bob Breen, *Mission Accomplished – East Timor: Australian Defence Force Participation in International Force East Timor* (Crows Nest, NSW: Allen & Unwin, 2001); Londey, *Other People's Wars*, 231–261.
7   Peter Cosgrove, *My Story* (Pymble, NSW: HarperCollins, 2006).

without homes. Sometimes you would see children who didn't appear to have parents. We sometimes collected all the candy and chocolates from our ration packs and then threw them out of the back of vehicles when we drove around Dili and into the mountains. The children were happy with this gesture.

I was there from day one of operations in mid-September until a few weeks before the handover to UNTAET [United Nations Transitional Administration in East Timor]; it was only one rotation. We didn't get the blue hats and INTERFET was considered to be a UN-sanctioned, multinational peace enforcement operation, rather than a formal UN-sponsored peacekeeping operation. UNTAET took over in February 2000 and there was a 50-day overlap between other UN missions that began and the conclusion of INTERFET. I can remember a few weeks before the transition to UNTAET because people were building up to the blue hats. It was only a matter of taking off your helmet and armband and putting on a United Nations beret. The second time I went to East Timor in 2003, I wanted to see how the country had grown with the handover of UNTAET to full government autonomy. I volunteered for a few months with a legal NGO and travelled all around the villages and cities. I even managed to get sick again from a mosquito in the jungles of Los Palos and had to be admitted into the UN military hospital with dengue fever.

I put my discharge in from East Timor when I was in Dili in early 2000. I knew I was going home and that I'd achieved what I wanted to achieve in the Army. I'd served overseas twice. I'd received three medals and a Meritorious Unit Citation; one of them is an Australian Active Service Medal [AASM]. I have two others – an INTERFET Medal and an Australian Defence Medal – but they're only your standard run-of-the-mill service medals; they weren't for any gallant or noble actions. I know of other people from my unit who definitely got medals of gallantry with INTERFET. There were some good soldiers who did some outstanding things, brave things, and earned higher awards. My medals were routine service medals like my grandparents received. I only have three for everything I ever achieved in the military. I put in my discharge because I didn't want to see any more destruction and death. I really couldn't face it anymore. I had experienced first-hand the depth of what conflict can bring out in humanity, and although I could have stayed in my unit for another four years and been promoted on my return from Dili, there was no future in just going from war zone to war zone for the rest of your life. I came back with the intention of discharging from Enoggera and then perhaps going to the University of Queensland and studying Peace Studies, which I did one year later.

I don't think my family would describe my transition from the Army as seamless, and I think there were a lot of difficult times in the initial stages. When I first left the Army I remember I used to be really angry, but I wasn't sure why. I could be pretty violent when pressed by other people, but I was only recently discharged and for the first few months I was very emotional. I think I was upset maybe at humanity itself – the level of depravity that people will go to. I was still only young. I started my first operation when I was 20. When I went to East Timor I was still only 23. I discharged when I was 24. I won't go into specifics, but there were some pretty ugly things I needed to deal with in the military. I didn't always sit behind a radio and pass orders to and from patrols; there were times when you'd have to jump on a chopper or a caribou to go somewhere or you'd have to drive into the mountains, or be attached to a team that did something. It wasn't pleasant and it wasn't healthy, but I think that's probably what a lot of soldiers have to face now when they come back and they say, 'That was a really unhealthy environment'.

The transition from the Army to civilian life was good from my perspective. I helped out my family quite a lot financially from time to time during and after the military. I remember I had over $20,000 saved from East Timor and it cost me $12,000 to start them off with a house deposit. I think they were only too happy to know I was part of something special between '96 and 2000, doing a good thing and a service to the country, as my dad did in the Army as a serviceman in the Vietnam days. Taking up the chalice was only the next generation going on from my grandparents, to my father, uncles and aunty, to me and perhaps my older brother for a short time, and then to the next generations. For the seven years I was in the military from March '93 to May 2000, when I was holding the chalice, I hope my family were proud to see that.

I haven't really caught up with any mates from the Army since I discharged; I know there are still friends who are in the military today. I don't know how they address some of the challenging environments they needed to be a part of, and still are. But for me, personally, it was academia and I also became an Anglican in late 2000. I wasn't a Christian before I left the Army, but I became a Christian after I left the Army. I'd definitely call myself a proper Christian now, although my thoughts are slowly turning towards secular, rather than ecclesiastic law. I think the Army was the reason why I started looking at religion. When I discharged, I didn't always have the intention of going to university and wandered around aimlessly for a few months, and was actually going to re-enlist in the British Army at one point. I had everything organised – I had a plane ticket, a working holiday visa, I had at least $5,000 saved and everything was ready. I even called a recruiting officer in Trafalgar Square. I discharged in May and I was pretty much ready to go a couple of months after, and my intention was to join the British Army in a parachute regiment. Perhaps it was something to do with my non-Indigenous ancestry. But that didn't happen and it was kind of lucky that I didn't go because I don't think going from one army to another, where you didn't have to deal with anything, was the answer. I was meant to fly out on a certain day, but I had a going away party the night before and had second thoughts. My flight was booked for London via Japan the next morning, and all of my relatives came around and everything was ready. I had my bags packed but I just didn't get on the plane. Some part of me still regrets at least not going there and doing a bit of time in the British Army, but another part says it was for the best and my role in Australia was far more important.

After I missed my flight I didn't do a lot; I just sat around on the couch and played a lot of ping pong. I did nothing for a good six months after I discharged. But then come early 2001, I did correspondence courses through Open Learning Australia [OLA], and it was mostly to do with morality and moral issues. As I said, when I discharged I didn't really have the intention of going to UQ specifically; I always had the intention of getting the education I never received in high school. I remember one of the subjects I did through OLA, 'The Meaning of Life', and the two others were to do with either philosophy or ethical and moral dilemmas. I just did a lot of thinking in that first semester and at the same time I didn't do so well at finding work. Employers would say, 'It's great you've done what you did, and you've achieved what you have, but we really can't apply that in our commercial business. It would be great if you are able to work on the sales floor, for instance. But how is getting your parachute wings or a roping course going to help you as a salesman?' One person said, 'Why don't you go back to school and get a degree or something like that, and then you'll be more employable'.

I started at UQ in semester two, 2001. I started with Ancient History and liked it so much that I ended up with a minor in Classics as part of my Bachelor of Arts program. It was the first time I'd been exposed to Ancient History, but I think that it was a really good start, getting into Rome, Egypt, Mesopotamia and Greece. I was pretty fortunate in that regard as well because I later travelled to Egypt in 2004 with my father. I think it's important to have memories of taking pictures with your family in front of the Sphinx. I stayed in Egypt for two months to round off my Classics in Egyptology, but my dad only stayed for the first few days to help me get my feet in the Middle Eastern culture. There are a lot of people who perhaps can't frame their experiences with any of their academia and once you start getting into Ancient History, you begin to realise these things have been happening for millennia. You don't need to go any further than Rome to know just how brutal and savage people can be, and then you bring that back to the twenty-first century and say, 'It's not healthy, and it's not good, but at the end of the day, this has been happening for a long time. You didn't create it, and it's certainly not going to finish in your generation. So just accept this is the reality of life and humanity, and that's the bottom line'. I did both part-time and full-time study, but I studied Arts, then Arts/Law, then Arts again. I'm now enrolled in an LLB (Hons) [Bachelor of Laws with Honours] program at UQ and looking to be a lawyer; that's my aspiration. I'm looking to work with the Indigenous community.

When I started doing some subjects at UQ, I can remember some of the titles, such as 'Moral issues in International Relations'. This type of subject led me to finish my BA [Bachelor of Arts] with an extended major in Peace and Conflict Studies and choosing a lot of elective subjects in religion, philosophy and languages as well. I must have completed or attempted at least 30 subjects for my BA. However, I think those two streams, Peace and Conflict Studies and Ancient History, spared me anything that would make me lie down and not want to get up again, and dwell in negativity for the rest of my life. I guess finding a purpose through serving the Indigenous community also played a big role – having a good future, looking to be a professional, and helping people on another front outside of a war zone. I had the chance to come to the University of Queensland and study Peace and Conflict Studies, which is a rare privilege for an Indigenous Australian who started with only a Sound in Year 10 English. I'd served in military environments and then studied hard to understand them from an academic point of view as well. PACS [Peace and Conflict Studies] contained a lot of formal studies on the UN and this helped with a lot of my questions. University is not a place where your emotions are running wild like when I first left the Army and had no support. It's a place that's contained in a safe, enclosed environment and structured through your professors and with your peers. You can discuss moral issues in tutorials, and I think I've done the right thing in terms of the books I've chosen to read. I've picked up autobiographies I know were written about the times I was directly involved as a soldier, when there were some difficult decisions regarding life and death, and I got to see other people's perspectives, like John Howard's through his book, *Lazarus Rising*.[8] I think he is really level-headed, and I'm glad that I read it from cover to cover.

Talking about post-traumatic stress, the Army has mechanisms. At the time, they had psychologists and they did address our unit in particular. They were looking at potential challenges for an individual. With some of the difficulties contemporary soldiers have to face when they discharge after serving on a few operations, they'd say, 'Well, you might not see that in the initial stages, but it might manifest itself a little bit later on'. I think I was spared a lot of this personally because of the disciplines I chose to study at UQ and my strong spiritual beliefs. I think there were times where my family would have a different opinion about post-traumatic stress. They'd say, 'It's affected you a lot'. And it did. It's taken me perhaps, I'd say, a good 10 years to understand what I went through and I think that I'm only now picking up the pieces, in the last couple of years and especially after I received my first degree. That's the reality of the military; it cost me 10 years of my life following my discharge to normalise again. There was some really tough stuff. I haven't looked for support,

8   John Howard, *Lazarus Rising* (Sydney: HarperCollins, 2010).

but I guess the thing is, I definitely wouldn't want to go back to the last 10 years and do it all over again without support. I don't think I'd have the strength to do it twice on my own.

If I were to give an emotional glimpse of the first few months after I discharged from the Army, it would be that I get back, I sit around and get really angry. It was just an explosive anger, not so much anything I could really understand. It's not with me anymore, but it was only those first few months after I discharged, after everything had finished and I was home again. I think studying Peace Studies is probably the best decision I ever made following my military service. You study peace for 12 years and only then have you earned and created this mechanism, I personally believe, is far superior to any of those feelings and emotions you can't control. So as much as there's raw anger and emotion from during and before the military, there's also a rational, reasoned approach developed from peace building and conflict resolution, built over the same period of time or longer. I guess it's all about developing the skills to be able to deal with those unhealthy environments without allowing your emotions to take over too much.

From time to time I do have my thoughts about the military. I wouldn't say I do anything special for Anzac Day and I wouldn't say I catch up with any friends from the Army to have a beer and remember all the good times. To be honest, I am only now finding a sense of closure. I'm starting a new identity and a new role as a community lawyer. It did take 10 full years to not so much recover, but I guess rewrite my military identity toward being fully civilian and have a completely new frame of mind, with a new career and everything rewritten. I'd say right up until a couple of years ago, I was still in that military mindset where I had my thoughts about re-enlisting. I did try and re-enlist a couple of times during university but didn't go through with it. I tried to get back into the Reserves and even tried out for the Navy. But now it's all gone. To be honest, I don't want to catch up with my old mates because it's something I've been trying to rewrite since 2001. I'm now a civilian and since 2013, a qualified peace builder through my Bachelor of Arts. From time to time you'll still have to address what you need to address when you come across a particular assignment or you'll read something. For instance, maybe I'll be doing an assignment in peace building and it will be a case study of East Timor. I'll have to look into things and say, 'Right, well in this particular case study, the first involvement by the United Nations in East Timor was with INTERFET following the independence vote'. You do a bit of research and you'd see something on a Dutch journalist who was killed by the TNI on day three, and you'd say, 'Well I was there as a peacekeeper, standing only a few metres away from his dead body'. Or you'd say, 'I was driving the second UN vehicle to that site behind General Cosgrove's'. It would play on your mind for a few days. You wouldn't do a lot during those periods; you'd just sit around home for a bit, maybe have a few beers, and then you'd get back to your studies. But it's constantly manifesting itself throughout that entire 10-year period. Sometimes you want to re-enlist, so you don't need to think about those things anymore. But I think now, today, it's settled in my mind and not a part of me anymore. I'm definitely looking to be a lawyer and study at UQ for the next five years until my second graduation in law.

I guess my primary motivation right now is to finish my LLB (Hons) program. Peace and Conflict Studies also has a direct application towards the Indigenous community in terms of Alternative Dispute Resolution. Although my life's been based mostly around study for the last 12 years, I found time to volunteer with Amnesty International as well. I've done some volunteer work with the UQ Student Union as the Indigenous student officer; however, I'd say Amnesty International was the most influential organisation for me personally. There was a time in which I was really involved, but it's now shifting from Amnesty International back to Indigenous-based issues. Over the last few years, I've also sought employment with other community organisations, like the Aboriginal and Torres Strait Islander Legal Service. ATSILS said they would be only too happy to employ me during my final year of law school and throughout my Practical Legal Training. My thoughts are mostly to do with justice and Reconciliation. I'm not necessarily looking so much at the international macro level and the United Nations; I'm bringing everything back to the micro level — all domestic issues at home in Australia these days.

I have been following the proposed referendum to recognise Indigenous Australians in the Constitution of Australia. An expert panel came to Brisbane a few years ago led by an Indigenous community leader, Jackie Huggins, the former co-chair of Reconciliation Australia.[9] I also spoke to a lawyer who was the president of the Law Council of Australia. When they were making these community consultations I remember making an opinion in front of an audience of mostly lawyers, and I basically stated that, 'I served in the Army. I'm entitled to make an opinion as a citizen'. If you're going to send people into conflict zones based on the premise of promoting democracy, yet don't promote these values within your own country first, such as section 25 of the Constitution, it's only saying to me, 'Look how undignifying it is to think you could actually serve your country, but still be under the jurisdiction of these archaic race laws that deny the very freedom that you fought for'.[10] I made an opinion to the expert panel based on the fact I was an Indigenous soldier. I felt earning an AASM is something that allowed me to make a legitimate opinion.

---

9   See Australia, Department of Families, Housing, Community Services and Indigenous Affairs, 'Recognising Aboriginal and Torres Strait Islander Peoples in the Constitution: Report of the Expert Panel', January 2012, online, available from, www.recognise.org.au/uploads/assets/3446%20FaHCSIA%20ICR%20 report_text_Bookmarked%20PDF%2012%20Jan%20v4.pdf, accessed 12 February 2014.
10   Section 25 of the Constitution allows states to disqualify citizens from the franchise on the grounds of race.

I contributed to the nation for seven years, and even saluted Prime Minister Howard in Melbourne during an Olympic function for the Atlanta games in '96. The basis for my contribution in the military was to promote the liberal values that are currently being denied to every single person outside of an Anglo-Australian background through race laws. My statement was received well by the whole audience, that's the thing. If you're some Aboriginal off the street you wouldn't have the same authority as having served your country. It's different when you are discussing these points of freedom and liberalism and democracy with somebody who hasn't contributed, or who wasn't required to bring those values into other countries. I said:

> If you are going to send soldiers overseas to promote those same liberal values, do it in your own country first and don't pretend you're a first-world nation and you have the right to be on the UN Security Council, but keep these archaic and valid race laws you don't even think could be wiped away with a referendum, because the population isn't mature enough to throw off the shackles of colonialism.

I always did Indigenous topics in both Peace and Conflict Studies and now in Law. I've done a lot of Indigenous subjects; I have a lot of friends who are now Indigenous lawyers and working for the same place that I hope to work for in native title,[11] and working to reform the same things as well. Some of them have been involved in other community reforms to complement constitutional recognition, but I'd like to think my influence has been something that's bettered their own understanding of freedom and cultural tolerance – two fundamental principles of neo-classical liberalism. I feel strongly about anti-race laws, and most Australians would agree they are terrible, outdated modes of thinking and often described as 'archaic notions, not relevant in the twenty-first century'. I'd like to think I've influenced a lot of people who are involved in community-based organisations, to try and promote Indigenous reforms like striking out sections 25 and 51(xxvi) of the Australian Constitution.[12] I certainly wouldn't feel as though I had the confidence to try and promote these national issues within civil society unless I received my AASM. Once I had those three medals, it gave me the entitlement to have an opinion about my country. It says you've contributed; it says that you're not only an Indigenous Australian who was born here, but you actually contributed something to the nation to entitle you to be a part of civil society and change things for the better. Without legitimacy from the military and my studies, I certainly wouldn't feel as though I could

---

11 He has since worked at Queensland South Native Title Services for three months as a Community Relations Officer in 2014.
12 Section 51(xxvi) of the Constitution gives the Commonwealth Parliament power to enact special laws for people of any race. The proposal for constitutional recognition of Aboriginal and Torres Strait Islander people would replace it with a new section 51 that would allow the Commonwealth to make laws for Indigenous Australians and a complementary section 116 which would outlaw racially discriminatory laws and require that laws under section 51 only be permitted for the betterment of Indigenous Australians.

ever put forward some of the points I have put forward. Both active service and a Bachelor of Arts has definitely legitimised my opinions and improved my standing in the community.

There's been Indigenous soldiers that I've worked with, and knowing the history of Indigenous involvement in Afghanistan and Iraq, World War II, in Vietnam, in Korea, in World War I, and even to some extent the Boer War, everyone has contributed, including the peacekeepers and peacemakers. To say that only white Australians served in Gallipoli is a lie. Indigenous people have fought for freedom and contributed. I know there were at least 5,000 Indigenous military personnel from Queensland alone who served in World War II. So if these people did contribute to the nation, I think their next generations they have sacrificed their lives for should be entitled to a degree of freedom that other Australians have received from their forefathers. To not acknowledge the Indigenous contributions in war is disrespectful, and I think it's something other Indigenous veterans wouldn't be happy with. That's something I'd like to correct in the future as a lawyer, not through retribution in any regard, but more through promoting an awareness of, I suppose, of needing each other's culture in a way. I think Australia needs their Indigenous heritage as much as Indigenous Australians need the technology and the advancements of colonisation. But it's not something I like to think of in terms of the Indigenous culture being slowly assimilated into an Anglo-Australian metropole, with their unique values being incrementally eroded. I think we can live together with the values both cultures cherish because of the contributions of Indigenous soldiers, who have done what they have done in order to preserve and keep their own culture alive, not just to preserve the mainstream Australian culture. It's definitely about looking to a path that's sustainable and promotes harmony between all communities within Australia, not only the descendants of European colonialists or first-nations people. A peaceful approach to constitutional reform, inclusion and Indigenous self-determination are all that matter to me. Perhaps future generations may even discuss the possibility of a treaty?

I don't look back at my time in the military with regret. I'd say that it cost me dearly; however, it shaped me a lot as well. To think these small instances I've discussed make up all of my life in the Army I'd say would be a distortion of the truth. I enjoyed my time in the military. Obviously there have been challenges and there have been trials. There have also been difficulties. I'd like to think the Army's evolving and getting better. Nobody ever looks at the military and believes they were bigger than the military, not even a general. The Army is a larger institution than any one individual, and I hope it's adapting to the twenty-first century. The values I learnt in the military are good, decent, traditional values. I wore an Australian flag on my uniform and we all worked together as soldiers, for Australia, towards the betterment of Australia. I wouldn't like to see that destroyed any more than I'd like to see the Indigenous community destroyed. I'm saying that things need to be reformed, but then again I'm not going to burn the Australian flag at the same time. That's some of the values that I got; I'm not going to hurt the system because I believe in the system and I also believe in working within the system. Having completed Peace Studies over the last 12 years, and having already started my second degree in a Bachelor of Law, with a third class honours in 2014, I know there's a way to move forward without necessarily destroying systems or cultures. You can work within systems and tap into the status quo, and see that even one person has the ability to shift community attitudes. Once those attitudes shift it will transform the nation as a collective. With the status quo shifting forward, I hope this Constitutional referendum gets momentum and successfully removes the last remnants of a disgusting and disgraceful history, through the protectionist policies of the early to mid-twentieth century. I'm positive, and I don't have any regrets in life. I'm not bitter; it's just taking a long time, that's all. I hope that perhaps a young Indigenous Australian might see this story and say, 'Well, maybe this is a good thing if I contribute to the nation by being a soldier, or a sailor, or an airman', and doing something constructive for once instead of just sitting around complaining.

Figure 13. Steven Maloney today
Source: Steven Maloney

Bibliography

Interviews

Harry Allie, 4 November 2011, Chester Hill, NSW.

David Cook, 20 January 2010, Raymond Terrace, NSW.

Sue Gordon, 25 November 2010, Perth, WA. Available from National Library of Australia, ORAL TRC 6260/5.

Neil Macdonald, 3 and 5 December 2009, Canberra, ACT.

Steven Maloney, 24 September 2012, Brisbane, Qld.

Mabel Quakawoot, 5 June 2011, Mackay, Qld.

John Schnaars, 23 November 2010, Perth, WA. Available from National Library of Australia, ORAL TRC 6260/1.

Chris Townson, 26 September 2012, Townsville, Qld.

Theses and published sources

Agostino, Katerina. 'Femininities and Masculinities in the Royal Australian Navy: Workplace Discourses'. Thesis for Doctor of Philosophy. Department of Psychology and Sociology, James Cook University, March 1997.

Angels of War. Produced and directed by Gavan Daws, Hank Nelson, and Andrew Pike. 54 min. The Australian National University, Research School of Pacific Studies, 1981. Videocassette.

Attwood, Bain and Andrew Markus. *The 1967 Referendum: Race, Power and the Australian Constitution*. Canberra: Aboriginal Studies Press, 2007.

Australia. *Royal Commission into Aboriginal Deaths in Custody*. 1991. Available online from www.austlii.edu.au/au/other/IndigLRes/rciadic/. Accessed 11 February 2015.

Australian Human Rights Commission. 'Review into the Treatment of Women in the Australian Defence Force'. 2 Vols. Canberra: 2011 and 2012.

Banivanua-Mar, Tracey. *Violence and Colonial Dialogue: The Australian-Pacific Indentured Labor Trade*. Honolulu: University of Hawai'i Press, 2007.

Barker, Lorina. '"Hangin' out" and "Yarnin"': Reflecting on the experience of collecting oral histories'. *History Australia* 5, no. 1 (2008): 09.1–09.9.

Bomford, Janette. *Soldiers of the Queen: Women in the Australian Army*. South Melbourne: Oxford University Press, 2001.

Brawley, Sean and Chris Dixon. 'Jim Crow Downunder? African American encounters with White Australia, 1942–1945'. *Pacific Historical Review* 71, no. 4 (2002): 607–632.

Breen, Bob. *A Little Bit of Hope: Australian Force – Somalia*. Crows Nest, NSW: Allen & Unwin, 1998.

——. *Mission Accomplished – East Timor: Australian Defence Force Participation in International Force East Timor*. Crows Nest, NSW: Allen & Unwin, 2001.

Broome, Richard. *Aboriginal Victorians: A History Since 1800*. Crows Nest, NSW: Allen & Unwin, 2005.

Burger, Angela. *Neville Bonner, a Biography*. South Melbourne: Macmillan, 1979.

Chaat Smith, Paul. *Like a Hurricane: The Indian Movement from Alcatraz to Wounded Knee*. New York: New Press, 1996.

Chesterman, John and Brian Galligan. *Citizens without Rights: Aborigines and Australian Citizenship*. Cambridge: Cambridge University Press, 1997.

Choo, Christine. 'Sister Kate's Home for "Nearly White" Children'. In *Many Voices: Reflections on Experiences of Indigenous Child Separation*. Eds Doreen Mellor and Anna Haebich, 193–207. Canberra: National Library of Australia, 2002.

Clarke, Mavis Thorpe. *Pastor Doug: The Story of Sir Douglas Nicholls, Aboriginal Leader*. Adelaide: Rigby, 1975.

Connor, John. *The Australian Frontier Wars: 1788–1838*. Sydney: UNSW Press, 2002.

Cosgrove, Peter. *My Story*. Pymble, NSW: HarperCollins, 2006.

Courtney, G.B. *Silent Feet: The History of 'Z' Special Operations, 1942–1945*. McCrae, Vic: R.J. & S.P. Austin, 1993.

Defence Abuse Response Taskforce. 'Report on Abuse in Defence'. Canberra: Department of Defence, 2014.

Dennis, Peter and Jeffrey Grey. *Emergency and Confrontation: Australian Military Operations in Malaya and Borneo 1950–1966*. The Official History of Australia's Involvement in Southeast Asian Conflicts 1948–1975. Vol. 5. St Leonards, NSW: Allen & Unwin and the Australian War Memorial, 1996.

Edwards, Peter. *Australia and the Vietnam War*. Sydney: NewSouth Publishing, 2014.

Evans, Raymond, Kay Saunders and Kathryn Cronin. *Race Relations in Colonial Queensland: A History of Exclusion, Exploitation and Extermination*. 3rd ed. St Lucia, Qld: University of Queensland Press, 1993.

Freire, Paulo. *Pedagogy of the Oppressed*. Trans. Myra Bergman Ramos. 30th anniversary ed. New York: Continuum, 2000.

Haebich, Anna. *Broken Circles: Fragmenting Indigenous Families*. Fremantle: Fremantle Arts Centre Press, 2000.

Hall, Robert. *The Black Diggers: Aborigines and Torres Strait Islanders in the Second World War*. 2nd ed. Canberra: Aboriginal Studies Press, 1997.

———. *Fighters from the Fringe: Aborigines and Torres Strait Islanders Recall the Second World War*. Canberra: Aboriginal Studies Press, 1995.

Hawke, Steve and Michael Gallagher. *Noonkanbah: Whose Land, Whose Law*. Fremantle: Fremantle Arts Centre Press, 1989.

Horner, David. *Australia and the 'New World Order': From Peacekeeping to Peace Enforcement: 1988–1991*, The Official History of Australian Peacekeeping, Humanitarian and Post-Cold War Operations, Vol. 2. Cambridge: Cambridge University Press, 2011.

———. *The Gulf Commitment: The Australian Defence Force's First War*. Melbourne: Melbourne University Press, 1992.

Horner, David and John Connor. *The Good International Citizen: Australian Peacekeeping in Asia, Africa and Europe, 1991–1993*, Official History of Peacekeeping, Humanitarian and Post–Cold War Operations, Vol. 3. Cambridge: Cambridge University Press, 2014.

Horton, Dick. *Ring of Fire: Australian Guerrilla Operations against the Japanese in World War II*. South Melbourne: Macmillan, 1983.

How the West Was Lost. Directed by David Noakes. Produced by Heather Williams and David Noakes. 72 mins. Ronin Films, 1987. DVD.

Howard, John. *Lazarus Rising*. Sydney: HarperCollins, 2010.

Hunter, Tamara. 'The myth of equality: The denial of citizenship rights for Aboriginal people in Western Australia'. *Studies in Western Australian History* 22 (2001): 69–82.

James, Jan 'Kabarli'. *Forever Warriors*. Perth: Scott Print, 2010.

Jordens, Ann-Mari. 'An administrative nightmare: Aboriginal conscription 1965–72'. *Aboriginal History* 13, no. 2 (1989): 124–134.

Keating, Paul. 'The Redfern Park address'. 10 December 1992. In *Reconciliation: Essays on Australian Reconciliation*. Ed. Michelle Grattan, 60–64. Melbourne: Black Inc, 2000.

'The Last Post'. *Message Stick*. Directed by Adrian Wells. Produced by the Australian Broadcasting Corporation (ABC). 2006. DVD.

Londey, Peter. *Other People's Wars: A History of Australian Peacekeeping*. Crows Nest, NSW: Allen & Unwin, 2004.

Lui-Chivizhe, Leah. 'Making history: Torres Strait Islander railway workers and the 1968 Mt Newman track-laying record'. *Aboriginal History* 35 (2011): 37–55.

MacGregor, Sandy, as told to Jimmy Thomson. *No Need for Heroes*. Lindfield, NSW: CALM Pty Ltd, 1993.

Maynard, John. '"Let us go"… it's a "Blackfellows' War"': Aborigines and the Boer War'. *Aboriginal History* 39 (2015): 143–162.

McLeod, Don. *How the West Was Lost: The Native Question in the Development of Western Australia*. Port Hedland, WA: Don McLeod, 1984.

Morgan, Anthony and Erin Lewis. 'Evaluation of the Queensland Murri Court: Final Report'. AIC Reports Technical and Background Paper 39. Canberra: Australian Institute of Criminology, 2010.

Murphy, John. *Harvest of Fear: A History of Australia's Vietnam War.* St Leonards, NSW: Allen & Unwin, 1993.

National Inquiry into the Separation of Aboriginal and Torres Strait Islander Children from their Families. *Bringing Them Home: Report of the National Inquiry into the Separation of Aboriginal and Torres Strait Islander Children from Their Families.* Sydney: Human Rights and Equal Opportunity Commission, 1997.

No Bugles, No Drums. Written and directed by John Burnett and Debra Beattie-Burnett. Produced by Seven Emus Productions in association with Australian Television Network, 1990. Videocassette.

Norman, Heidi. *'What do we want?': A Political History of Aboriginal Land Rights in NSW.* Canberra: Aboriginal Studies Press, 2015.

Ollif, Lorna. *Colonel Best and Her Soldiers: The Story of 33 Years of the Women's Royal Australian Army Corps.* Hornsby, NSW: Ollif Publishing Company, 1985.

Osborne, Elizabeth. *Torres Strait Islander Women and the Pacific War.* Canberra: Aboriginal Studies Press, 1997.

Reynolds, Henry. *Forgotten War.* Sydney: NewSouth Publishing, 2013.

Riseman, Noah. 'The curious case of Mervyn Eades: National Service, discrimination and Aboriginal people'. *Australian Journal of Politics and History* 59, no. 1 (2013): 64–80.

——. *Defending Whose Country? Indigenous Soldiers in the Pacific War.* Lincoln, NE: University of Nebraska Press, 2012.

——. 'Enduring silences, enduring prejudices: Australian Aboriginal participation in the First World War'. In *Endurance and the First World War.* Eds David Monger, Katie Pickles and Sarah Murray, 178–195. Newcastle upon Tyne: Cambridge Scholars Publishing, 2014.

——. 'Equality in the ranks: The lives of Aboriginal Vietnam veterans'. *Journal of Australian Studies* 36, no. 4 (December 2012): 411–426.

——. 'Racism, Indigenous people and the Australian armed forces in the post-Second World War era'. *History Australia* 10, no. 2 (2013): 159–179.

——. 'The stolen veteran: Institutionalisation, military service and the Stolen Generations'. *Aboriginal History* 35 (2011): 57–77.

Rumble, Gary, Melanie McKean and Dennis Pearce. 'Report of the Review of Allegations of Sexual and Other Abuse in Defence: Facing the Problems of the Past'. Canberra: Department of Defence, 2011.

Saunders, Kay and Helen Taylor. 'The reception of black servicemen in Australia during World War II: The resilience of "White Australia"'. *Journal of Black Studies* 25, no. 3 (January 1995): 331–348.

Scarlett, Philippa. *Aboriginal and Torres Strait Islander Volunteers for the AIF: The Indigenous Response to World War One*. Macquarie, ACT: Indigenous Histories, 2012.

Schwarzkopf, H. Norman with Peter Petre. *It Doesn't Take a Hero: The Autobiography of General H. Norman Schwarzkopf*. New York: Bantam Books, 1992.

Sharp, Nonie. *Stars of Tagai: The Torres Strait Islanders*. Canberra: Aboriginal Studies Press, 1993.

Stevenson, Clare and Honor Darling (eds). *The WAAAF Book*. Sydney: Hale & Iremonger, 1984.

Strelein, Lisa. *Compromised Jurisprudence: Native Title Cases since Mabo*. 2nd ed. Canberra: Aboriginal Studies Press, 2009.

Thanks Girls and Goodbye! The Story of the Australian Women's Land Army 1942–45. Ed. Sue Hardisty. Ringwood, Vic: Viking O'Neil, 1990.

Thomson, Donald. *Donald Thomson in Arnhem Land*. Compiled and introduced by Nicolas Peterson. Rev. ed. Melbourne: The Miegunyah Press, 2005.

Thomson, Joyce. *The WAAAF in Wartime Australia*. Melbourne: Melbourne University Press, 1991.

Westheider, James E. *The African American Experience in Vietnam: Brothers in Arms*. Lanham, MD: Rowman and Littlefield, 2008.

———. *Fighting on Two Fronts: African Americans and the Vietnam War*. New York and London: New York University Press, 1997.

Winegard, Timothy. *Indigenous Peoples of the British Dominions and the First World War*. Cambridge: Cambridge University Press, 2012.

Internet and unpublished sources

'About IPRC'. Indigenous Pre Recruitment Course. Online. Available from iprc. aboriginallearningcircle.com/about-iprc. Accessed 12 January 2015.

Australia. Department of Defence. 'Australian Defence Force Indigenous Employment Strategy 2007–17'. Online. Available from www.defence.gov. au/fr/publications/ADF%20IES%20-%20External%20Version_04Dec08. pdf. Accessed 3 July 2012.

——. 'Defence Reconciliation Action Plan 2010–2014: Reconciliation through our people'. December 2009. Online. Available from www.defence.gov.au/ CODE/_Master/docs/drap/DRAP2010-14.pdf. Accessed 14 September 2015.

——. 'Department of Defence Census 2011 public report'. Canberra: Roy Morgan Research, May 2012.

Australia. Department of Families, Housing, Community Services and Indigenous Affairs. 'Recognising Aboriginal and Torres Strait Islander Peoples in the Constitution: Report of the Expert Panel'. January 2012. Online. Available from www.recognise.org.au/uploads/assets/3446%20 FaHCSIA%20ICR%20report_text_Bookmarked%20PDF%2012%20 Jan%20v4.pdf. Accessed 12 February 2014.

Australia. National Native Title Tribunal. Online. Available from www.nntt. gov.au. Accessed 25 February 2015.

Australia. NTER Review Board. *Northern Territory Emergency Response: Report of the NTER Review Board*. October 2008. Canberra: Australian Government, 2008. Online. Available from www.nterreview.gov.au/docs/report_nter_ review/default.htm. Accessed 11 February 2014.

'Australian and New Zealand Somali Veterans Association'. Online. Available from www.anzsva.org. Accessed 25 February 2015.

'Australian Peacekeeper & Peacemaker Veterans Association'. Online. Available from www.peacekeepers.asn.au. Accessed 25 February 2015.

'BARK: Brothers Act of Random Kindness'. Online. Available from brothersactofrandomkindness.wordpress.com. Accessed 25 February 2015.

'Indigenous commemoration for the Centenary'. Australian War Memorial. Online. Available from www.awm.gov.au/1914-1918/indigenous-commemoration/. Accessed 13 February 2015.

'Indigenous cultural events and commemorative events'. Department of Veterans' Affairs. Online. Available from www.dva.gov.au/i-am/aboriginal-andor-torres-strait-islander/indigenous-cultural-events-and-commemorative-events. Accessed 11 February 2015.

'Indigenous Pre-Recruitment Course'. The Centre of Diversity Expertise: Indigenous Affairs. Online. Available from www.defence.gov.au/code/indigenous/career/adf/iprc.asp. Accessed 12 January 2015.

National Congress of Australia's First Peoples. Online. Available from www.nationalcongress.com.au. Accessed 1 August 2014.

'Queensland Government Action Plan: Australian South Sea Islander Community'. Brisbane: Queensland Government, Department of Premier and Cabinet, 19 July 2001. Online. Available from www.datsima.qld.gov.au/resources/datsima/publications/archived/qld-govt-assi-action-plan.pdf. Accessed 10 February 2015.

'South Sea Islander Honour Roll'. Online. Available from www.mackayhistory.org/research/war_memorials/SSI_memorial.html. Accessed 25 February 2015.

www.ingramcontent.com/pod-product-compliance
Lightning Source LLC
Chambersburg PA
CBHW061217270326
41926CB00028B/4674